# Ending the Computer Con:
## The Thinking Person's Guide to Succes

CW01460419

# Ending the Computer Conspiracy

## The Thinking Person's Guide to Successful Systems

Colin Corder

McGRAW-HILL Book Company (UK) Limited

**London** · New York · St Louis · San Francisco · Auckland
Bogota · Guatemala · Hamburg · Johannesburg · Lisbon · Madrid
Mexico · Montreal · New Delhi · Panama · Paris · San Juan
São Paulo · Singapore · Sydney · Tokyo · Toronto

Published by
McGRAW-HILL Book Company (UK) Limited
MAIDENHEAD · BERKSHIRE · ENGLAND

---

**British Library Cataloguing in Publication Data**

Corder, Colin
    Ending the computer conspiracy: the thinking
    person's guide to successful systems.
    1. Business—Data processing    2. System design
    I. Title
    651.8'4    HF5548.2

    ISBN 0-07-084795-9


**Library of Congress Cataloging-in-Publication Data**

Corder, Colin R.
    Ending the computer conspiracy.

    Bibliography: p.
    Includes index.
    1. System design.    2. Electronic digital computers.
    I. Title.
    QA76.9.S88C67    1985        004.2'1        85-18025
    ISBN 0-07-084795-9

Copyright © 1985 McGraw-Hill Book Company (UK) Limited. All
rights reserved. No part of this publication may be reproduced,
stored in a retrieval system, or transmitted, in any form or by
any means, electronic, mechanical, photocopying, recording, or
otherwise, without the prior permission of McGraw-Hill Book
Company (UK) Limited, or of the original copyright holder.

12345    CUP 865

Filmset by Eta Services (Typesetters) Ltd, Beccles, Suffolk
Printed and bound in Great Britain at the University Press, Cambridge

# Contents

# Foreword

Most books about computers are the unreadable in full pursuit of the unteachable. Written by technical experts, they dwell lovingly on bits, bauds and BASIC while largely ignoring the day-to-day problems facing the average manager; the problems he hopes a computer will help him with.

When Colin Corder sent me an initial manuscript of *Ending the Computer Conspiracy* he asked me merely to read the first two or three chapters. I took him at his word and set off to read the introductory pages. I stopped reading when I got to the last page. It is rare praise to be able to say of a book about a subject as complex, not to say arid, as computers, that 'It is as readable as it is instructive'.

It does not descend into the cartoon style currently affected to liven up otherwise turgid texts. It is readable because it is literate. The author draws on examples from many different disciplines to illustrate his theme that problem-solving in business is not exclusively the domain of the computer expert. The initial chapters show clearly why computers have always been thought to be difficult and therefore unusable by the non-expert; and why this no longer holds true. Thereafter a realistic case study, with a frustrated user mouthing exactly the questions that we all want to ask, convincingly shows two things:

First, that there are many areas, traditionally viewed as the domain of the technical expert, where the user not only can, but must, participate.

Second—and a most useful and timely corrective to the more extravagant claims of computer salesmen—that there still remain many activities where unthinking self-reliance courts disaster. In these areas the expert is needed. What the intelligent manager requires is the ability to distinguish between the two areas. To know when, and how, to do it himself but equally to know when to involve others. In both areas he wants to know how to retain *control*.

Anyone reading this book will emerge with a much clearer view of the many choices open to him in using computers—and with a much enhanced ability to make the right ones.

Antony Jay
Chairman, Video Arts Limited

# Preface

*Plus ça change, plus c'est la même chose.*

A survey on the use of computers carried out by the British Institute of Management in 1971 concluded with the following advice:

> stop looking at computers and start looking at your business—don't regard the computer as a panacea for the problems of your organization.

A review of a more recent survey conducted in 1984 on the use of information technology by management concluded:

> for those upon whom the light does not break information technology will allow bad managers to make bad decisions, more quickly and in greater numbers.

This book is an attempt to spread some light—not over new ground, but over ground that is familiar to computer people but less so to laypeople. As personal computing spreads, so more and more users come into direct contact with data processing systems. There is no prospect of enough systems analysts to advise on the disciplines of systems work. In many respects, users will become their own analysts. Even when using prewritten packages, such as spreadsheets and file management systems, someone still has to decide what data the system is to hold and what calculations must be performed. It is therefore of the utmost importance and urgency that users become aware of the methods, skills, and disciplines of systems work. A knowledge of how to specify requirements and analyse problems is a prerequisite of using computers effectively; an appreciation of how systems are built is a prerequisite of control. Without this, new users will reproduce the mistake made by an earlier generation—implementing solutions without defining the problem.

The systems field is so wide and complex, the techniques used in systems development so diverse, that a book of this length must have strictly limited objectives. The first is to persuade you of the necessity to analyse problems before rushing into solutions; the second is to show ways in which you can turn this principle into practice.

One of the most important messages in the book is the need for consultation in systems work. This is no less true in writing about systems, and I am therefore pleased to acknowledge a considerable debt to my colleague Grahame Stehle, who has vastly increased the pill-to-sugar ratio of the text, and to Tom DeMarco, the originator of many of the methods described and a coruscating but constructive critic of early drafts. Both have taken a tolerant view of my attempts to simplify complex material.

Another theme of the book is the iterative nature of systems work—the successive refinement of an initial rough draft of a system. Again, this applies equally to writing. Technology, in the form of word processors, helps, but iteration is hard on the typist. I am therefore pleased to record my gratitude to Vera Jones and Wendy Chalker, both of whom can recite the text by heart.

# 1. The conspiracy theory of computing

*All professions are a conspiracy against the laity.*
George Bernard Shaw

What characterizes 'the professions'? First and foremost, protection of the livelihood of their members. They do this by making every effort to ensure that people requiring the particular service are forced to come to them. This is achieved where possible by establishing a legal monopoly; where not, by persuading outsiders that the skill and knowledge required to practise is so great that users must go to an expert.[1] Solicitors check deeds, conduct some standard searches, give it a long name—'conveyancing'—and charge the earth for it. Accountants confuse us with mysterious initials such as DCF and NPV to express what we well know—that a pound in the hand is worth two in the future.

To protect the monopoly they make entry difficult—lengthy exams, long apprenticeships often on low pay—in order to keep membership smaller and reduce internal competition. Once you have been accepted into the profession it is important that this is clear to all, so you are granted letters to put after your name. In many countries, courtroom lawyers dress up in wigs and gowns to give visible proof of their separation from the common man. The reward for all this is high pay, status, and job security. It is hardly surprising that so many aspire to 'enter the professions'.

During the last decade the computer industry has assumed the trappings of a profession. Entrants have been selected by aptitude testing, despite the tenuous empirical evidence of what aptitudes to look for; salaries have been kept high owing to the excess of demand over supply consequent upon restriction of entry; learned bodies devised professional examinations leading to meaningless letters to put after

---

[1] As Milton Friedman has pointed out, in his book *Free to Choose* (taken, without attribution, from an article by Robert Reid in *World Medicine*, July 1973), the Hippocratic Oath contains examples of restriction of entry: 'I will hand on precepts, lectures, and all other learning to my sons, to those of my teachers and to those pupils duly apprenticed and sworn, and to none others'; and, for leaving things to the experts, 'I will not cut, but will leave such procedures to practitioners of the craft.'

one's name; and, though possessing no distinctive uniform, computer people have tended to dress casually and male practitioners have a statistically significant tendency to have beards. In sum, the industry has successfully persuaded outsiders that systems development is a black art whose secrets are revealed only to the initiated. As Robert Townsend said in *Up the Organisation*, 'Computer people are complicators not simplifiers—they are trying to make it look difficult'.

Just as accountants talk in initials and use opaque expressions like 'sum-of-the-years method' for calculating the depreciation of fixed assets, so computer people employ 'computerspeak'. This sub-language consists of acronyms, initials, numbers, and plain long words.

> The program is a general-purpose, multiprogramming, communications-oriented operating system designed for interactive use in a distributed data processing environment. (Extract from an announcement of a new computer system)

Most people's reaction to something they do not understand is to opt out—'leave it to the experts'. As a direct consequence, computer systems have been developed at arm's length. The user has initially indicated what he thinks he wants while remaining in ignorance of what computers are, and are not, good at; the computer person, for his part, has never been behind a line manager's desk in his life: what he possesses is a good technical knowledge of computers. The end result is often an elegant system, but one bearing little relation to the user's problems. Whether this failure to communicate, this mystique surrounding computers resulted from a conspiracy is open to debate. What is certain is that the mystery is hard to sustain when your ten-year-old child is demonstrating advanced keyboard skills—even if it is only at playing Space Invaders.

But if the so-called conspiracy is ending, the problem of communication will never completely disappear. Users still need to be able to describe their problems and articulate their requirements. Much of this book is therefore about communication: communication methods that are at once sufficiently free-form for the non-technical person to understand and use, and sufficiently rigorous for the computer person to implement. A common language.

The effect of such a medium of communication is revolutionary. It means that the skills and experience of the ordinary manager are immediately relevant. Users can fully participate in—indeed, drive—the development of their own systems. No longer are they at the mercy of technical experts.

Everyone is familiar with systems. Our rights are protected and circumscribed by legal systems; we elect our governments by different voting systems; they take our money by tax systems. A system is merely a set of linked procedures aimed at producing a specified end result.

If there is a difference in the design of systems in which computers are involved, it arises from the fact that computers are incapable of thinking for themselves. All eventualities must be foreseen. The most cursory examination of legal systems, tax systems, or voting systems shows how difficult this is. Legal systems overcome it by designing as precise a system—statute law—as possible but then dealing with unforeseen circumstances by case law. The requirement of computers to have everything cut and dried in advance, in a world where few things are, is essentially what makes computer-based[1] systems so complex.

Systems do not suddenly become different or uniquely difficult because a computer is involved. When a new industry such as data processing is born, it is natural that in its early years it regards its problems as different from everyone else's. But with age should come wisdom and humility. We can now see that all systems problems have more that is in common than is different. Consequently, lessons learned through the ages by engineers, architects, lawyers, and philosophers are both relevant and useful when it comes to developing a computer system.

This observation would be of mild academic interest were it not for developments in the computer industry which are freeing the user from dependence on the expert. In the hardware field the micro-revolution has put computing power in the hands of everyone; in the software field advances in the ways in which computers are instructed to perform their tasks—the development of so-called 'user languages'—are increasingly enabling users to install their own systems.

In *Le Bourgeois Gentilhomme* by Molière, Monsieur Jourdain, having learned to compose verse, turns his attention to learning prose. When his professor informs him that anything that is not verse is prose, he exclaims: 'Good heavens! For more than forty years I have been speaking prose without knowing it.'

---

[1] I use the expression 'computer-based systems' to indicate that what the computer does is only ever a part of the total system. Having once made this qualification, I shall from here on, in the interests of conciseness, use the shorter expression, 'computer systems'.

The same is true of systems work. For years, non-computer people have been specifying, analysing, designing, and implementing systems. 'Without knowing it', they were in all probability transaction-processing systems using indexed access to distributed data with graceful degradation thrown in. The fact that to them it merely appeared to be a straightforward stock-recording system only shows their failure to speak the language.

Let me not spoil my case by overstating it. In computers, as with medicine, the law, and other professions, there are technical matters requiring extensive training and many years' experience. One reviewer of an early draft of this book described a later, and more technical, chapter as 'Hints on how to remove your own appendix'. (I have since modified it.) His point was that, while he accepted my basic thesis of user participation, there remain areas where this is still impractical. My acceptance of this point means that this book has two aims.

The first concerns those areas—analysing current problems, specifying requirements, identifying benefits, approving changes in company policy and procedures—where users can, and must, involve themselves. They fund such projects, and retain the final responsibility for ensuring that any new system contributes to corporate efficiency. In this area I endeavour, first, to persuade you of the necessity for involvement and, second, to show you how to achieve it in practice.

The second aim is about those areas, such as cost estimating, detailed file design, and program coding, where technical expertise is essential. The problem here is not one of involvement, but one of control. How do you control an activity that you cannot understand? If an expert tells you it will cost £50 000 to develop a system, what confidence can you put in that figure? In these areas, reading this book will enable you to understand what is going on, and how people go about their different tasks, to a level where you can exercise your own judgement about how well they are being accomplished. It will teach you the right questions to ask.

# 2. What is a user?

*War is much too serious a thing to be left to military men.*

Talleyrand

The computer industry is a model of clear thinking and precise definition. Many large companies have 'Data standardization committees' who, like medieval scholiasts, ponder over the exact definition of commonplace user terms such as 'quantity on hand'. How odd, then, that the most commonly used term, 'the user', should itself be so ill-defined. For 'users' run from managing directors contemplating a ten-year computer strategy up to clerical staff entering data at terminals. If one were to attempt to define the normal usage of the term one would have to do so in negative terms; a 'user' is anyone who is not a computer person—the 'them' as against 'us'.

The 'user' to whom this book is addressed is anyone, with minimal or no computer training or experience, who wishes to use a computer to assist in solving business problems.

Now for a second piece of linguistic analysis. What this book is concerned with is the development of 'good' systems. The appropriate starting point is therefore to ask what we mean by a good system. Defining a good weedkiller is not hard; a definition along the lines 'kills a high proportion of common garden weeds, without adversely affecting non-weeds' would be widely regarded as acceptable (provided one can distinguish 'weeds' from 'non-weeds'). Defining what makes a person, or an action, 'good' has kept philosophers in work for centuries.

Goodness, like beauty, is often in the eye of the beholder. To a programmer, a good system may be one whose execution time on the computer has been optimized to an irreducible minimum; to the auditor, it will be one that has clear audit trails, reconciliations, and controls; to the line manager, one that provides the right information at the right time; to the finance director, one that did not exceed budget. As always, a community of different users look for different things. For our purposes, I will define a good system as one that:

- solves the user's problems by achieving the business objectives set for it;
- is easily maintainable;
- is cost-effective;
- is secure and auditable.

5

Devising a system requires that you have a clear idea of what you are aiming at. The first thing is for the person specifying the system to define what will constitute an acceptable end-product. The system designer will then endeavour to get as close to that specification as possible. But it is an essential intellectual perception that one never produces the perfect system in any field where systems deal with people. The perfect production control system is as elusive as the perfect husband.

Churchill once described democracy as 'the worst form of government except all those other forms that have been tried'. To say that systems work consists in designing 'least bad' solutions may not be an inspiring clarion call, but is an essential truth. Indeed, it has been well argued that it is a more easily definable task to eliminate badness than to introduce goodness, since it is always easier to find agreement about problems than about solutions.

Should the user get involved in developing systems? Isn't this a case of buying a dog and barking yourself? The answer to this is simple. It is not possible to imagine non-involvement. As soon as the user makes the statement, 'I want a new payroll system' (as opposed to 'I want a new invoicing system'), he is involved. He has already defined the area of change. Thereafter it is a question of the extent of his involvement. Minimal involvement might be the statement, 'I require a new purchase ledger system. Come back in six months with one but don't bother me in the meantime.'

One of the few situations where one might give a specification to an expert of the type, 'Don't consult me at all: just get it done', would be commissioning a hit man—a situation where the commissioner has a vested interest in remaining in ignorance of how the job is done. At the level of program coding, this attitude is defensible; at the systems level it is a recipe for disaster.

It may be argued that other pressures of time allow only a low level of involvement by the user. This may just be an adequate excuse for a senior manager (although in this case I would expect him to delegate the user role to an immediate subordinate). What is not an excuse is 'I don't understand all this computer stuff.'

Computer-based systems affect every aspect of most organizations. They are central to their administration and profitability. Users cannot afford to opt out. Whether the user is a manager in a multinational with a large internal computing department or the proprietor of his own small company, he dare not entrust the fortunes of his department or business to outside experts. This is as inefficient as it is dangerous: inefficient because the user is pre-eminently in the best position to identify and analyse his own problems; dangerous because, without his involvement, the wrong solution could waste thousands of pounds and jeopardize years of goodwill.

The penalties of non-involvement will become clearer as the book progresses. But the stumbling-block in the past has been not so much a lack of will as a confusion about how the non-technician could involve himself. Don't you need to be a technical computer expert before you can start designing systems? Let me answer that by an analogy.

# 3. The time machine

*Civilisation advances by extending the number of important operations we can perform without thinking of them.*

Alfred North Whitehead

The opening chapter of this book implies that computer people have deliberately made things difficult for the user. In reality, this is too conspiratorial a view for an infant industry. The actual explanation has more to do with the life-cycle of any technological invention.

Let us imagine that an inventor has developed a time machine, allowing its user to travel back in time. We can immediately make some observations about such a machine.

- First, it has obvious potential. Historical disputes such as the identity of the Dark Lady in Shakespeare's sonnets, or whether Richard III was responsible for the murders of the princes in the Tower, can at last be definitively resolved.
- Second, until such time as it goes into mass production, it is likely to be expensive.
- Third, it will in all probability be prone to mechanical malfunction. (The press will be full of disaster stories—'Time explorer stuck in Jurassic Age . . .'.)
- Fourth, it will be difficult to use—you will need a six-month conditioning programme prior to going, plus a grasp of Middle English to know what's going on when you get there.

However, if the potential of the machine is sufficient, engineers will work on the problems. Machine enhancements will improve reliability and range as well as the price/performance ratio. Other problems, such as getting you to the time and place specified—and understanding the language in use—will be solved by what may be termed 'manufacturer's support', i.e., the provision of specially trained experts to navigate and interpret. For as long as they can, time machine manufacturers will force you to use experts supplied by them. Gradually, market forces will break this restrictive practice and produce a new support industry for time exploration. Because the capital cost of the hardware is still high, few individuals will own their own, preferring to go to a Time Travel Bureau.

Ultimately, continuing improvements will solve almost all technical problems. Hardware costs will fall, bringing the machines within reach of more and more people. The problems of navigation and·interpretation, previously solved by supplying expensive experts, will increasingly be solved by logic built into the hardware itself. An automatic pilot will guarantee to get you within ten miles and ten minutes of your chosen time/place; computerized headphones will translate from the vernacular. Both developments will have been greeted with cries of 'deskilling' from the experts.

In short, most of the technical problems will have been resolved. The type that remain will be those of specification—'I went to Moscow in October 1917, but only then realized that to understand the Communist Revolution I should first have gone there in March.' In other words, technical problems of machine-functioning will have been replaced by 'managerial' problems of how to get the best out of the technology.

Reviewing the development of our time machine, we can identify three broad stages in what I term the 'technological development cycle':

1. *Technological trail-blazing*   The machine is new and largely untested. It has frequent operational failures, but these are tolerated in view of its perceived potential and because of the pioneering aspect. However, these problems restrict its use to a small number of enthusiasts. Its commercial application is highly limited.

2. *Dependence on experts*   Technological enhancements broaden the market beyond that of the enthusiast. Mass production brings prices down. The new users thus attracted are more interested in the uses of the machine than in its technical features. They therefore employ other people to facilitate its use. A support industry emerges. Because the machine is complex, only the new experts know how to get it to work. Users become dependent on the technical experts. Because of the technical newness the 'experts' make it up as they go along, and invent their own jargon which is unintelligible to outsiders. As knowledge is pooled, improved methods emerge and are codified into standards.

3. *User friendliness*   A variety of factors—pressure from the users, expensiveness of the experts, engineering ingenuity—leads to the development of yet more sophisticated machines in which solutions to many user problems are built into the machine. The machine becomes

accessible to an even wider market because users are increasingly freed from the constraint of the requirement for technical expertise.

This process can be seen at work in most technological developments. Early radio users needed the skill to cope with crystals in order to get garbled and indistinct messages from 100 miles away. Now you press a button to tune into a live broadcast from La Scala. The history of telephones and polaroid cameras follows the same lines.[1]

More importantly to us, so does that of computers. In the early days, say pre-1965, their usage was restricted by hardware limitations. The severe constraints on design resulting from these meant that it was impossible to specify a system without detailed technical knowledge of the computer hardware on which it was to be implemented. Knowledge is power. Users had to put up with what they were told they could have. They had no ground on which to challenge the technical expert.

In the second stage, roughly from 1965 to 1980, hardware limitations were increasingly removed. Dramatic reductions in cost lead to the proliferation of computers throughout commerce, industry and government. It became a matter of debate whether a systems analyst needed to have been a programmer. Finally, the debating question was resolved in the negative as the ever-growing number of new developments—database, structured programming, micros—made it impossible for any one person to be expert in them all. Thus, like accountancy and engineering before it, the industry split into many different jobs—business analyst, systems designer, database administrator, programmer, etc.

The computer industry is now at stage 3 of the technical development cycle. Contrary to the extravagant claims of many computer salespersons, this does not mean that you can get a computer to do anything you like with zero effort and minimal discipline. There remain many constraints on the use of computers, and the effect of these constraints is to force the user to devote time and effort to the tasks of defining and developing systems that meet his particular requirements. So we return to the necessity for user involvement. And the prerequisite for involvement in any activity is the knowledge of what the activity comprises; what special terms it uses—in short, the ability to communicate.

[1] I do not regard the absorption of technical complexity into the hardware as a universally 'good thing'. Some of us still prefer the challenge of the conventional piano keyboard to electric organs programmed to provide one-finger chords.

In most organizations a manager's knowledge of computers is an inverse function of his position in the organization (which is merely a pretentious way of saying that, the higher up he is, the less he knows about them). At one extreme we have top management, who know a lot about return on capital employed but little about binary subtraction; at the other, we have programmers who are never happier than when writing the re-entrant code for a multi-tasking system, but have difficulty naming the products the company makes.

The systems development problem is how to translate a high-level statement by the former—'We need to reduce work-in-progress by 15 per cent'—to the many thousands of program instructions written by the latter.

This type of problem is not unique to computers. A managing director may say to his legal department, 'Make sure that our employment contracts conform to the new legislation', a similarly high-level requirement likely to cause much browbeating down the line. Galbraith, in his book, *The New Industrial Society*, argues that senior management is increasingly reduced to rubber-stamping the recommendations of subordinate experts—the technostructure. And there is a shrewd suspicion that, in the realm of government, the executive is manipulated by the permanent civil service.

The problem stems from the increasing complexity of modern life. In primitive societies most people understand the implements they use in their everyday lives. In the developed world this is no longer possible. Every day we use things we do not understand. This need not be a matter of great concern—how many people understand how the mind works?—provided that our lack of knowledge does not impede our usage.

In general terms, the solution employed is to regard any complex piece of equipment as a 'black box'. The user treats the equipment as a predictable machine which, given certain inputs, will produce certain outputs. He does not concern himself with its inner workings. Computer people use the terms 'logical' and 'physical' to describe this approach. By 'logical' they mean concentrating on *what* something does, as opposed to 'physical', which is *how* it does it. This approach is forced on them by the sheer complexity of the modern computer compared with its predecessor, the tabulator, where you could actually watch the wheels go round.

The logical–physical distinction is central both to this book and to the problem of dealing with technology generally. The world is divided

11

into logical people and physical people (or, as *Zen and the Art of Motor Cycle Maintenance* would have it, 'romantic' and 'classical').

I personally am a 'logical' extremist. I try never to open the bonnet of my car for fear of being confronted with the distasteful sight of the dirty, oily, noisy, physical things necessary to accomplish the purely logical task of getting me from A to B. This is not a value judgement. When my radiator seizes up through lack of anti-freeze I wish I was more physical. It also makes me vulnerable to the physical experts—mechanics—since I have no idea whether a knocking sound should cost £5 or £500 to put right.

It is important to realize that the logical–physical distinction is not black and white: it is a continuum. My view of electricity is predominantly logical. If I turn a switch, the light goes on. If the light fails to go on, my physical awareness extends to changing the bulb. If this does not work, I give up. My wife, being slightly more knowledgeable about physical things, may investigate the fuse box. Beyond that we are both in the dark. These objects, i.e., bulbs and fuses, are our respective physical boundaries. If these solutions fail we must call in a person with a wider physical boundary—an electrician. But even his physical knowledge falls short of a detailed understanding of the behaviour of electrons. He knows the dangers of allowing negative and positive wires to touch—a very physical flash—but probably does not have the theory as to how and why this happens.

This progression gives us a clue to how we overcome the problem of the complexity of computer systems. We can identify a *Hierarchy of Views*[1] dependent upon the perceiver (see Fig. 3.1). What this hierarchy shows is, first, the length of the progression from completely logical to completely physical, and, second, the impossibility of any one person's view encompassing the complete spectrum. One no more expects the average managing director to understand solid-state physics than the physicist to run a warehouse.

The minimum requirement is that each person can communicate with the persons above and below him in the hierarchy. Thus developing computer systems is an exercise in good communication between users who know what they want and technicians who know how to give it to

---

[1] I have always been envious of people whose fame is enshrined and perpetuated eponymously in phrases such as 'Blake's Grid' or 'Maslow's Hierarchy of Needs'. Hence the capital letters. I look forward to the day when the sun never sets on lecturers showing slides of 'Corder's Hierarchy of Views'.

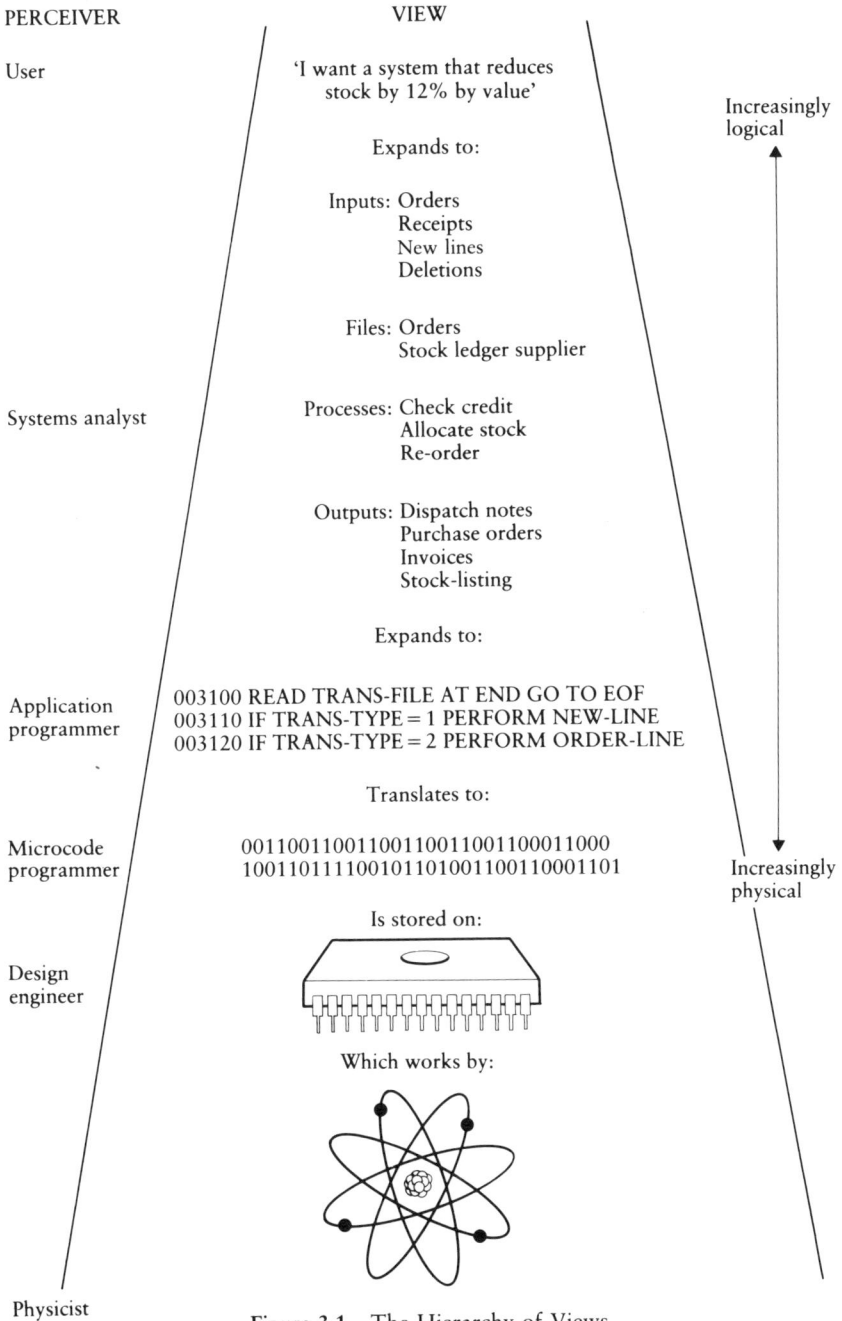

**Figure 3.1** The Hierarchy of Views

PERCEIVER

User

Systems analyst

Application programmer

Microcode programmer

Design engineer

Physicist

VIEW

'I want a system that reduces stock by 12% by value'

Expands to:

Inputs: Orders
Receipts
New lines
Deletions

Files: Orders
Stock ledger supplier

Processes: Check credit
Allocate stock
Re-order

Outputs: Dispatch notes
Purchase orders
Invoices
Stock-listing

Expands to:

003100 READ TRANS-FILE AT END GO TO EOF
003110 IF TRANS-TYPE = 1 PERFORM NEW-LINE
003120 IF TRANS-TYPE = 2 PERFORM ORDER-LINE

Translates to:

0011001100110011001100110001100 0
1001101111001011010011001100011 01

Is stored on:

Which works by:

Increasingly logical

Increasingly physical

them. Let me give an example of the logical–physical distinction in practice.

To the user, a personnel records system is a set of procedures and information concerning company employees. A requirement of such a system may be to display names of all female employees earning over £20 000 a year, or information about a specific employee.

Here are two entirely different physical solutions to this logical requirement. Both achieve the same end—namely the speedy retrieval of required information. Under the solution depicted in Fig. 3.2, the information is held on a floppy disk sitting next to the user on his desk. If he is the sort who likes to takes his work home with him, he can do so, because the computer comes in its own suitcase.

In Fig. 3.3 the information is shown to be stored on the head office's multi-million-dollar computer on the other side of the Atlantic, and the data does a round trip of some 7000 miles. In theory, which of these physical solutions is involved should be 'transparent' to the user; that is computerspeak for saying that there should be no discernible difference

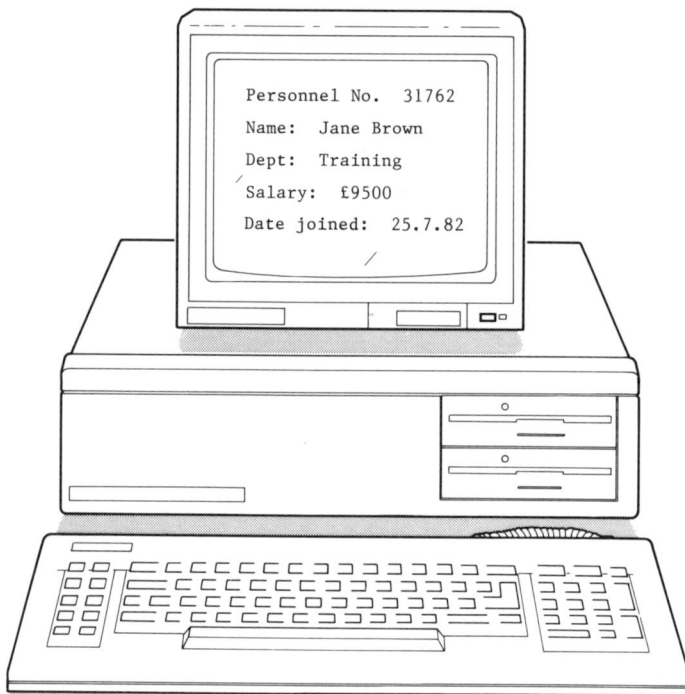

```
Personnel No.   31762
Name:   Jane Brown
Dept:   Training
Salary:   £9500
Date joined:   25.7.82
```

Figure 3.2   Microcomputer system

LONDON

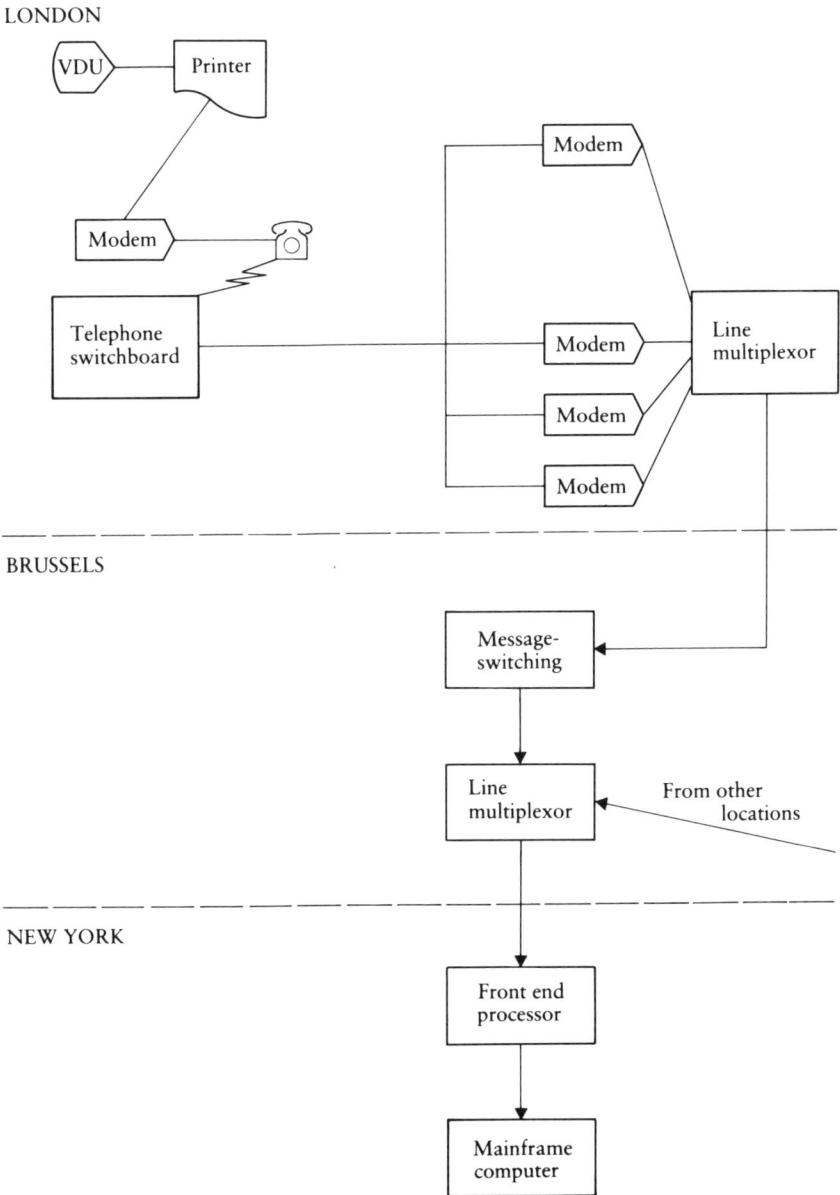

BRUSSELS

NEW YORK

**Figure 3.3**  Remote mainframe

in the result—in this case, the way in which the information is displayed on the screen.

Provided that the user can specify his requirements, can describe a proposed system or set of business rules in logical terms, the physical implementation of that specification can be left to the technicians. What the user then requires is a control mechanism to monitor progress and the quality of work done—even though the details of how it is being done are a closed book.

# 4. Is systems development difficult?

*A computer is a device to turn a clerical error into a corporate disaster.*
Anon.

Computer systems have always suffered a bad press. Stories abound of systems developed late or scrapped altogether. To a large extent, this is attributable to what I term the *fallacy of the notional ideal*. This consists in comparing some project, product, or service not with the general run of other projects, products, and services—good, bad, and indifferent—but with some non-existent ideal. My wife is always complaining about my life-style, which involves lecture tours overseas followed by periods 'under her feet' at home. 'Why can't you be like other husbands?' is her stock question. However, when I ask which particular 'other husband' among our acquaintances she has in mind she has difficulty in naming one. It transpires that no one particular person is in mind so much as a composite notional ideal husband made up of the best points of a number of them.

So when users complain of the unique unsatisfactoriness of computer projects, I must first ask them to point to those other projects which serve as the model against which the computer projects are being adversely compared. Where are all these projects that were completed on time, within budget, to the total satisfaction of the user?

However, this is what my old Latin master used to call a 'tu quoque' argument, i.e., answering the accusation by saying that others are just as guilty. There is clearly a problem, and since much of this book is about problem-solving it is as well if I follow my own advice about how to go about it.

*First, define the problem.* Computer systems have a marked propensity to be delivered late and over budget. The end-product is seldom to the users' complete satisfaction, and considerable costs are incurred in maintaining and enhancing the system once operational.

As we shall see subsequently, much of the art of problem-solving consists in arriving at a clear definition of what the problem actually is. If you do not recognize this definition it is unlikely that the solution propounded in this book will appear relevant.

*Second, quantify the problem.* Before embarking upon some expensive new solution, it is always as well to satisfy oneself that the problem as defined not only exists but is significant. Are we talking in the context of minor overruns or of disasters of epic proportions?

This is a difficult field in which to discover hard facts. Few companies like to cost accurately their own disasters let alone release such figures to outsiders. However, a study conducted by the Atlantic Systems Guild of New York estimated that approximately 15 per cent of all projects are cancelled before delivery of any useful product. Study of the cancelled projects showed that virtually all had used up their budgeted money before cancellation.

Given a total US expenditure of $15 billion per annum on data processing, this would give a figure of $2.25 billion in the US alone.

*Third, analyse the problem.* What are the causes of the problems referred to? This book will endeavour to look at this at both the macro-level and micro-level. In this chapter I want to answer it at the macro-level by relating it to the stages of what, in the previous chapter, I termed the 'technological development cycle'.

Systems development is an attempt to meet certain defined systems objectives within specified constraints. The computer industry is not perverse: it desperately wants to deliver an excellent product on time. But it has been hampered by the difficulties implicit in the technological development cycle.

In Stage 1—technological trail-blazing—we were learning our trade. Hardware was unreliable, software primitive, and development standards non-existent. The latter reflected the fact that standard procedures are the collation and codification of individuals' experiences. At this stage, no such base of experience existed. The limitations of the hardware imposed such constraints on the ultimate system that it was not possible to develop a system without detailed hardware knowledge. Dependence on the technicians was total, and the participation of the user strictly limited. Suggestions, and requests for additional facilities, were met with the response, 'You can't get that on to the machine.' Since the user was in no position to dispute this, his role was restricted to that of specifying his requirements and then being told which he could or could not have.

By Stage 2—dependence on experts—the situation had improved.

The worst hardware constraints had eased; the software to operate the computer was less unreliable; some experience in managing projects had been gained and pooled. Nevertheless, problems remained. Two can be identified as crucial:

- lack of good programming techniques leading to complex and unmaintainable programs;
- relatively primitive file-handling facilities leading to inflexible storage of data.

These very constraints meant that a system, once developed, was difficult to modify. *You therefore had to get the system design right first time.* This is a virtually impossible task. In almost every field of human endeavour, progress is made by trial and error.

But during the 1970s, virtually the whole of systems development was based on the myth of the 'frozen specification'. The user was asked to specify his requirements, sign on the dotted line, and promise not to change his mind for the next five years. Failure so to do was met with frantic attempts to 'educate users' into the straitjacket imposed on them. User involvement—which in practice meant users coming up with new ideas halfway through the development process—was to be discouraged, as inevitably leading to design changes and missed deadlines.

The method of systems development militated heavily against user involvement. The design process was still intrinsically 'physical'. The systems analyst was typically an ex-programmer and often was thinking in hardware terms from an early stage in the project. Design options were presented in physical terms, with the accompanying jargon of record formats, file accessing methods, and operating systems. A language common to computer people and users did not exist. Users employed narrative as the basic medium of communication; computer people turned these into flowcharts. Since there was no easy way for the user to check the work, his main recourse was to keep his fingers crossed and hope that the analyst knew what he was doing.

The adverse, and well-documented, results of this approach were that management discovered what it really wanted only after the system had been installed; that systems were technically elegant solutions to the wrong problem; and that they imposed irksome operational restraints on the end-users.

However, as the computer industry has progressed to Stage 3—user-friendliness—the constraints of the previous stages have disappeared or been markedly reduced. Among the most significant developments are:

- the tremendous reduction in hardware costs which has largely eliminated the constraint of fitting the system into the available hardware: if in doubt, buy more hardware;
- improved programming methods—so-called structured programming—which have dramatically increased the ability to maintain and modify programs;
- improved file-handling techniques, which have made possible—via databases—significantly more flexible storage of information;
- improved communication techniques between user and computer person, which have resulted in the user being able to understand better, and therefore to contribute to, the development of his own systems;
- the new phenomenon of the second-time user who has built up an experience of computer systems;
- developments in user programming—so called 'fourth-generation' languages—which give the user the ability to set up, update, and interrogate his own files;
- 'packaged', i.e., pre-written, systems, which have improved in quality and come down in price to the point where building any system from new is questioned.

The impact of these developments upon the way in which systems are developed is significant. The word 'engineering' has been appropriated in the phrase 'software engineering' to attest to the fact that systems no longer have to be built on the basis of a set of successive checkpoints, each of which marked a point of no return, but can be developed on an iterative basis.

An initial model or prototype of the desired system can be developed so that at an early stage users have a reasonable idea of what it is they are asking for. This can then be successively refined until a clear definition of the desired system is arrived at.

The effect of the evolution of new techniques is to enable users to participate more actively, and to a much later stage, in a systems development project. Where before the user role was limited to describing his output requirements and leaving everything from then on in other people's hands, now he can help to define files, specify procedures and the sequence in which they should occur, and oversee progress throughout the development life-cycle. Indeed, at the level of personal computers, the pendulum is rapidly swinging to the other extreme. Instead of computers being seen as remote and mysterious, the danger now is of the disciplines necessary to use them being neglected. User-friendliness is being sold as the cure for all ills.

# 5. The convivial computer

'User-friendliness' is a vogue word in the computer industry. I personally prefer the French equivalent, 'convivialité'. How pleasantly Gallic to think of your computer as a convivial beast! Whichever word we use, the concept is important in representing Stage 3 of the technological development cycle. What, then, does it actually mean in the context of computing?

The most common expression to describe what computers do is *data processing*. This is an excellent expression, because in essence all computer systems development can ultimately be reduced to:

– describing the data;
– describing the processes.[1]

**Figure 5.1**  *Convivialité*

Computers are remarkably simple. They take in data, store (or file) some of it for future reference, process it, and 'output' it. They are not only simple, they are unchanging. Today's micro does exactly this, as did the first postwar computer, or for that matter Babbage's difference engine. All that has happened is that some physical changes have occurred—chips for valves, diskettes for punch cards. These have had

---

[1] It is so clear a description that computer people have had to invent the new term, 'information technology', in order to keep one step ahead.

tremendous effects in improving performance and reducing cost. But the functions input, file, process, output remain the same.

It follows from this that the specification of computer system consists in:

- defining the data, both input, stored, and output;
- defining the processes which convert the data you feed in into the data that comes out.

Building the system then consists in taking these descriptions and writing the appropriate instructions to implement them on a given machine. User-friendliness is important because it is the key to allowing the user's participation in these activities. Because it *is* the key, this chapter is devoted to explaining what user-friendliness actually is, its emergence in the technological time-cycle, and its likely evolution. To do this I will look first at data, and then at processing.

## Data

### 1. INPUT

In the context of user-friendliness, there is not much to be said about input. The most significant development here has been that of screen-based systems where the data can be entered directly into the computer rather than captured on an intermediary device such as a punch card or diskette.

The significance of this is that errors in the data can be detected by the computer and rectified by the user at the time. This is a considerable improvement on poring over long error printouts some days after you have submitted the original data.

### 2. OUTPUT

There is little more to be said about user-friendliness of output. A printout is a printout is a printout. Again, the most significant development has been screen-based enquiry systems. Computer systems were always accused, with some justification, of burying the user in reams of paper. This was not perversity on the part of the systems designer; nor did he have shares in a computer stationery company. It stemmed from the typical user's need to answer *ad hoc* questions about random stock items or customer accounts. With a screen-based system you can get at the specific record that you want. Before this facility was available, the only means by which a computer system could give the user information about any one product or customer was to give him information about *all* products or customers. Hence the foot-deep computer printouts.

3. FILES

The above facility—of getting at one specific record on a file—results from the way in which data is stored within a computer system. It is here that improving technology has had the greatest impact. In the early days, the sole medium for the storage of data was magnetic tape. The physical characteristic of magnetic tape—that it comes in a long reel—meant that you could process data only sequentially. To get to a record near the end of the tape, you had to go through all preceding records.

Magnetic tape was also a slow device, so that updating a file of 20 000 stock items could well take an hour. As a result, the file was likely to be updated only once per day. All possible types of transactions affecting the file—issues, receipts, new lines, deletions, price changes—had to be collected together to go into the one daily run. The large number of different inputs lead, of necessity, to large, complex, and unmaintainable programs.

The emergence of disks, and consequent dramatic improvements in the ability to store large volumes of data and retrieve it at speed, is the key to modern file-handling. The mechanism of reading or writing to a disk—'read/write' heads which move in and out while the disk continually revolves—brings with it the ability to access data anywhere on the disk surface. Provided the system knows where a particular record is located, it can retrieve or update it in a few milliseconds. To do this it merely needs to set up an index, or indexes, telling it that product 70651 is physically located on track 87 of the disk.

Originally the computer software set up only one index. The file would be physically arranged in a given sequence, i.e., a stock file in product code sequence, or a sales ledger file in customer number sequence, and the index would give you the location respectively of either the product or the customer. Nowadays multiple indexes give much greater flexibility. Although the file is still set up in one physical sequence, e.g. by product number, indexes may point you to suppliers as well as products.

Now, in addition to obtaining an immediate answer to the question, 'How many bottles of Glenfiddich do we have in stock?' we can also more speedily retrieve information such as, 'Which products are supplied by Distillers?'

The ability to access data in a number of different ways is what characterizes a database. The data can be stored in one central file with each user having his own 'views', i.e., accessing just that information that interests him.

This concept is neither mysterious nor new. It is the basis of any library. Librarians sequence books in one, and one only, physical sequence. The sequence universally used—by subject—reflects the fact that this is how the majority of readers use a library. They usually go in looking for a book on a particular subject. However, at other times they may want to access the same store of books differently. They may be searching for a specific title, or for books by a specific author. To cater for both these requirements, separate indexes or catalogues are set up which cross-reference from the author's name to the subject code, from which the physical location of the book can be determined. The only real difference between a library and a computer database is that a database stores only one copy of any record, whereas a library holds multiple copies of popular books. But then, users accessing databases 'borrow' the records for only a few seconds at a time.

As we shall see in Chapter 9, users can specify their own databases by describing simply the data they wish the system to hold, the modes of access they require to it, and the provisions necessary to keep the data secure.

There may still be problems in being sure exactly what data one does want to hold, but these are specification problems, not technical ones. And one further caveat should be entered. The fact that a computer system *can* hold and retrieve large amounts of data does not mean that it *should*. Cost constraints still exist. A £3000 microcomputer will not hold a large corporate product database of 150 000 items—at least, not at the time of writing.

## Processing

If user-friendliness with respect to data means that the user need concern himself only with what is stored and not with how it is stored, the equivalent in processing data is to specify *what* has to be done, leaving the 'how' to the systems builder. Bricklayers tend to get annoyed if you start advising them about the correct mix of sand and cement.

In general terms, the higher up the Hierarchy of Views one is, the more one adopts this approach. However, with micros and terminals proliferating, users want to be able to manipulate their own data—in effect, by writing their own small programs.

This does not mean that highly paid marketing directors will be well employed writing inefficient BASIC programs. It does mean that accountants should have the facility to produce their own reports without having to go cap in hand to a programmer every time they want to re-format one. User-friendliness in the processing of data is just that: reducing the complexity of the art of programming. Indeed, a standard complaint of programmers over the last few years has been that programming is being 'deskilled', which is just their view of the transition to Stage 3 of the technological development cycle. To see how this has happened, and its impact on the user, it is worth tracing this transition.

A company I once worked for had a really brilliant programmer. You could tell he was special. His admiring peers spoke in hushed tones about the programs he wrote—'You should try to read them—they're impossible to understand!' The computer operators had his home telephone number so that, if a program of his failed in the middle of the night, they could ring him up for him to tell them how to correct it.

Early programmers were like early aviators—conspicuous in dress, devil-may-care in attitude, and a danger to themselves and all around them. Fortunately, early programmers bear as little resemblance to present-day program coders as early aviators to a 747 pilot. The technological development cycle has seen to that.

The way in which data is processed by a computer is determined by a program. Programs have not changed conceptually since programming first started. The basic commands of computer programming are the same; what has changed is the language in which these commands can be expressed. The major classes of instructions available in any programming language are:

1. input/output instructions;
2. arithmetic instructions;
3. conditional statements:
$$if\ a = b\ then \ldots$$
4. branching instructions.

A programming language is just a prearranged convention for writing computer-followable recipes. Just as a recipe describes first the ingredients then the instructions, so a program describes first the data, then its processing. The language a person uses to describe a particular process—how to calculate a telephone bill—is too abstract for the machine; the machine's internal language is too detailed for the human. The processing part of the computer is only a mass of on/off switches (known in the trade as 'bits'). The internal language of the processor—the machine code—consists of unique patterns of 'bits', just as Morse code consists of unique patterns of dots and dashes.[1]

The earliest programs—at the 'trailblazing' stage—were not unlike a complex instruction manual written in Morse code. Imagine an operating manual for an automatic camera written in Morse: now the manufacturers of the camera wish to make 'just a minor change' to the specification—perhaps the addition of a flash unit or an increase in the range of shutter speeds. . . . You now know why programmers were reluctant to change programs once written, and why users had to swear on all that is holy not to change their mind once they had signed on the dotted line.

Clearly, such a state of affairs acts as a considerable brake on the development of computer systems. There is little advantage in being able to mass-produce personal computers if nobody can master their use. Consequently, the evolution of 'software'—specifically, programming languages—has been, and continues to be, towards making them easier to use. The easier they are, the more maintainable and flexible the end-product becomes, and the wider the market of people that can use them. The key to the development of easier programming languages is the use of the computer itself to undertake the translation from the abstract language of the human to the detailed language of the computer.

The Hierarchy of Views (Fig. 3.1 on page 13) shows the gap to be covered. The computer's internal machine code is the series of noughts and ones—itself a representation of the two possible physical states of a switch. This is what a program 'looks like' inside the computer. This is also how the earliest programs had to be coded. The crucial step is to interpose a translator between programmer and computer.

The translator may be called an interpreter, assembler, or compiler; the programmer's language may be BASIC, COBOL, PASCAL, or any one of

[1] One of the perils of lecturing internationally is the permanent possibility of unintentional *double entendres*. *Le bit* is French slang for the male sexual organ. I also heard of an English company, owned by a family named Jones, whose telegraphic address was 'Cojones'. This creates amusement in Spanish-speaking countries.

27

a dozen others. But the principle is the same. The key to understanding how to use computers is this: *the more powerful the translator becomes, the less skill is required for programming and the more accessible computers become to the layperson.*

One piece of computer jargon is the expression 'high-level' language. What this means is that one instruction written by a programmer generates a number of machine code instructions. In a 'low-level' language there is a one-for-one translation between the programmer's language and the computer's language. The difference between a high-level and a low-level language is like the difference between an experienced secretary and a 'temp'. The former can translate one statement, 'I have to visit our Paris office on Thursday', into a large number of detailed instructions to book plane tickets, arrange hotel accommodation, currency, and so on; a 'temp' would need to have everything spelled out in detail. Just as the boss is more productive with an experienced secretary to help him, so is a programmer using a high-level language.

To show what this means in practice, Fig. 5.2 shows the same program—for calculating the average of a series of numbers—written in five different languages. It can be seen what is meant by the transition to higher-level languages. Of those shown, only NOMAD is readily usable by the non-computer, or the non-mathematically-minded. NOMAD is an example of a user language. Not only is it extremely concise; it is also user-friendly, in the sense that it uses common English verbs as opposed to the mathematical notation of APL and the pseudo-English of COBOL. If we extend the instructions contained in NOMAD to include those for setting up and updating files, then we can see that it is possible for users to create their own systems independent of technical experts.

It is also possible for people to build a shed in their back garden; this does not mean that they are then well advised to tackle a 30-storey skyscraper, even though the latter performs basically the same function as the former—protecting whatever or whoever is inside from the external elements.

This comparison is meant to imply that, although small programs are built of the same logical components as large ones, there are nevertheless complexities of scale which mean that 'professional' programmers are not yet obsolete. Whereas a user may, in a small application, write his own programs or use some standard program, with larger and more complex systems he is unlikely to do so.

1. ASSEMBLER

```
        TITLE AVERAGE NUMBER PROGRAM
        EXTERN READ,PRINT              ;SUBROUTINES
        NO = 15
        SUM = 1
        CTR = 2
START:  RESET
        JSR READ
        JUMPL NO,FIN                   ;EXIT IF NUMBER ZERO OR LESS
        MOVE SUM,NO                    ;COPY TO SUM
        MOVEI CTR,1                    ;SETUP COUNT OF NUMBERS
REP:    JSR READ                      ;GET NEXT NUMBER
        JUMPL NO,PRIN                  ;GOTO PRINT IF ZERO
        ADDI CTR,1                     ;INCREMENT COUNTER
        JRST REP                       ;GO FOR MORE
PRIN:   IDV SUM,CTR                    ;DIVIDE TO FIND AVERAGE
        MOVE NO,SUM
        JSR PRINT
FIN:    TTCALL 3,[ASCIZ" END OF PROGRAM"]

        END START

        TITLE INPUT NUMBER
        INTERN READ
        FLAG=0
        AC=17
READ:   EXIT
        SETZ NO,
        SETO FLAG,
        TTCALL 3,[ASCIZ" NUMBER PLEASE ?"]
REPT:   TTCALL 0,AC                    ;INPUT A CHARACTER
        CAIGE AC,"0"                   ;GREATER THAN OR EQUAL TO 0
        JRST NOTNUM
        CAILE AC,"9"                   ;LESS THAN OR EQUAL TO 9
        JRST NOTNUM
        SETZ FLAG,                     ;CLEAR FLAG
        SUBI AC,60                     ;CONVERT TO INTEGER
        IMULI NO,^D10                  ;SHIFT 1 LEFT
        ADD NO,AC                      ;ADD NEW DIGIT TO NUMBER
        JRST REPT
NOTUM:  CAIE FLAG,0                    ;IF FLAG IS 0 THEN A NON
                                        NUMERIC 0
        JRST REPT
        JRST @READ                     ;RETURN VIA ENTRY
        END

; SUBROUTINE TO OUTPUT A NUMBER
        TITLE OUTPUT NUMBER
        INTERN PRINT
        FLAG=0
        AC=17
        NO=15
        NOREM=16
        TENS=13
        TENREM=14
PRINT:  EXIT
        CAILE NO,^D                    ;SINGLE DIGIT ?
        JRST MAIN
        ADDI NO,60                     ;CONVERT TO CHARACTER
        TTCALL 1,NO                    ;OUTPUT CHARACTER
        JRST @PRINT                    ;RETURN
MAIN:   MOVE TENS,[^D10000000000]      ;TEN TO THE POWER TEN
        SETO FLAG
REPT:   IDIV NO,TENS
        CAIE FLAG,0                    ;LOOK OUT FOR LEADING ZERO
        JUMPE NO,ZERO                  ;CONVERT TO CHARACTER
        ADDI NO,60                     ;OUTPUT THIS CHARACTER
        TTCALL 1,NO                    ;CLEAR FLAG
        SETZ FLAG,                     ;DECREASE POWER OF TEN
ZERO:   IDIVI TENS,^D10                ;FULLY DIVIDED YET?
        CAIN TENS,0                    ;RETURN
        JRST @PRINT                    ;IDIV REMAINDER TO NO
        MOVE NO,NOREM
        JRST REPT
        END
```

2. COBOL

```
00010   IDENTIFICATION DIVISION
00020   PROGRAM ID                    CALCULATE-MEAN
00030   AUTHOR                        COLIN CORDER
00040   DATE-WRITTEN                  OCTOBER 1985
00050   ENVIRONMENT DIVISION
00060   CONFIGURATION SECTION
00070   SOURCE-COMPUTER               ICBM-99
00080   OBJECT-COMPUTER               ICBM-99
00090   INPUT-OUTPUT SECTION
00100   FILE-CONTROL
00110   SELECT INPUTFILE              ASSIGN TO DISC
00120   SELECT PRINTFILE              ASSIGN TO PRINTER
00130   DATA DIVISION
00140   FILE SECTION
00150   FD INPUTFILE
00160   BLOCK CONTAINS 20 RECORDS
00170   RECORD CONTAINS 6 CHARACTERS
00180   LABEL RECORDS ARE STANDARD
00190   01 DATAREC.
00200   03 NUM                        PIC 9(6)
00210   FD PRINTFILE
00220   BLOCK CONTAINS 1 RECORD
00230   RECORD CONTAINS 132 CHARACTERS
00240   LABEL RECORDS ARE OMITTED
00250   01 PRINT-REC
00260   03 FILLER                     PIC X(17)
00270   03 PRINT-MEAN                 PIC Z(5)9.99
00280   03 FILLER                     PIC X(106)
00290   WORKING-STORAGE SECTION
00300   01 TOTAL                      PIC 9(7)   VALUE ZERO
00310   01 N                          PIC 9(6)   VALUE ZERO
00320   01 MEAN                       PIC(7)V99
00330   01 EOF                        PIC X
00340   88 END-OF-FILE                           VALUE "Y"
00350   PROCEDURE DIVISION
00360   OPEN INPUT INPUTFILE
00370   OPEN OUTPUT PRINTFILE
00380   MOVE "N" TO EOF
00390   PERFORM READ-FILE UNTIL END-OF-FILE
00410   DIVIDE TOTAL BY N GIVING MEAN
00420   MOVE MEAN TO PRINT-MEAN
00430   WRITE PRINT-REC AFTER ADVANCING 2 LINES
00440   CLOSE INPUTFILE PRINTFILE
00450   STOP RUN
00460   READ-FILE
00470   READ DATAFILE AT END MOVE "Y" TO EOF
00480   IF NOT END-OF-FILE ADD 1 TO N
00490   ADD NUM TO TOTAL
```

3. BASIC

```
10  DIM A(100)
20  LET SUM=0
30  INPUT "How many numbers ";N
40  FOR I=1 TO N
50  INPUT "Number Please ";A(I)
60  LET SUM = SUM + A(I)
70  NEXT I
80  PRINT "AVERAGE = ";SUM/N
```

4. APL

$$+ / X \div \rho \ X - \square$$

5. NOMAD

```
READ DIGITS LIST AVG (DIGITS)
```

**Figure 5.2**  Programs to calculate arithmetic mean

The problem then becomes that of the user communicating precisely what a given program has to do, in a form that is unambiguous and intelligible to the programmer. In many instances a systems analyst will act as an intermediary in this process. How far down the Hierarchy of Views an individual user is prepared to go in the development of a system will depend on a number of considerations—the size and complexity of the particular application, the user's own attitude, and the cost he puts on his time.

Enough of the theory. To see how it works in practice I shall take a typical business problem and follow the development of a system to solve it from initiation to implementation. For our purposes we will take an order-processing system in a wine merchant's; it could equally well be a personnel records system in a government department or a billing system for a public utility.

The initial survey of World's Wines as depicted in this book would probably take an experienced systems analyst about four weeks. To keep the text readable I have drastically cut down on detail and thereby oversimplified the problem. The intention is to show how systems are developed rather than make you an expert in the specific problems of wine retailers, or in the minutiae of analysis and design techniques.

One final point. My thesis is that, as computers become more user-friendly, so the skills required to use them change and many come within the layperson's sphere of competence. The book's main emphasis is on the techniques and skills of systems analysis. These skills are present in any person of reasonable intelligence. Nevertheless, the innate ability to do something should not be confused with experience and training in the particular discipline. In the case study, the user has (wisely, in my view) chosen to employ an experienced analyst to assist him. But 'assist' is the operative word. The analyst helps the user to define his requirements and write them down in a way that is clearest to those whose job is to build the system; he helps him in spheres—such as cost estimation, or systems building methods—where the user could never attain competence without giving up his own job to become a systems analyst himself.

Ultimately, however, the user is responsible. The responsibility is discharged by ensuring, through full involvement, that the specification for the system is correct, and by sufficiently understanding how systems are built (or selected) to be able to control progress and quality.

# 6. Case study: World's Wines

World's Wines is a wine and spirits retailer. It was founded in 1970 by Andrew Patterson as a company importing French and German wines. Although originally just an extension of his personal hobby, Patterson's ability to locate good but 'inexpensive' wines led to the company growing well beyond his early expectations. In 1974 he opened his first retail outlet in north London and these have now grown to sixteen. The original handful of trade accounts has increased to 600, all within a radius of 100 miles of the company's head office.

Along with this expansion of the company's market has gone diversification into different product lines, so that now the company's catalogue features some 1200 different products in five categories: wines, spirits, soft drinks, tobacco, and miscellaneous. World's Wines own retail outlets ('branches') send in daily orders to head office. Other orders are received from outside customers.

At head office the orders go first to Don Chichester, the order processing manager and one of the company's longest-serving employees. He credit-checks customer orders before passing them, and branch orders, through to Ted French, in charge of stock records. Here the orders are posted to stock cards by Ted and five clerks. The buying department is advised when any product reaches re-order level. The orders are then passed to Maureen Jones in despatch control. Her section types up a clean copy of the order and runs off six copies which are distributed to various other departments. Two copies go to the warehouse for order assembly. The goods are delivered and an invoice sent to the customer. All procedures are manual, and approximately 200 orders a day are handled, averaging 15 lines each.

Andrew Patterson no longer involves himself in the day-to-day running of the company. He has recently reverted to his initial role of locating good wines. This activity has involved him in periods of increasing length spent in Burgundy and the Rhône Valley. His longstanding connection with local vignerons has culminated in his being elected into Les Compagnons du Beaujolais (motto: *Vuidons les tonneaux*) at Lacenas near Villefranche.

In order to perpetuate this agreeable life-style he has appointed

George Wynne to take over the day-to-day running of the company. George is less of a wine buff and more of a 'scientific' manager, who believes that computerization would help improve the company's order processing and stock control procedures, whereas Andrew Patterson has always distrusted automation.

George calls in a consultant, Stan Breagan, to assist and advise him, while resolving to stay in ultimate control of a project that is central to the company's profitability. Stan Breagan is an independent consultant with no attachment to, or interest in, any supplier of computer hardware or software.

**Extract from conversation between George Wynne and Stan Breagan**

GW   . . . of course, until recently the company's chairman was always opposed to computers. Didn't think them necessary. But now with the new management team—and with computers so cheap these days—I feel it's time we went ahead and got one. The trouble is we know very little about them and how you go about selecting one.

SB   Well, the first thing to do is to define why you think you need one. What problems do you have at the moment that you think a computer might help you solve?

GW   In our view the most urgent problem is with order processing. We're losing sales because the current system cannot get the goods out as fast as we would like. That's the area that needs looking at first. But before we actually get on to that, what I'd like to know is how do we go about it? And if we decide to go ahead with the project how do we control it? You hear so many disaster stories. . . .

SB   Well, different companies go about these things in different ways. What makes most difference is probably the size of the company, and the size of the particular project. But to answer your question, let me draw you a generalized diagram of how any new system is developed.

Any system, whether computer-based or not, goes through three main phases. First of all, somebody has to specify what is required; second, somebody has to design a solution; third, somebody has to build it. For a simple system the same person may do all three. For a complex computer system each of the three phases may be broken down into many individual tasks performed by a large number of different people. In your own

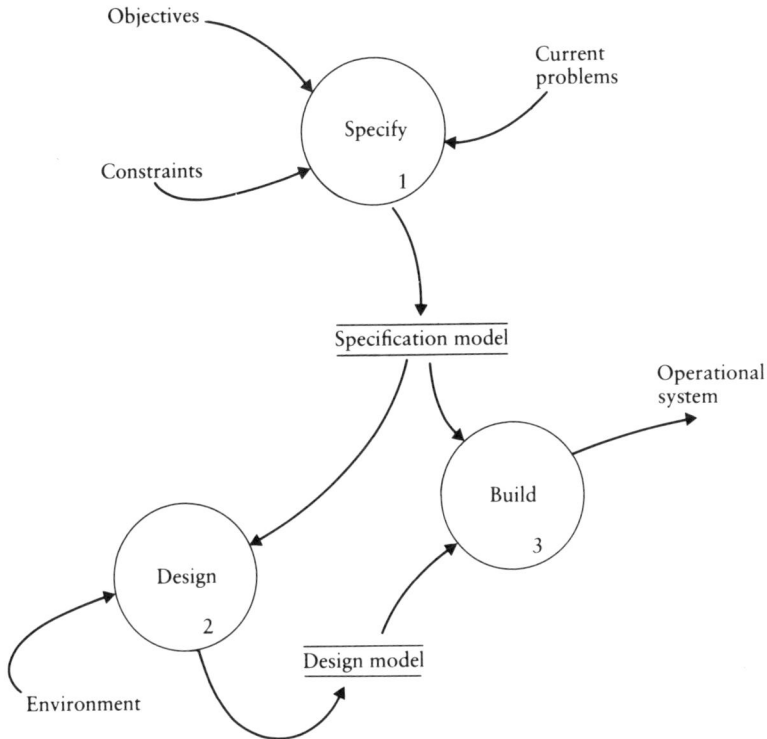

**Figure 6.1** The development framework

case I will certainly rely heavily on you and your managers to specify what you require from the system; I shall also need to work very closely in conjunction with you to design it. After that, we may well go to some third party to build the system for us.

GW These specification and design models on the diagram—what are they?

SB Well, obviously, that is something we're going to come to, but for the moment let us say that the specification model describes what the system has to do, and is therefore expressed mainly in business-orientated terms; the design model, on the other hand, describes in some detail how the system is going to work, and it is from this that the programmers in our case will actually build the system.

GW And what's meant by 'environment'?

SB     Well, by that we just mean the particular set of operating conditions within which the system has to work. This may mean such things as the system having to be installed in many branches, or indeed in many countries; it may be that a particular type of computer hardware is already dictated; it may mean something about the particular aptitudes of the people that are going to be responsible for working the system once it has been installed.

GW     I take it from what you've said that it's mainly up to me to come up with what I want out of the new system. This is what the arrow marked 'objectives' means.

SB     Exactly. The first thing I want to do is to define carefully the scope of the project. Do you want me to undertake an overall review of your data processing requirements over the next decade, bearing in mind convergent technology and the electronic office (GW *faints*)—or just find you a payroll package (*revives*)?

GW     Don't forget that this is our first foray into computers. I don't want to bite off more than we can chew. How much is it going to cost? And there's a lot of non-technical considerations like the impact on staff. . . .

SB     Those are the sort of things we mean by 'constraints'. In specifying the new system, it's just as important to tell us what *can't* be done—i.e., make people redundant, spend more than £50 000—as to define what has to be done. We can take care of all these considerations by drawing up an initial project request. This will be the first stage in the specification phase.

GW     How long will it take to do that?

SB     Probably not more than a couple of days.

GW     OK. Let's go. Can I start you off, or do you want me to call in a couple of my line managers?

SB     Let's start with you and see how it develops. . . .

# 7. Project request

*. . . meet it is I set it down. . . .*

*Hamlet*

Let us start by asking a question: *Is there always one right solution to a given systems problem—or at least one solution that is demonstrably superior to all others?*

If we ask teams of aeronautical engineers working independently in three different continents to design a supersonic aircraft, it is likely, and has been shown to be the case, that their designs—their solutions to the problem—will exhibit striking similarities. The aeroplanes will tend to have slim fuselages and delta-shaped wings. There will be few designs for supersonic bi-planes. The reason for this is obvious. In searching for a solution, the designers are constrained by the laws of aerodynamics. These laws push them towards a certain solution.

What of other types of systems—systems that are not in the scientific field, but in the human field? We observe here a completely different phenomenon. No two countries have identical systems of voting; no two countries have identical tax systems; no two countries have identical legal systems. The reason for this is that such systems are not governed by anything analogous to the physical laws of aerodynamics. Therefore such systems exhibit quite wide diversities, based on history or different cultural or ethnic settings.

What of business, or a computer system in one company? Again, empirical observation suggests that there would be a great variety, as there is a wide diversity of different stock recording, accounts payable, and payroll systems in many different companies. On the other hand, the increasing prevalence of 'packaged', i.e., pre-written, systems leads one to the view that there must be an underlying similarity.

Reverting to one particular company, let us pose the question, If a company identifies a problem with its invoicing or stock control and this problem is presented to three independent groups of analysts, would they come up with identical solutions? Again the answer is 'No'; but it is instructive to see what it is that causes different groups of analysts, faced with the problem, to come up with different solutions. What causes what I term 'systems divergence'? The answer is that divergent solutions may result from a variety of factors: perhaps one group is more experienced, or cleverer, than the others; perhaps one group discovers a key fact that the others have neglected, or makes different assumptions about the future.

If one pursues the argument to its conclusion, it would appear that the system that is implemented as a solution to the user's business problems is a matter of pot luck.

This phenomenon is by no means uncommon with complex systems. If you ask 20 different economists to design a system to run a country's economy, you will get 20 different solutions. However, this is clearly not totally satisfactory from the user's point of view. It would be comforting to think that there is a best, if not perfect, solution to a given problem; and that different experts would ultimately converge upon this solution, provided the problem is accurately and exhaustively defined. We can term this process 'systems convergence'.

Systems *divergence* results from inadequate specification or faulty analysis of a problem, together with superficial investigation and arbitrary design; systems *convergence* results from clear definition, good investigation, and close consultation with the user during the design phase. In our study of World's Wines we shall see this process at work. We will see that the more clearly both the current problems and the user's requirements for the new system are specified the more we home in on one solution.

A comparison often made is that between the development of a computer system and the construction of a house or factory. The systems analyst is the architect. A well-known architectural axiom is 'Form follows function.' To paraphrase this school of thought (with apologies to its founders), if you are a 6 ft 7 in. energy conservationist, married to a naturist wife with a teenage son who likes to play rock music at a large number of decibels and an elderly relative confined to a bath chair with gout, then the design of your house will be determined by these. Giving your set of requirements to three different architects would result in highly convergent systems (solar energy, high doorways, misted windows, soundproofing and lack of stairs). By analogy, if users exhaustively define all the functions of a given computer system, designers will converge on similar solutions.

The first area where we see this happen in a computer project is the *project request*. This will initially specify the system, as one can specify any system, as a set of objectives to be met within a given set of constraints. Identifying these and agreeing them with the user is a clear step towards systems convergence.

The project request defines the problem to be solved. It is a written statement by the user of his current problems and system objectives. The reason for this document is two-fold. It forces the user to become involved, and it ensures that his requirements are down in writing. The document may be known by a variety of names in different companies—'statement of requirements' and 'problem definition' are common. What it does is to define the area of initial survey and what is to be studied.

The systems task is to alter the environment within which the user conducts his business, or runs his department. It is sensible, therefore, to specify the desired end state. This is done formally under a set of headings that experience has shown to be essential. Definition of the current state then serves to delineate the area of the problem. We may usefully define the problem area as the difference between the existing state and the desired state.

The project request formally defines this area, and can therefore be regarded as the terms of reference for the feasibility study. Writing the project request should consume only a couple of days. It is possible that this may be the end of the story. If there is contention for resources to undertake feasibility studies in an organization, there may have to be a sifting process at this stage. For this reason, many companies demand an outline statement of anticipated benefits even this early.

The contents of our project request will be:

Study area (systems boundary)
Current system
   Data
   Processes
   Problems
Desired system
   Objectives
   Constraints
   Time-scale
Future business environment

The project request is manifestly the province of the user. He is the only person who can properly originate such a document; George Wynne has got Stan to assist and guide him, but it is for George to determine in business terms what he wants. He will start by defining the boundary of the project.

## 1. Boundaries

You decide to strip out and replace the wiring system in your house. You have promised your spouse that it will all be completed over one holiday weekend. Unfortunately, in the process of carrying out the work, you come across some problems with the plumbing. As you have already got the floorboards up, you decide it would be sensible to fix the pipes at the same time as the wiring. Taken by itself, this is a perfectly rational decision. The problem is that in so doing you increase the work to the point where the wiring is not done by the time your important house-guests arrive. Your plea of good intentions falls on deaf ears.

Any computer person will recognize the scenario. You start off on a simple payroll system to be implemented within 12 months; you end up with a personnel records system three years later. Systems grow like Topsy. This fact is often highly convenient for those involved in the development work (particularly if on a fixed-price contract), as it supplies the perfect answer to the question as to why the original estimates of time and money were exceeded by a factor of two. But it is no way to run a project.

If users keep adding new requirements, or involving other business areas in the end system, project control becomes impossible. Our intention must be to define as carefully as possible the boundaries of the system at the outset, recognizing that any major changes to these can only result in a modification of the project plan, usually by extending the time-scale and increasing the cost. That is not the same thing as saying that we 'freeze' the specification at this stage: this is clearly impractical. It means that we recognize that changes are likely to incur penalties, so we try as hard as possible to establish boundaries and stick to them. However, one's method of project control must recognize that some such changes—changes also to objectives and constraints—will occur, and must be able to cope with them. Our methods of actually doing the work—analysis, design, and building—must be flexible enough to minimize the penalties.

Note that, although the boundaries that are being defined are of the area of the company's activities where a new system will be installed— the so-called 'domain of change'—the feasibility study itself will extend beyond this to examine the impact of any such change on those other systems that interface with it. In fact, from the user standpoint it is often easier to think in terms of a guaranteed 'domain of no change', beyond which any changes resulting from the new system will not impact.

## 2. Current problems

Having defined the area of study, the obvious starting point is the problems which exist in the current system and which have brought about the survey. (If you feel that 'problems' is too negative a word for your well-run department, then you may care to refer to them as 'opportunity areas'.) It is clearly exclusively the province of the user to identify his problems. Beyond that they must also be defined. A problem clearly and accurately defined is well on the way to being solved. Subsequently the user will quantify the problem and then analyse it to determine its exact causes. The nature of problem analysis will be discussed in depth later.

Here is an early example of the process:

(a) *Identify*: 'Control of finished stocks is becoming an increasing problem for us.'

(b) *Define*: 'Finished stocks are items cleared by production and awaiting despatch to customers.'

(c) *Quantify*: 'Stocks have increased from £1.2 million to £1.8 million over the last twelve months.'

(d) *Analyse*: 'The increase is due to two factors:
  - production schedules have been based on over-optimistic sales forecasts;
  - our customers are reducing their own stock holdings in response to their own increased costs.'

## 3. Objectives

These comprise the formalization of what has been said earlier about the need to define what one is trying to achieve. The systems objectives are the most important of the set of variables that describe, or make a model of, the proposed system. Until these have been defined, the analyst or user has a blank canvas before him, just as an architect does until one starts to describe the sort of house one wants. Until this time there is an infinity of solutions open to the systems designer. Each objective, constraint, or other limiting descriptor reduces this infinity, first to a large finite number, and then, as more detailed requirements are established, to the one system that best meets the user's objectives within the constraints imposed by him.

Sherlock Holmes used to work on the theory, when seeking a murderer, that you should first identify all possible suspects, then eliminate them one by one: the one that remains is the murderer. This process of elimination can be seen at work in the designer's role. He starts off knowing that he is looking for an inventory management system. Immediately prior to defining the project request, the appropriate solution could be anything from a loose-leaf folder of stock records to a complex computer-based system comprising 200 terminals linked to a massive centralized data base, complete with Trigg Tracking, Box-Jenkins coefficients, and exponential smoothing. Definition of the systems objectives narrows down the search.

Objectives should be clear, quantified and realistic. Here is a good example:

> I propose that before the end of this decade this nation should put a man on the Moon and then return him safely to Earth. (President J. F. Kennedy)

Note the completeness of the definition. Sending a man to the moon without getting him back safely is an altogether different proposition. The statement includes a clear time-scale but no cost constraints. It is wonderful what you can do without the latter.

Objectives should be non-conflicting. Where a system cuts across departmental boundaries, and one is dealing not with one user but many, it is easy to set objectives that potentially conflict with each other. Conflicts emerge between production and sales, finance and production, requiring the analyst to devise a system that reduces stocks by 20 per cent while at the same time increasing the service level to the customer from 75 to 90 per cent. Though this is theoretically possible (i.e., if the company had its money tied up in the wrong product lines), it is more likely that one advantage is a trade-off against the other. This trade-off is a managerial, not technical, decision.

It is advisable strictly to limit the number of objectives that any system is to pursue. My experience is that for practical purposes three is the maximum. Above this number I usually find either conflicts among the objectives or confusion between means and ends.

The latter, which is very prevalent and betrays sloppy thinking, can be illustrated by the following example. The systems objectives are:

1. to reduce value of finished stocks by 10 per cent;
2. to cut staff costs by 15 per cent;
3. to reduce paperwork;
4. to standardize stock issue procedures.

The first two of these are valid objectives. The third and fourth (quite apart from their vagueness) are two of the possible means by which the real objectives may be attained. A simple test will normally suffice to show the difference. Compare these two statements made about a system resulting from the above objectives:

'We reduced stocks and cut staff costs by the required amount; unfortunately, we were unable to reduce paperwork or eliminate many of the non-standard procedures.'

'We reduced paperwork substantially and streamlined many of the procedures; the bad news is, we didn't manage to reduce either stockholding or staff costs.'

If you ask the user which of these two statements he prefers, you quickly discover the difference between means and ends.

The argument about means and ends is one that I frequently encounter. You can argue perfectly logically that 'reducing staff costs' is itself a means to the higher end of 'increasing company profitability'. This is true. It is equally true that 'increasing company profitability' is not an end in itself. The question, Why do this?, always requires a higher-level objective as an answer. Continuing this line of questioning ultimately leads to a statement of the type, 'to maximize the sum of human happiness'. Admirable though it is to question all assumptions, the objective 'maximize human happiness' is of questionable usefulness to the designer of a company general ledger system.

What this shows is that the level of the objectives must match the level of the project. A stock control system will require objectives about the level of stockholding and about customer service. Objectives to improve corporate return on capital employed are too high to be directive; objectives to reduce form-filling are too low to be relevant.

Following my theme that the best way to become a systems analyst is to study systems and not computers, I suggest that the reader examine systems such as tax and education systems, which are political footballs. Where there is a lack of agreement between the parties on systems objectives, the designer's job is impossible, and the operational systems are subjected to continual re-design and maintenance. The observation that Mussolini made the trains run on time is merely an illustration of how much easier systems design is when one is freed from constraints— in this case, those of a democracy.

## 4. Constraints
Objectives define what the system has to achieve. Constraints are what

41

it *cannot* do. Some constraints apply to the project—'The development cost must not exceed £50 000'; others to the system—'No staff are to be made redundant.' Whichever applies, they serve the same function as objectives in narrowing choice. If an objective of overnight turn-round of orders limits the area of possible solutions, so too does the injunction, 'The system must not cost more than £50 000 to develop and implement.' In many cases the objectives may turn out to be unattainable within the constraints (a familiar position for any manager or politician), but it is for the feasibility study to determine this. At the moment we are still dealing with the project request, i.e., with what the user wants; the actual feasibility of the requirements will be examined at the next stage. But it is a meaningless exercise to define objectives without at the same time defining constraints.

## MONEY

The most obvious constraint is that of money. It is essential to have at least a 'ballpark' figure for the anticipated one-time cost. Frequently, however, this is not made explicit at this stage, the user preferring to leave financial constraints implied. This may be because he genuinely has no yardstick by which to measure this type of project, or because he has an innate feeling that any figure he mentions is going to serve as the minimum cost, much as a government-supplied norm for wage increases rapidly becomes the starting point for union negotiations. Equally, any figure quoted for return on investment or payout period will merely serve as the analyst's target to which to 'back-fit' the figures when he comes to the cost–benefit analysis.

The most reasonable position is for the user to ask for a range of solutions covering a range of costs. The user has made no commitment (even implied) by asking, 'What system would I get for £50 000? for £75 000? What additional advantages accompany each increment in cost?'

## PEOPLE

Increasingly, people have to be recognized as a constraint on the freedom to design systems. Any system has to be acceptable to, and workable by, those who will be involved with it on a day-to-day basis. These two points can be summarized by referring to people's *attitudes* and their *aptitudes*.

The aptitude of people using the system, or supplying data to it, dictates, for example, that source documents must not be so complex as to exceed the capacity of the person required to complete them. This constraint is particularly felt where the originators are the general public and therefore outside the range of training in the system. It may well be a significant consideration if we are designing a system to be installed in many different countries.

Consideration of people's attitudes towards a new system is equally fundamental. Computers bring change. Resistance to change may be personal or institutionalized. Trade unions may impose tight constraints on the redeployment of staff, or demand additional payment for new responsibilities. In one system in my experience the designer was precluded by the unions from putting terminals on managers' desks. Company policy may preclude redundancies, in which case the system cannot be cost-justified on staff savings unless the displaced staff have been genuinely redeployed.

HARDWARE

When designing a system within a company that already has a computer, one is usually constrained by the existing hardware. The best solution to the problem may be to install a minicomputer in the particular department concerned, dedicated to that department's work. However, if the company has already invested a large amount of capital in a mainframe computer, it is likely that there will be pressure—most probably from the accountant—for any new system to be implemented on this computer. If the technical case for the minicomputer-based system is strong or overwhelming, then we have a political battle on our hands.

Such battles are by no means uncommon. Most large companies have large mainframe computers, often with spare capacity. A holding company in a conglomerate with smaller operating companies may lay down a company policy that all systems are to be implemented on the central computer. This clearly brings about systems convergence (by reducing options), although not necessarily convergence on an optimal system. It is an example of the axiom that designers are invariably in the position of designing not the *best possible system*, but the *best system possible*, i.e., designing the best system that one can get within the restraints imposed by management.

PRIVACY AND SECURITY

Since computers are basically information-handlers, the question of access to information arises. Many countries have legislation for data protection with which systems must comply. Stringent design measures may need to be taken if the system has to maintain strict privacy. Allied to this is the matter of security. Are there any particular security considerations that must be borne in mind when examining potential solutions? One can formulate a general rule that the complexity of systems increases—in most cases, exponentially—with the need for security. This is at its greatest where an end-user or outsider has a financial incentive to beat the system, i.e., an inducement to fraud. Betting systems, such as tote systems or football pools, are inherently simple, involving the most trivial matching and arithmetic processes. That they are, in practice, the most complex of systems is because anyone succeeding in placing a bet after the matches have been played, or the race run, stands to make himself substantially better off. And there are many things that a potential beneficiary of £500 000 will do— including splitting it three ways with the operations manager and maintenance programmer!

Consider income tax. Here we have a system which virtually every single end-user is trying to defeat. If every taxpayer paid up with a glad heart, pleased to do his bit towards funding government expenditure, the system would be extremely simple; with everyone trying to beat it, it becomes unmanageably complex.


## 5. Time-scale

The time-scale within which a system must be operational is also a constraint on its development. It is to underline the importance of this particular constraint that I have given it a separate heading. More computer projects fail as a result of highly optimistic, if not plain impossible, deadlines than from any other single cause.

If your objective is a highly complex seat reservations system for an international airline, it will not be ready in less than two years—not even if you thump the table and insist that it must be. The type of manager who imagines that an order given, and repeated with sufficient force, will be self-implementing is like the person in a foreign country who thinks the natives will understand him if he speaks louder.

As with costs, one can argue that it is not necessary to include it in the project request. Why not examine the systems objectives and other constraints and then come back with a proposed system plus time-scale for implementation? The first answer to this is that some guidance is better than none. There is no point in coming up with some perfect solution which can be implemented in ten years' time.

Second, when dealing with computers a golden rule is to make things *explicit* rather than *implicit*. In some projects the time-scale may be the most important single variable to be taken into account. As I write, the European Space Agency is engaged on a project to send a satellite to intercept with Halley's Comet in 1986. If the 'launch window' is missed, they will have to wait 76 years for another chance! With a computer system this would occur, for instance, if the system—or system modification—had to be completed by a specified deadline such as the start of a financial year. If this leaves you with only six months to do a complete systems re-write, the delivered system will perforce be a simple one, meeting only the most critical user requirements. Those of lower priority will have to be introduced afterwards.

However, an immutable deadline is the exception rather than the rule. A desired time-scale should be indicated, with particular attention paid to times of the year when the system cannot be implemented, e.g., pre-Christmas, and then these can be taken account of in the feasibility study without the project being doomed by an impossible deadline before it has even started.

## 6. The future business environment

Any new system that we implement is unlikely to be in operation in under six months and will be expected to have a life of at least five years in order to recover the investment in it. When we come to systems design, we shall therefore be required to build a system that will meet the company's needs not only now but for a period of up to possibly ten years in the future.

It follows from this that a view must be taken about the future—a view, or set of assumptions, that can only be provided by top management. We shall make every effort, by exhaustive analysis of the business data, to build a flexible system, but this itself involves forecasting.

It is axiomatic that, the further ahead one attempts to forecast, the greater is the likelihood and extent of error. Other disciplines confront the same difficulties as computer people, frequently in worse form. Traffic planners have to look decades ahead. People planning social policy may have to base their decisions and plans on predictions of the birth rate. Unanticipated variations in the latter can cause unemployment among schoolteachers after a time-lag of ten years or more. And both traffic and educational systems are considerably less easily modifiable than business systems.

Any system that requires a lead-time for development, and that then has to have a systems life of at least five years, cannot be designed without formulating assumptions about the future. It helps to have a checklist of headings under which to consider the problem. The most important of these are as follows:

GROWTH

The number of the various entities—employees, customers, products— and the number of transactions that relate to these are both of paramount importance. In some cases assumptions about the growth of numbers may dictate the decision between a manual and computer solution, or between a micro and a mini. They will certainly affect the cost–benefit analysis.

In general terms, the higher the volume of transactions, the more attractive the cost–benefit analysis will appear, because the one-time development cost will be spread over a greater level of business.

ORGANIZATION POLICY

Corporate policy changes. It does so in response to external changes in the economy—in the price of supplies, in government legislation or pressure group activity, in the search for better products and new markets. Computer systems dislike change. Research has shown that it can be up to 200 times more costly to make a change to a system that has gone live than to make it at the specification stage. The cost rises exponentially through the various phases of the systems development cycle.

We should therefore strive to identify any changes of corporate policy that may affect the system both during and after implementation. These vary from one company to another, and the user is best positioned to predict them in his own operations. Typical will be such things as diversification into new product areas or new markets, company reorganization such as the decentralization of functions previously retained in head office, new policies such as a shift in modes of payment from cash or cheques towards credit transfers or charge accounts.

In the case of World's Wines, the type of decision that would drastically affect any new system would be a decision to change from having one central warehouse to holding stock at a number of decentralized depots. The question as to whether or not to design this option into a new system should be resolved at an early stage.

EXTERNAL CHANGES

We have seen that changes in the external environment occasion changes in company policy that impact systems design. There is normally a considerable time-lag, except in the most dynamic companies, between the external change and the company's reaction to it. But many changes in the environment affect the system directly and quickly. Many of these are technological; most reflect some change in relative costs. As energy costs escalate and the costs of data transmission fall, it becomes cheaper to move data than people. This is bound ultimately to affect the way we do business. Why catch the 7.45 to town every morning to get to your data when it is easier and cheaper to get your data to you? Just as an increase in the price of oil affects operational investment decisions by making previously uneconomic energy sources profitable, so falling computer hardware costs and rising people costs dramatically affect systems decisions in data processing.

There are innumerable instances at the company level of external changes drastically affecting the company's business. My personal favourite is the company that manufactured plastic drinking straws. The managing director turned on the radio one morning to discover that the new Conservative Minister for Education, a certain Mrs Thatcher, had, at a stroke of the ministerial pen, abolished state-supplied school milk for the over-sevens, thereby eliminating 50 per cent of the company's market. A rapid diversification into plastic straw dollies ensued. A second was the effect of the ending of the Vietnam war on Hong Kong brothels—an equally dramatic market erosion, with more limited opportunities for diversification.

The same thing happens with systems. With manual systems, which adapt more easily, there is not the same compulsion to get the system right first time. With computer systems there is a case for employing a clairvoyant to formulate a set of assumptions on anything from consumer behaviour to the price of oil, from developments in voice recognition systems to the winner of the next election.

The secret of running a successful business, and equally of designing a successful system, is to identify as clearly as possible all the various considerations prior to making the decision, but then to keep them constantly under review. The implication of this for project control of

47

computer systems is fundamental, but is inadequately observed in practice. The feasibility study is merely the first look at the assumptions, leading to the first draft of a solution. All assumptions, all problem analysis, all design decisions must continue to be reviewed formally at preset checkpoints in the systems development cycle.

The second observation that results from our analysis of predicting the future is this. The further into the future that we attempt to predict, the more wrong we are likely to be. The conclusion that this leads to is two-fold. First, we must accept that changes to the system are the norm, not an aberration from the norm. We must therefore go about the design task in a way that recognizes this fact and constructs the system accordingly, i.e., so as to design inbuilt flexibility.

The second conclusion is that we should design *modest* systems. The usual adjective is 'simple'. Having failed to find a 'simple' computer system in 15 years of looking, I prefer the word 'modest' to describe systems that have carefully prescribed boundaries, encompass limited objectives, and can as a result be implemented within a reasonably short time-scale.

Again, we are adopting conclusions already arrived at in the other spheres. Just as 'small is beautiful' and vast bureaucracies and centralized organizations are increasingly seen as obsolescent, so we need smaller user-orientated systems to replace the massive all-singing, all-dancing systems of the seventies. The next ten years in computing, fuelled by the spread of cheap data processing, will bring about a revolution. Its chief manifestation will be that users will appreciate that they are in charge of their own destiny, and that success or failure will be largely a function of the effort that they apply to this.

Let us return to the problems of World's Wines. After a day's discussions, Stan Breagan has drawn up the following document.

---

### World's Wines—Project request

#### 1. Boundaries
The feasibility study will cover all procedures from origination of order through to delivery and invoicing. This investigation will examine the associated applications of sales ledger and purchase ledger although it is not envisaged that these will be computerized in Phase 1. Any new system will incorporate stock recording while leaving decisions on stock

control in the hands of the buyers. Such decisions will be assisted by the management information specified in 2(c) below.

## 2. Outline of current problems

The existing order processing system processes daily orders from own retail outlets and external customers. The processes involved are:

credit checking,
stock recording,
order assembly,
delivery,
invoicing.

The system deals with approximately 3000 order lines per day, peaking to 4000 at certain times.

The problems identified in the current system are as follows:

(a) DELAYS IN TURN-ROUND

Branch orders, which receive precedence, take from two to four days to deliver. This causes overstocking by branch managers, with a consequent reduction in the number of different lines stocked. This is causing loss of sales.

External orders are taking from two to eight days to deliver. Owing to increased competition, this is beginning to result in erosion of market position.

(b) EXCESSIVE COSTS

Although no precise figures are currently available, the clerical cost of processing orders is considered excessive. This is attributed to the manual system, which is highly labour-intensive. Second, inefficiencies have been identified in the flow and quality of information to the order assembly and distribution functions. These are held to result in higher warehousing and transport costs than necessary.

(c) LACK OF MANAGEMENT INFORMATION

In the past, the company has been run with an informal management style relying heavily on personal contact at all levels of management. With pressure on profit margins, there is now a demand for more regular, statistical information, particularly in the areas of sales analysis and stock profiling.

## 3. Objectives of new system
(a) IMPROVE ORDER TURN-ROUND

Turn-round is defined as the elapsed time between origination of an order and receipt of the goods. The desired turn-round is:

Branch orders:    36 hours; i.e., an order placed on a Monday evening would be delivered prior to shop opening on Wednesday at the latest

External orders: 48 hours

N.B. In both cases it is assumed that orders posted within the company's area of operations before 8 p.m. will arrive at the head office the following morning.

(b) REDUCE OPERATING COSTS

Although precise figures have not yet been established, it is hoped to effect cost savings of at least 20 per cent in the processing of orders, and 10 per cent in both order assembly and distribution.

(c) IMPROVE MANAGEMENT CONTROL

Better statistics are required in order to assist management in its overall objective of improving company profitability.

The two areas where the investigation will be concentrated are those of sales and stock reporting.

*Sales reporting*

Monthly figures for sales and profit broken down by product category within branch or sales territory.

*Stock reporting*

A monthly stock valuation at cost and sales price, with breakdown by product category; detailed movement statistics for buyers; provision for immediate information on specified product lines.

## 4. Constraints
(a) COST OF SYSTEM

The proposed system should be delivered within an overall budget of £60 000. This figure is to include all hardware costs, systems development, training, and implementation. The operational system, after allowing for all associated costs including systems maintenance, should show a discounted return on investment of not less than 40 per cent.

(b) HARDWARE

The company has no computer at present. It is assumed that it will acquire its own computer to be installed on-site. No constraint exists on choice of manufacturer.

(c) SYSTEMS SECURITY

Order processing is at the heart of the company's business. It is therefore essential that the system should not be non-operational for any extended period without an adequate fall-back system.

(d) PERSONNEL

It is essential to take account of the fact that, with the single exception of the company payroll, which is processed by a bureau, the company has no experience of computer systems. This means that full allowance must be made for retraining, and that the initial system should not be over-complex. The company has a history of good labour relations, and full consultations with unions and staff will be held as appropriate.

## 5. Time-scale

Any new system requiring extensive procedural changes should be implemented immediately after the company year-end in January, or in the period May–October. Because of the existing pressures on the order processing system and increased workload in the coming year caused by new branch openings, it is imperative that the new system enabling us to process orders, produce dispatch documentation, and maintain stock records is operational within 12 months at the latest. It is desirable that procedures for invoicing and for management information are implemented as soon after this date as possible.

## 6. Future business environment

For the purposes of the initial study, the following assumptions will be made:

- The policy of one centralized depot will be maintained.
- The number of product lines will be increased from 1200 to 1600 over the next five years without major diversification of product types.
- The area of operations for external customers will be expanded to a radius of 150 miles from head office.
- New retail outlets will be opened at the rate of one a year.

51

## 7. Project outline
For further discussion.

Let us take a checkpoint. The user, in consultation with a systems analyst, has specified what the ultimate system should look like. It has not taken up a great deal of time, nor is it precise in every detail. But it is sufficient to enable a feasibility study to be carried out and a range of options to be studied.

# 8. Systems investigation

*Time spent on reconnaissance is never wasted.*

Military maxim

GW    Well, Stan, I've had a look at the project request. I've also shown it to one or two other people, and there seems to be pretty general agreement. I see that you put 'subject to further discussion' under the heading 'Project outline'. . . .

SB    Yes. Although we identified the boundaries of the system as a whole, I wanted to be sure that we agreed upon how far I am to go in the next stage and what you expect from it. Some people regard the next stage as merely producing a functional specification and outline cost–benefit analysis; others expect it to include systems design and selection of computer.

GW    Well, I'm a great believer in the Latin tag, 'festina lente'.

SB    'Festina' what?

GW    Lente—it means 'hasten slowly'. You computer people are so illiterate. . . . What I'm saying is that everything I've heard about computers convinces me that it is a high-risk undertaking. What I want to know is, how can I limit the extent of the risk to which my company is exposed at any one point in the project?

SB    You limit your risk by not rushing your fences, which is presumably what your quote meant. At each stage we will agree on what I like to call a 'model' of the system. As we go on, so the models will get increasingly detailed. But at each checkpoint you will approve the work done so far and commit yourself only up to the next agreed checkpoint. That way you don't sign a blank cheque. Let's go back to the diagram we looked at last time [Fig. 6.1].

As I said at the time, the diagram is a very high-level view. Now that I've had a preliminary look at your business and got an idea of the size of the particular project, I can draw up a more detailed model [Fig. 8.1]. We've just done the initial project request and now, provided you agree with it, we will go on to the next two steps, which are to do an investigation of the current system and at the same time to talk to your managers to identify their information requirements in greater detail. The first of these

53

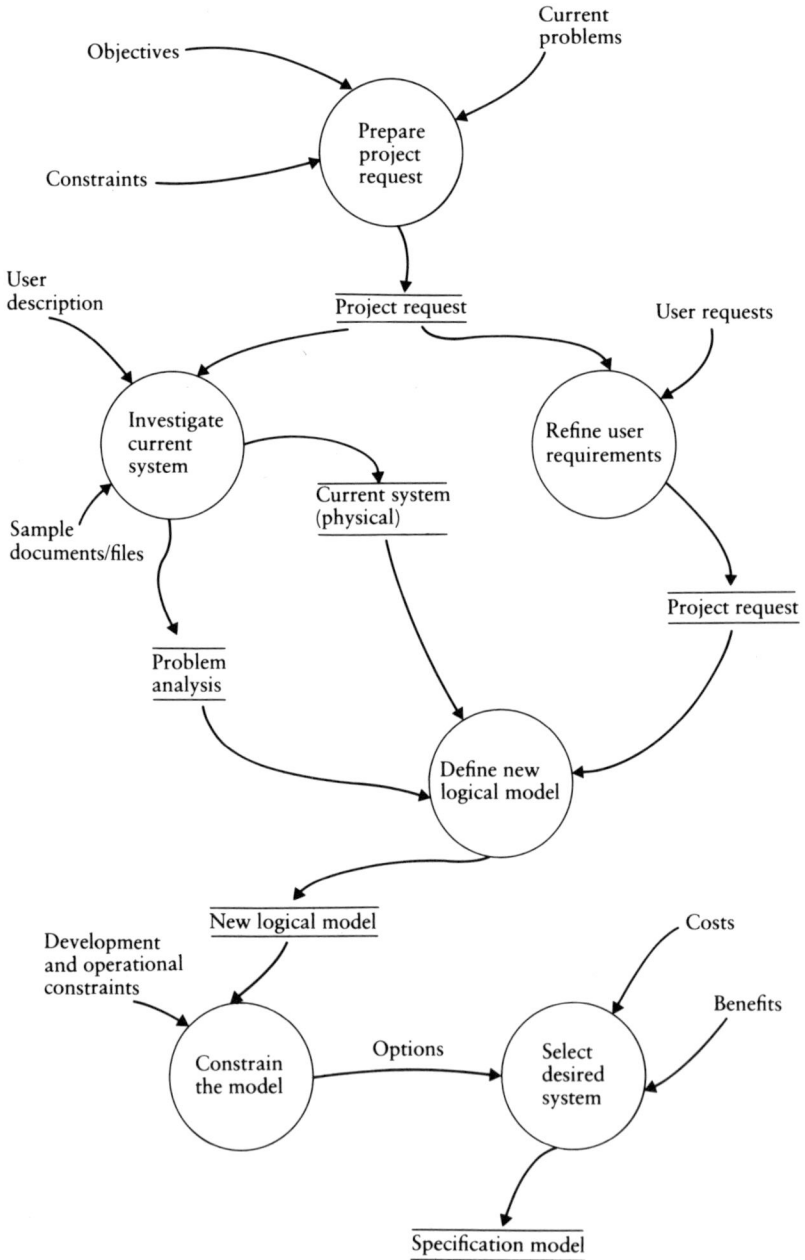

**Figure 8.1**  Producing the specification model

will result in a documentation of the current system in terms of a physical model, that is to say, a model of how it works. Working from that we can then see the problems in the current system and, by taking these, together with any new requirements, we can consider what shape the new system will take.

GW  Is that what you mean by 'Define new logical model'?

SB  That's it. This new logical model will be a clear representation of what you, the user, want the new system to do.

GW  But how can I do that? Surely you need some level of expertise in computers to be able to design a new system?

SB  Of course. But I didn't say 'design' new logical model; I said 'define' new logical model. We are defining what we want the new system to do, not how it is going to do it.

GW  But isn't that all a bit academic? I mean, it is no good defining something that's going to require 20 man-years to build.

SB  Obviously not. And that is why the next activity shown on the diagram is to constrain the logical model. In defining the logical model we work on the premise of 'perfect technology'. This enables us to define what the user would have in a perfect world.[1] We can then come back and look at all the various constraints of cost, time-scales, equipment, etc., which force us into design compromises. These will be expressed as a range of possible physical solutions. We can then examine these from the standpoint of costs and benefits in order to see which should form the basis of the specification model.

### Systems investigation

The essential prerequisite of designing any new system is a thorough knowledge of the system which it will replace. This is true even if your approach is to go for a 'package' system as opposed to developing your own.

At the general business level, it is important to be familiar with the environment within which the system operates. Who are the users?

---

[1] For this very useful concept see S. M. McMenamin and J. F. Palmer, *Essential Systems Analysis*, Yourdon Press, 1984. The idea of 'perfect technology' is analogous to an economist's use of 'perfect competition'—that is, a state which does not exist but which enables us to be very clear about what would ideally be the case, and against which we can then measure the compromises enforced by the real world. Such a model would maximize both costs and benefits. The subsequent trade-offs can then be evaluated much more clearly.

What are the characteristics of staff, customers, suppliers, contractors? At the detailed level, it is essential to identify all the quirks of the current system, all the hidden *exceptions* on which a computer system will founder unless they are identified and either incorporated in the new system or abolished. Much of the information will be quantitative—how many documents, how long to process; some will be qualitative—why things are done in one 'way in preference to another.

The important thing about any investigation is to know what you are looking for. There are innumerable pieces of data in any system ranging from the almost certainly relevant—the number of products on the stock file—to the almost certainly irrelevant—the date of birth of the warehouse manager. Since it is an impossibility to gather all the facts, one must select those which appear most pertinent. This judgement can only be made by asking what problem we are trying to solve. This is true in all disciplines. One of the best groundings for systems analysis is philosophy. Here is Brian Magee summarizing Karl Popper's theory of 'Objective Knowledge':

> One learns to work hard and long at the formulation of problems before one switches one's main attention to the search for possible solutions; and one's degree of success in the latter is often determined by one's degree of success in the former.

We will conduct our investigation first by understanding the workings of the current system, then by examining where the problems are occurring and what is causing them.

There is a variety of ways of investigating a system. The most widely employed is that of interviewing the people who are directly involved in its running. As a back-up or extension to this, we may circulate questionnaires (if the views of a large number of people are required); we may employ work study methods of observation, counting of documents; in desperation, we may even put our trust in the company's procedure manual. One need hardly add that, whatever method, or methods, are used, it is of the foremost importance to check the accuracy of all information.

Let us start our investigation of World's Wines. An obvious starting point is to decide whom we wish to talk to. The company organization chart will show us who does what (see Fig. 8.2). From this, it appears that those people most directly involved are the order processing manager, the warehouse manager, the sales manager, the head buyer, and their various subordinates. As we are concerned with order

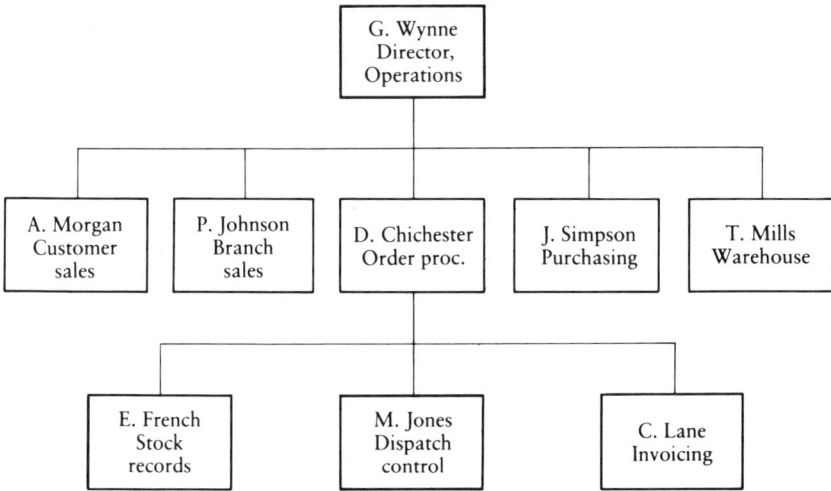

**Figure 8.2** World's Wines: organization chart

processing, the manager of the department of this name seems an obvious starting point.

### Transcript of part of interview between Stan Breagan and Don Chichester, Order Processing Manager

DC Most orders come in through the post. Occasionally a 'rep' may phone in an order to the sales office, and they will write it on our standard order form and send it through to me.

SB Do you have a sample of your standard form? (*takes one*) Do all orders come in on this?

DC All branch orders and those customer orders that are taken by the reps. Otherwise customers' orders may come in any form.

SB Does this cause you any problems?

DC Only if they haven't quoted the product code.

SB And what happens to the orders?

DC Well, first of all I do a credit check on any large customer orders. If there's any problem I pass it to accounts to look into. Otherwise I pass them all on to Ted.

SB Ted, that's Mr French.

DC Yes.

SB What does he do with them?

DC   Well, he's got himself and half-a-dozen stock clerks. Their basic function is to keep the stock records up to date. They post all orders to the stock cards and at the same time write the price of the individual products on to the order form.

SB   And what would happen if you were out of stock?

DC   Normally the clerk would make out a back order which will be filed and satisfied when fresh stock arrives.

SB   What next?

DC   After the orders have been posted to the ledger, they go to dispatch control. This section, which is really just a typing pool plus photocopier, types a master copy of the order and runs off copies for the warehouse, transport department, invoicing, sales, and buyers. The warehouse gets two copies—the delivery note and advice note—which are used first as picking documents. The transport copy is used for scheduling the vans—when the orders are delivered, the customer keeps the advice note but signs and returns the delivery note. This is then sent to the invoicing section. They have filed their copies of the order, as invoices are not extended and sent out until the goods have been received and signed for by the customer.

There is obviously much more to the system than this outline sketch.[1] But whatever its shortcomings, we may take the above interview as reasonably typical of its kind. It is how a user would describe what occurs in his department. If we analyse the description of the system, we can see that the system comprises the two elements we have discussed before,

– data (grouped in documents and files) and
– processes (things done to the data),

together with physical items, such as goods.

---

[1] In passing, let me point out that for interviewing style Stan scores well for his unobtrusive prompting, but badly on supplementaries. Anyone can get an overall impression of how a system works, because the user will tell him. But ultimately we will want not an overall impression but detailed knowledge—which means spotting the exceptions. How do you do this? By listening. The word 'normally' (just like 'for the most part', 'generally speaking' and a host of others) is a giveaway. The stock clerks 'normally' make out a back order: the next question should have been, 'What else might they do?'

The processing part of the system is a series of transformations of input data to output data.

This view is true of both the current system and of any new system. In a very small system one person can handle all data and keep the rules for the transformations in his or her own head. In larger systems, particularly very large systems (for example, airline seat reservation systems), there will be hundreds of documents, files, messages, screen displays, and processes, and many people would have to be interviewed to document the system.

### Documenting the system

Before we contemplate making changes to a system, we must have a complete understanding of how that system works. This is the *raison d'être* of any systems investigation. Since this is mostly carried out by interviewing, the common method of describing systems is by means of narrative. However, narrative falls down either when there is a very large system or when there are many conditional statements, i.e., statements of the nature, 'if this is true then do this'. Most disasters in systems, particularly in computer systems, stem from failures of communication between users and analysts and between analysts and implementers. Clearly, what we need is a means of communication which is both intelligible to the user and sufficiently rigorous for the technical expert. Again, this is a problem that existed well before the advent of computers. A study of how other disciplines have overcome this shows that there are four common methods:

1. by giving an overview or general description before descending into detail (a process referred to in the computer industry as 'top-down');
2. by then partitioning the large problem into a set of small, interrelated parts;
3. by using pictorial techniques to draw a model of the system;
4. by iteration and feedback. It is not sufficient merely to listen to Don Chichester: you also need to document your understanding so that he can set you straight if you have gone wrong.

Figure 8.3, showing the precise location of the village of Fontevraud, where Richard the Lionheart is buried, is a familiar example of the top-down approach to communication.

59

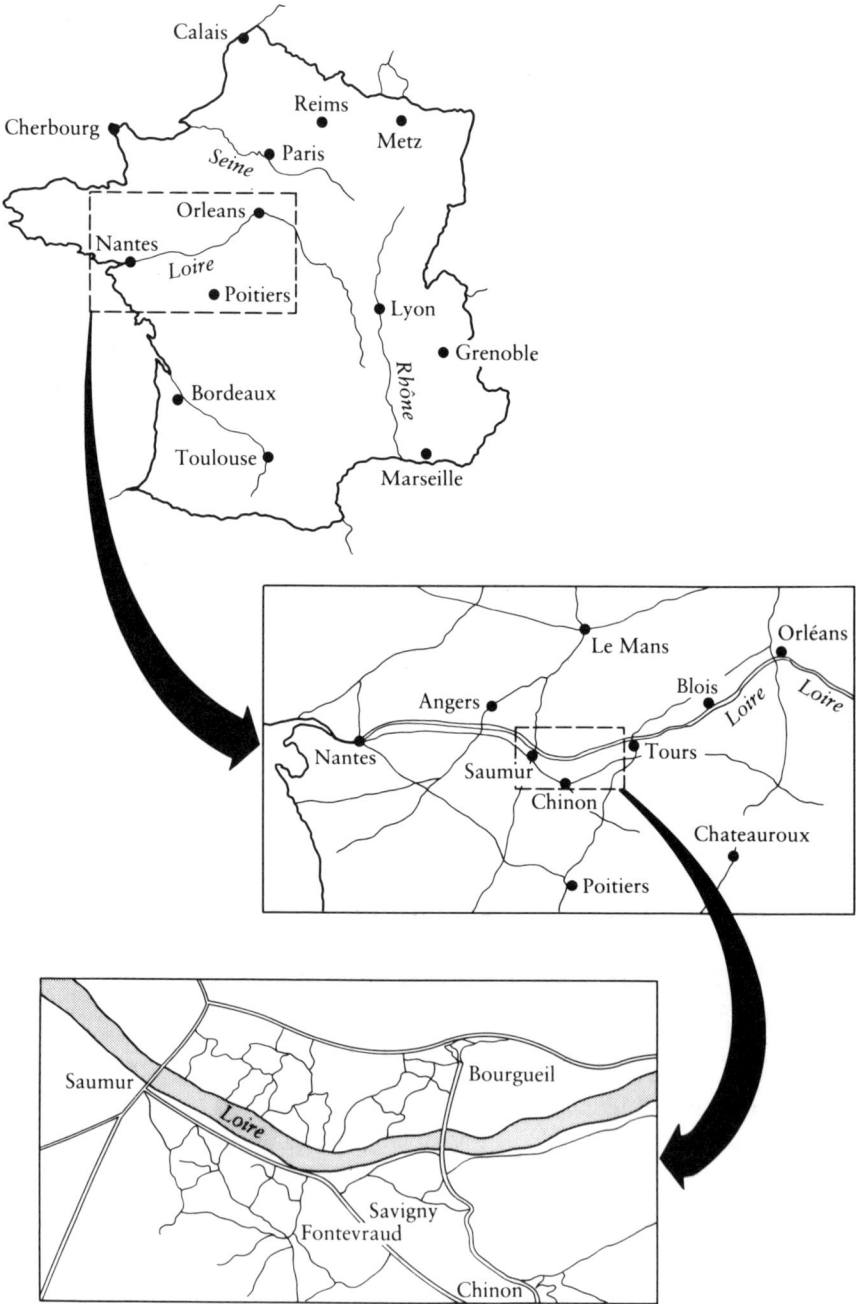

**Figure 8.3** Location of the grave of Richard I

In our investigation of World's Wines, we started at the top by talking to the director of operations. He gave us an overview, the details of which are being filled in through interviews with progressively lower levels of management and clerical staff. What we now need is an agreed set of tools whereby we can pictorially model a system.

As an example of what I mean by a model or representation of a system, let us examine a map of part of the London Underground (Fig. 8.4).

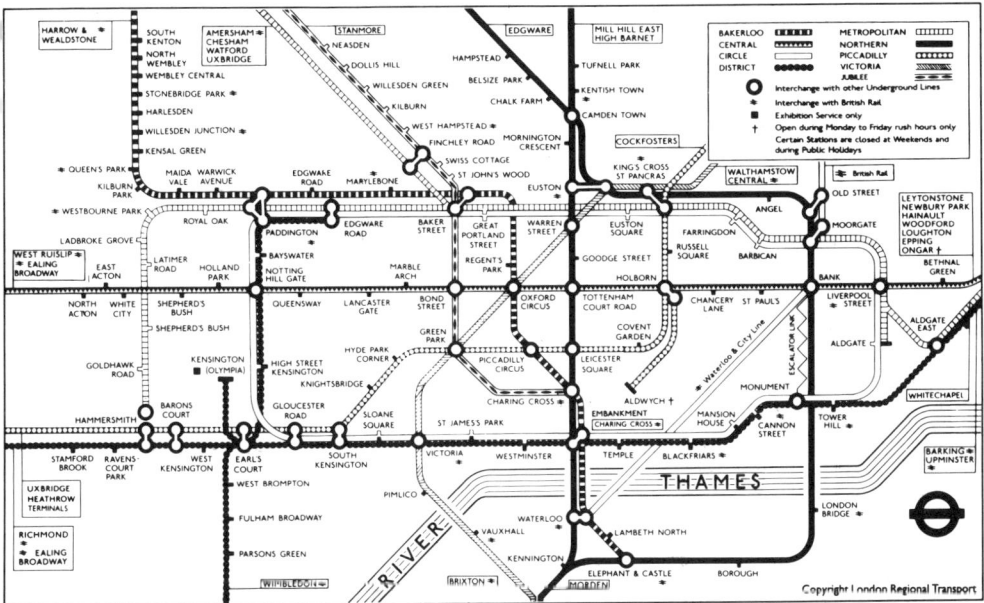

**Figure 8.4**  London central underground map

The evidence suggests that this model of the system is intelligible to its users. There are several instructive points about charting techniques to be derived from it.

1. The model is logical rather than physical—no one draws the conclusion that all tracks run in straight lines and at right angles or that it is strictly to scale.
2. It displays what the user needs to know (how to get from Hyde Park Corner to Oxford Circus) and conceals what he does not need to know—e.g., that in parts of the system lines are overground not underground.
3. It uses a minimum of notational conventions.

Since in many walks of life we are confronted with modelling techniques, it is instructive to note that, in anything which is a summary of reality, either pictorial or verbal, there is a trade-off between the intelligibility of the end-product and its accuracy as a descriptor. The more accurate and comprehensive that one endeavours to make a model, the greater number of different notational conventions are required and the more complex it becomes.

*Summarization invariably involves distortion.* If asked to précis the Bible in a thousand words, one would inevitably feel unhappy with the end result. In the trade-off between intelligibility and accuracy I shall err on the side of intelligibility. The audience for this book is the user; if I were writing for would-be practitioners, I would err on the side of accuracy.

### Data flow diagrams

Stan Breagan has already used the notation of circles and lines when talking to George Wynne. Let us refer to this as a data flow diagram and define some conventions:

———————  A line indicates a flow of data.

◯  A circle shows a process which effects some transformation of the data.

▢  A box shows a source or destination (terminator).

Using just these three conventions, we can define the boundaries of our current study (see Fig. 8.5).

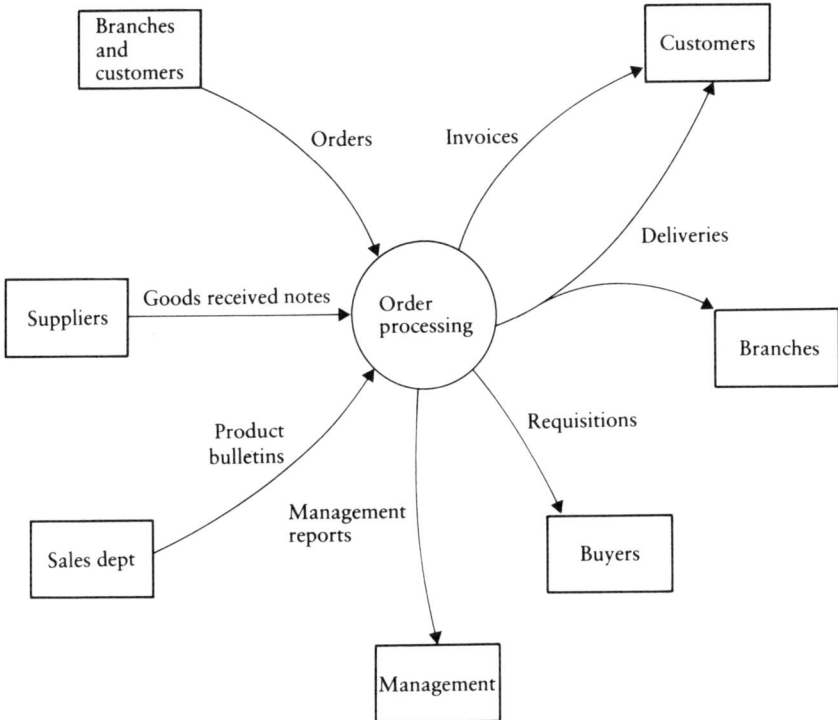

**Figure 8.5** World's Wines: context diagram. Product bulletins are inputs such as new products, price changes, and deleted products. In the interests of simplification, both these and the management reports are omitted from future diagrams.

Let us introduce another notation:

A double line shows a
file of stored data.

We can next take a look inside the circle marked 'Order processing' to see what happens to some of the individual documents. Figure 8.6 shows that customer orders are credit-checked—with failed orders being rejected—before merging with branch orders to be recorded on the stock cards. Multiple copies are generated and passed to the warehouse (for order assembly), to transport (for vehicle scheduling), and to the invoicing department. After delivery, the signed delivery note is matched with the Invoicing Department's copies and customer invoices are produced.

63

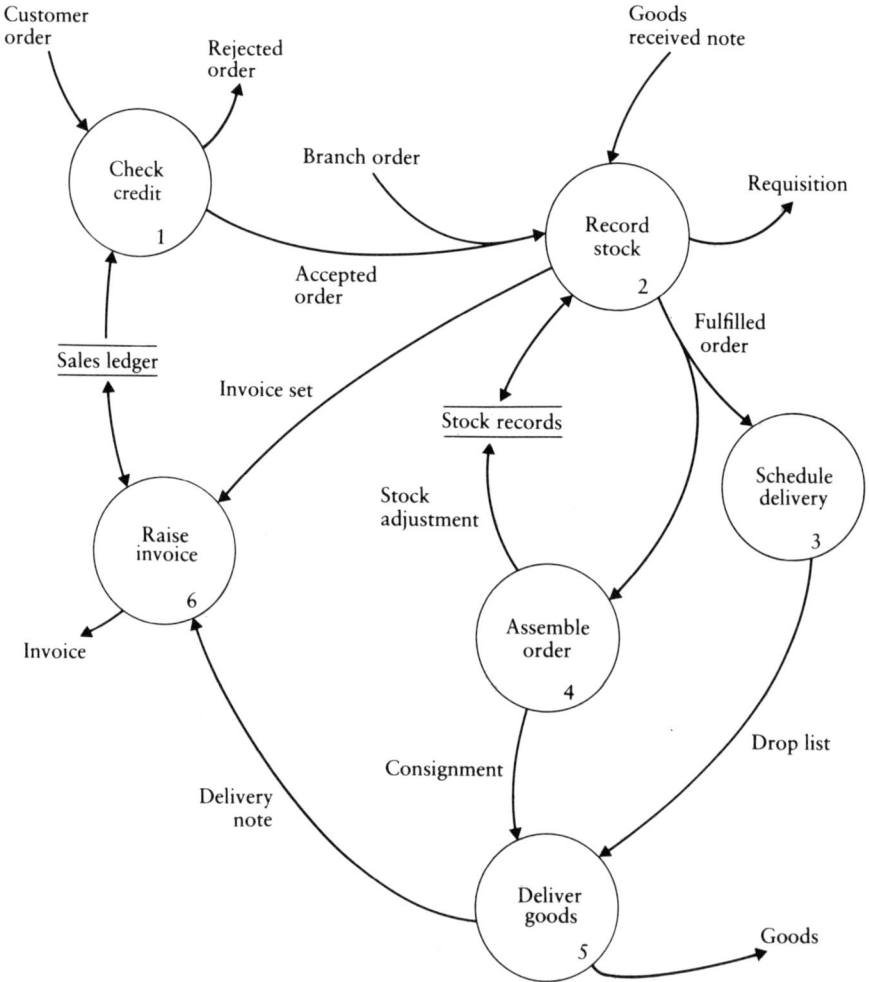

**Figure 8.6** World's Wines: current physical system

Simplicity—and therefore clarity—is achieved by deliberately con-cealing what is inside the circle (or 'bubble'). It is a high-level view. To get a more detailed—lower-level—view, we will 'explode' or 'level-down' the bubbles. Figure 8.7 shows Bubble 2 levelled down to show the detail of 'Record stock'. This lower-level diagram reveals the existence of a back order file. Not all incoming orders can be completely filled ex-stock. Where they cannot be, a back order is made out and filed,

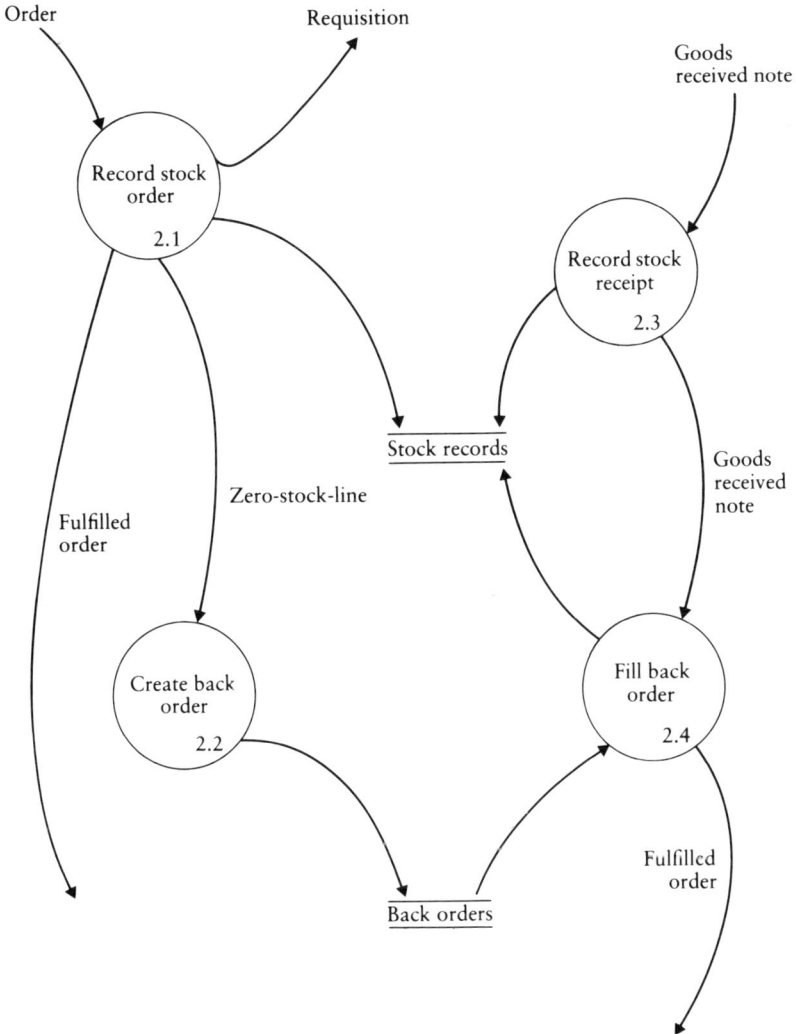

**Figure 8.7** World's Wines: stock recording

awaiting the delivery of more stock. When a 'goods received' note arrives to signal fresh stock, the back order is released into the system.

Our data flow diagram can be broken down to lower levels containing successively greater detail. This solves the problem besetting many documentation techniques, that of overwhelming the reader with detail.

Our data flow diagram, as the name implies, traces the flow of data through the system. It is obviously necessary for us to know something about the data. What does an order consist of? What is in a 'goods received' note?

One way of answering such questions is to include samples of all documents in our documentation. Figure 8.8, for example, illustrates World's Wines order form.

Documentation of the existing system, if not already available, is a necessary step in confirming our understanding of how it works. To this extent, the collection and filing of all existing documents within the system is a standard activity. However, our major interest lies in designing a new system. It is likely that existing source documents contain redundant or duplicated items and so may well have to be redesigned. Our major forward-looking interest therefore is in what any source document needs to contain rather than in what it actually contains at the moment. We are also after a more concise way of putting together systems documentation than using large working files of current forms.

### Data dictionary

The solution to both of these problems is to compile a data dictionary. Initially, this can be used to describe precisely the existing documents within the system: subsequently we can omit any redundant data. Our dictionary will then rigorously define what data *has* to flow between the various processes, or bubbles, in our data flow diagrams. This will be invaluable for whoever is building the new system. In common with data flow diagrams, the data dictionary is not specifically computer-oriented and can be originated by the user; at the same time, it is both concise and precise and therefore is an ideal communication tool.

If we examine the World's Wines' order form, we find that some items of data, for example the order number and the customer number, are present once only. Other items, such as the order lines, may occur more than once. Let us define some notations to represent these. We will use the expressions

=    to mean 'composed of'  
+    to mean 'and'  
{}    to mean 'one or more'.

We can now write a data dictionary entry for an order form:

ORDER = ORDER-HEADER + {ORDER-LINE}.

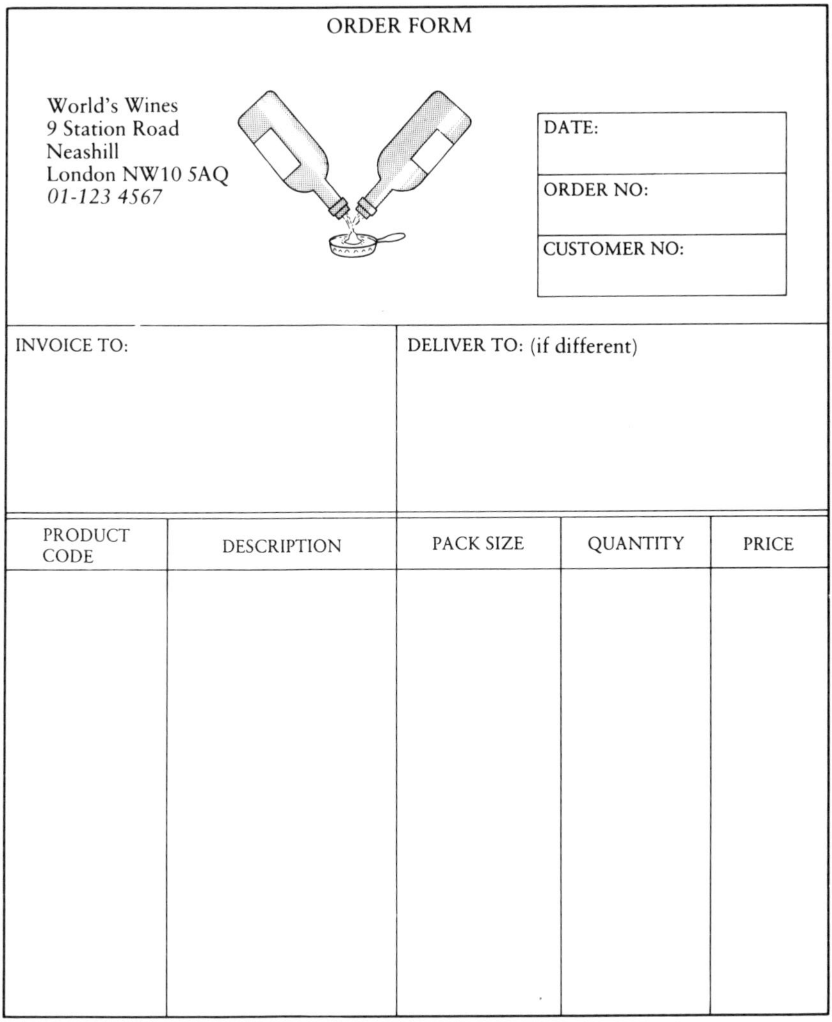

| | ORDER FORM | |
|---|---|---|

World's Wines
9 Station Road
Neashill
London NW10 5AQ
*01-123 4567*

DATE:

ORDER NO:

CUSTOMER NO:

INVOICE TO:

DELIVER TO: (if different)

| PRODUCT CODE | DESCRIPTION | PACK SIZE | QUANTITY | PRICE |
|---|---|---|---|---|
| | | | | |

**Figure 8.8**　World's Wines: order form

This says that an order consists of a header together with a number of lines. We can now define the order-header:

ORDER-HEADER = ORDER-DATE + ORDER-NUMBER + CUSTOMER-NUMBER + INVOICE-ADDRESS + (DELIVERY-ADDRESS).

We have introduced a new symbol—that of parentheses—to indicate an *optional* piece of data. A separate delivery address is filled in only if it differs from the invoice address. Thus we can define

( )   to mean 'this may or may not be present'.

Let us write our entry for ORDER-LINE:

ORDER-LINE = PRODUCT-CODE + PRODUCT-DESCRIPTION + PACK-SIZE + QUANTITY-ORDERED + (PRICE)

And, continuing our entries,

PRODUCT-CODE = PRODUCT-CATEGORY + PRODUCT-NUMBER

PRODUCT-CATEGORY = ["WINE"/"SPIRIT"/ "CORDIAL"/"TOBACCO"/"MISCELLANEOUS"]

We have introduced another notation:

[A/B/C] means 'Select one of the enclosed' or, alternatively, 'is either . . . or. . . .'

The technique of defining the data in terms of its constituent elements is invaluable for documentation purposes. Many documents within the World's Wines system contain the product code. Having defined this once in writing our entry for the order form, we do not need to repeat it when we come to the goods received note or purchase order. The principle is that of non-redundancy. Data is described once and once only. This will be invaluable for us should we in the future decide to change any data item, say by the addition of a suffix code to the product code to designate pack size. We shall then have only to amend the one entry:

PRODUCT-CODE = PRODUCT-CATEGORY + PRODUCT-NUMBER + **PACK-SIZE-CODE**

Failure to update documentation when changes are made to a system is one of the prime causes of systems becoming unmaintainable (as, after a time, no one is completely confident of the exact significance of any given piece of data). Any technique which facilitates keeping documentation current and correct saves companies large amounts of money.

The data dictionary is an invaluable tool because of its clear definition of the data necessary for the system. Ultimately, of course, we are interested in a new *physical* system. In any physical system data flows in different ways and in different time scales. Some data is contained on documents, some transmitted verbally, some on screen displays; other data is stored for periods within the system in files.

All information processing systems, manual or computer, use files. We can define a file as a collection of records concerning one specific type of entity such as customers, products, or suppliers. The data that each record holds is of course defined within the data dictionary. The stock ledger may be thought of as a set of stock records, with the contents defined as under:

STOCK-LEDGER     = {STOCK-RECORD}

STOCK-RECORD     = PRODUCT-CODE + PRODUCT-
                                       DESCRIPTION
                                   + PACK-SIZE + UNIT-QUANTITY
                                   + RE-ORDER-LEVEL + SALES-PRICE
                                   + COST-PRICE
                                   + QUANTITY-ON-HAND
                                   + (QUANTITY-ON-ORDER).

## Data modelling

Files are at the heart of both the current and the new system. The physical design of computer files is something we leave to the technical expert. This is because it is machine-dependent; that is to say, the exact way in which the files will be set up and updated will differ from one computer to another. The amount of time it will take us to get information from our files on to a screen, the flexibility to allow us to add new items easily, will be critically dependent upon the physical file design. This in turn will depend upon the speed of the hardware and the facilities of the file management system being used. If one throws in some technical concepts such as whether the file management system is using network, hierarchical, or relational data, the average user will rightly decide this is an area where he will wish to apply the 'Black Box Principle'.

However, the file management system exists to store his data, and to allow him to get at it as quickly and conveniently as possible. Only the user knows what data he needs to hold and what sort of queries he will want the system to be able to answer for him—questions such as:

'How many cases of Beaujolais Villages 1981 do we have?'
'Which Australian white wines do we stock?'

'What alternative suppliers are there of Yugoslav Riesling?'

Therefore, having once described our file data, we now need to describe the *relationships* between the data. What do we mean by 'relationships'? What possible relationships exist?

Let us start with an everyday example. Most Western societies practise monogomy; i.e., a man is allowed only one wife (at a time). The converse is also true. We may represent the *one-to-one* relationship thus:

```
┌──────────┐                ┌──────┐
│ HUSBAND ├────────────────┤ WIFE │
└──────────┘                └──────┘
```

In a polygynous society the relationship, man-to-wife, is *one-to-many*, and may be depicted:

```
┌──────────┐                ┌──────┐
│ HUSBAND ├──────────<─────┤ WIFE │
└──────────┘                └──────┘
```

A polyandrous society, man-to-wife, is *many-to-one*:

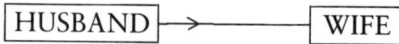

```
┌──────────┐                ┌──────┐
│ HUSBAND ├──>──────────────┤ WIFE │
└──────────┘                └──────┘
```

Using the same conventions, we can draw a model of the data within World's Wines (Fig. 8.9). What the model depicts is that a customer may have one or more orders outstanding. An order contains one or more order lines, each of which relates to one pack size. A product can have more than one pack size. An order results in one or more deliveries, each of which has a number of lines being delivered. Each delivery line refers to one pack size. Each delivery results in an invoice, which in turn consists of one or more invoice lines.

Drawing these relationships is called *data modelling*. It is a key tool in documenting systems.

### Process specification

Our data flow diagrams have described how data flows through the system. We have rigorously but simply defined the content of the data in our data dictionary and the relationships in our data model. It remains to describe *how* the data changes as it goes through the system. What are the rules for calculating an invoice? When, and how, is a requisition made out?

Once we have completed our set of data flow diagrams—i.e.,

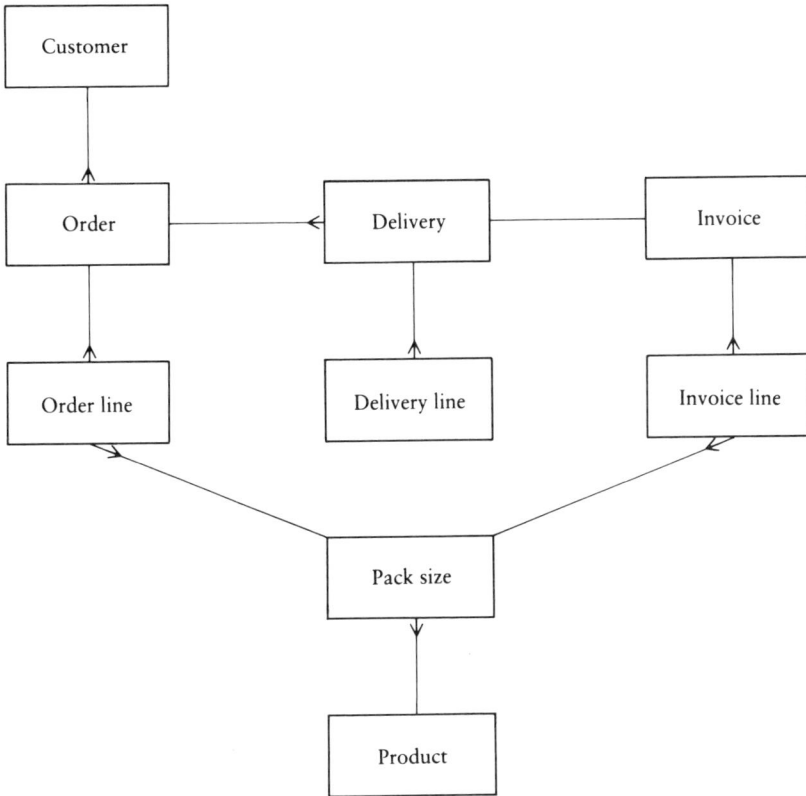

**Figure 8.9** World's Wine: Data model

levelled-down to a point where we can easily describe the particular process within any bubble—we can define the procedures by which that process is carried out. Let us suppose we have levelled-down Bubble 6, 'Raise invoice' (Fig. 8.6), to the point where we can specify the rules for allowing discount. To do this we identified the procedures with the invoicing superintendent. She described it thus:

Having matched the delivery note with the invoice set, we extend the invoice, taking care to include any adjustments for short delivery noted on the delivery note. This gives us a total amount for the invoice. If the total comes to £2000 or more and the customer has a good payment history or is an 'approved' customer, we allow a discount to the invoice total to give the net invoice amount. Unless, of

71

course, it is to our own branch—obviously, we don't bother to apply discount to them.

Assuming that these rules will continue to be applied in the new system, we shall need to include them in our specification. Before doing so, let us examine the statement regarding discount more closely. It illustrates the potential for misunderstanding caused by the ambiguity of common speech.

First, the most fundamental test—own branch or external customer has been mentioned last. In reality, this is the first test that is applied. Second, the status of 'or is an approved customer' is ambiguous. Is this a *sufficient* condition for receiving discount, or must the invoice also be over £2000?

The use of the expression, 'sufficient condition' is deliberate. It is an expression that a philosopher or lawyer might use. Both their jobs demand clarity of meaning. Since this type of ambiguity is not unfamiliar to them, they have invented terminology that sorts it out. To ask whether being an 'approved customer' is a sufficient condition is to ask whether that alone qualifies the customer for discount. If not, it is because it is a *necessary* (though not *sufficient*) condition that the invoice be over £2000.

Any discipline that demands unambiguity develops ways of clarifying such problems. In the field of mathematics, the sequence in which expressions in a formula are to be worked out is made clear by use of brackets. With the above example we can sort out the ambiguity by the simple expedient of inserting the word 'either' and adding some punctuation. Thus the original statement could mean:

'If an invoice is over £2000 and *either* the customer has a good payment history, *or* is an approved customer, discount is allowable.'

or

'If *either* an invoice is over £2000 and the customer has a good payment history, *or* the customer is an approved customer, discount is allowable.'

The example is somewhat laboured but illustrates the problem. We have solved it by 'tightening up' the English. We could go a bit further than this:

### Rules for customer discount

If INVOICE-TOTAL is less than £2000 then
no DISCOUNT

*Otherwise*:
If PAYMENT-HISTORY is 'OK', then
allow DISCOUNT

*Otherwise* (PAYMENT-HISTORY not OK):
If 'CUSTOMER-STATUS is 'approved' then
allow DISCOUNT

*Otherwise* (not 'approved') then
no DISCOUNT

Two comments on this should be added. Words in capitals are those that have entries in the data dictionary. In the final specification, terms such as 'approved' would need defining, as will the exact rates of discount to be applied.

The above technique is one which 'structures' narrative so as to eliminate ambiguities and bring out implied conditions. Alternatively, this can be achieved by decision trees or decision tables. Figure 8.10 (overleaf) shows the same set of discount rules expressed using these tools. The user pays his money and takes his choice. Their common denominator is that they allow business rules—whether for customer discount, calculation of bank interest, or issuing of renewal premiums—to be specified unambiguously.

An important characteristic of the four simple but powerful tools outlined above, i.e.:

data flow diagrams,
data dictionary,
data models,
process descriptions,

is that they demand no technical computer knowledge. Consequently they are capable of origination by users either in conjunction with an analyst or after appropriate training. The end-result is a clear, easy-to-maintain, specification of what the system does or has to do.

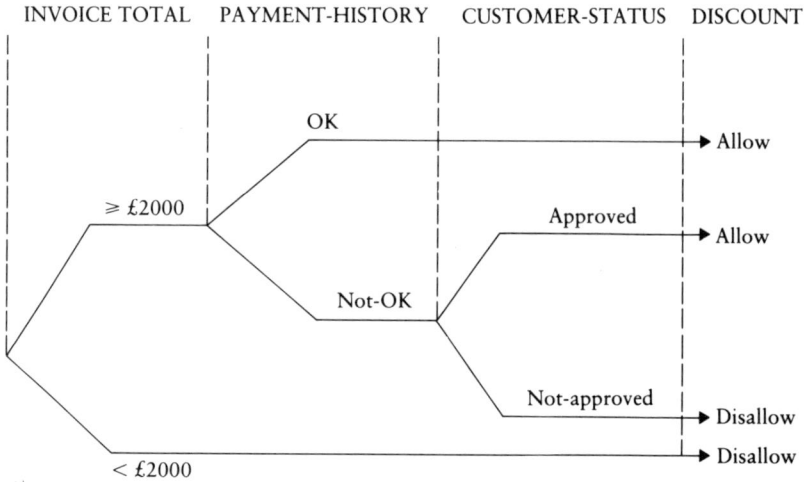

INVOICE TOTAL    PAYMENT-HISTORY    CUSTOMER-STATUS    DISCOUNT

```
                            OK                              ─────► Allow

            ≥ £2000                        Approved
                                                          ─────► Allow
                            Not-OK

                                           Not-approved
                                                          ─────► Disallow
                                                          ─────► Disallow
            < £2000
```

(a)

| Invoice > £2000 | Y | Y | Y | N |
|---|---|---|---|---|
| Good payment history | Y | N | N | — |
| Approved client | — | Y | N | — |
| Allow discount | X | X | | |
| Disallow discount | | | X | X |

(b)

**Figure 8.10** (a) Decision tree (customer discount). (b) Decision table (customer discount). The hyphen—a so-called 'indifference' symbol—indicates 'either Yes or No'.

# 9. Analysing information needs

*Information technology is an amplifier and it may amplify not only good but bad management.*

Paul Strassman, VP Xerox Corporation

The diagram drawn by Stan Breagan to explain how he would conduct the survey (Fig. 8.2 above) showed a process described as 'Refine requirements of new system'. What he meant by this was that, while talking to users to find out how the current system works, he would, at the same time, be asking them what additional information they want the new system to give them.

The World's Wines case study is of a system affecting the company's day-to-day operational running. All but the smallest companies already have such systems operational on a computer (though they could well be in the process of re-writing them). A high proportion of systems being developed today are to provide management with information on which to make decisions. Such systems have long been extremely weak, reflecting inadequate analysis of the type of information required. Communication between analyst and user is usually at its worst in this area. Defining what information has to appear on a payslip is easy; specifying management information requirements is bedevilled by the analyst's frequent lack of first-hand experience of management, and by the user-manager's difficulty in deciding precisely what information he is going to require. As a result, such systems have frequently been computer-driven; i.e., they have produced reams of information in the hope that something in there will help someone.

A recent research project on the use of computers as aids to management decision-making has come up with some interesting findings. The latest computer 'flavour of the month' is the so-called 'decision-support system'. These systems are promoted as the panacea for mediocre management, in that managers will make better decisions if they have faster access to better information. A confirmed sceptic such as myself derives wry satisfaction from the report's conclusion that, improperly applied—i.e., without proper analysis of information requirements—all that such systems do is enable poor managers to make more bad decisions faster. It appears that it is not the technology that makes the difference, but the quality of the management using the technology. It is very reassuring for me to see such authoritative backing for a rule I have long preached in much simpler terms:

If you computerize a mess, you get a computerized mess.

In the past I have applied this brilliant insight mainly in the field of computerizing operational-type systems. It is now obvious that there is a corollary to this in the field of information-providing systems:

If you don't know what you want, you can't ask a computer to give it to you.

How, then, can management improve its ability to specify information needs? And, second, how can the analyst assist in relating these to the technical questions of file and program design?

The first rule to lay down is this:

'Producing management information' should never be an objective of any system. Information is a *means*, not an end.

Once this is accepted, a lot of things fall into place. Crucially, management is forced to specify why they require the information, and what decisions or actions they will take consequent upon the figures provided. I once discussed at some length a project monitoring system which produced statistics on the productivity of individual workers—typical 'nice-to-know' stuff. Unfortunately, since the user-manager had no powers to sack or otherwise discipline the poor performer, the information was largely useless.

Focusing attention on decision-making leads naturally to another good analytical question: How will you interpret the figures?

Figure 9.1 reproduces a set of statistical data. It has the virtue of a clear connection to a particular set of decisions—namely, where to put your crosses on this week's football coupon. The problem is, what conclusions do you draw from the tables? Does the fact that Bolton have gone 42 games without a score draw mean that they have a propensity to win or lose, or does it mean that by the law of averages (layman's version) it is their turn for a draw?

If a set of sales statistics informs you that a given line of products is selling better in the North than in the South, do you bump up your marketing budget in the South to increase sales there, or concentrate on

**Figure 9.1** Pools information

the area where there appears to be a higher level of product acceptance?

A further complication is that a large proportion of high-level decisions are based on information totally outside of any computer system, e.g., knowledge of a competitor's strategies, or on inspired guesswork. In the latter case, what managers need (and can occasionally get through computer modelling or simulation) is the ability to ask 'what-if? type questions.

A competent analyst, such as Stan, might be expected to devote a considerable proportion of any investigation to turning a systems objective such as 'Reduce work-in-progress by 12 per cent' into the precise information which will enable management to achieve, or at least monitor, this aim.

It is not good enough to ask vague questions such as, 'What information do you require out of the system?' Information can be subjected to analysis as much as operating procedures. The most important analysis is that which receives least attention: Why does the user need this information, and what is he going to do with it?

Assuming that the information requested has a legitimate purpose sufficient to justify the cost of its production, how can we then turn a general statement, e.g., 'I need to know where our capital is tied up in stock', into the detail necessary for a good specification?

The key to this is that information from computer systems almost universally comes from data that is stored on files. Our knowledge of how filing systems work can therefore be utilized to produce the following checklist when specifying information requirements of a system:

1. *Content*   What actual information does the user require?
2. *Access*   What form will a request for information take:
    - a simple listing of all information from a given file?
    - a random enquiry on one specific record?
    - a search for all records meeting certain criteria specified by the user?
3. *Currency*   How up to date does the information have to be:
    - as at month-end?
    - as at close of business on previous day?
    - as at last transaction?
4. *Response time*   What is the time-frame within which the information is required:
    - regular basis such as each month-end?
    - within 24 hours of request?
    - within five seconds of request?
5. *Distribution/privacy*   Who is authorized to have access to the information, and what is the level of security required to protect it?
6. *Format*   How is the information to be presented:
    - printed or displayed on a screen?
    - tabulated or graphic?

By breaking down information requests in this way, it is once again easy for the user to specify his requirements without worrying about the physical system necessary to meet them. At this stage we are content to record the requirements as specified. When later we start to design a system to meet them, we may have to go back and negotiate the trade-off between the totality of the users' requirements and the design constraints imposed by available hardware and cost.

To illustrate the use of the above checklist, we can see how different requirements are specified using them.

### 1. Fixed assets register
- *Contents*  ITEM CODE + DESCRIPTION + PURCHASE DATE + ORIGINAL COST + DEPRECIATION RATE + DEPRECIATION METHOD + WRITTEN-DOWN COST
- *Access*  Requirement for quarterly printout of complete register with ability to look up any particular item at random.
- *Currency*  Position as at last month-end.
- *Response time*  Not more than five working days after the month-end.
- *Distribution/privacy*  Information restricted to Accounts Department and all managers above Grade 3.
- *Format*  Printed report. Useful if all items with written-down value of zero are highlighted.

The characteristics of this information need is that it is non-time-critical. This fact may well mean that the physical solution does not necessarily involve a computer. If one is used, then the simplest solution appears to be to produce a monthly listing. This would meet all requirements (the 'random access' one is met by the person finding the relevant item on the printout) except that of searching for classes of items. This would be done manually if the register is small; if large, then some form of query facility through a computer seems indicated.

### 2. Bank current accounts system
- *Content*  CUSTOMER ACCOUNT NUMBER + CUSTOMER NAME + CURRENT BALANCE + OVERDRAFT LIMIT . . . (etc.)
- *Access*  Requirement to look up status of particular customer's account at random.
- *Currency*  Position as at close of business on the previous day.
- *Response time*  Less than ten seconds (customer is presumed to be waiting for the information).
- *Distribution/privacy*  Information may be divulged only to customer in person.
- *Format*  No special requirement.

The significant feature of this request is the currency of the information. The bank is content with its being up to date only as at the previous day's close. This almost certainly results from a trade-off against the cost of a 'real-time' system that would reflect the last transaction made. The latter would necessitate (as some smaller banks do) the immediate posting to a customer's account of any debit. Since most of these are in the form of cheques, and we are talking of very large numbers of transactions, it becomes more cost-effective to capture these debits by magnetically coding the bottom of the cheque. This leads to all cheques being sent to the central computer department where the equipment to read them is situated. As a result, accounts in such a system can be updated only after the event. This is done overnight, so that at the start of the next day's trading customer accounts are up to date with respect to yesterday's business. Since, however, they will not be further updated until the next evening, it makes little sense to go to the expense of on-line enquiry systems at all branches. The information is therefore disseminated on microfiche. Where one does see an 'on-line' element is with the bank's Cashpoint systems, when debits are immediately recorded.

The most complex system results from the requirement for random access with minimum response time to data that is constantly up to date and where the distribution of this information is widespread. This is what airline reservation systems do. As technology improves, and performance costs drop, so more installations are able to justify this type of system, previously the province of only the biggest organization.

To reiterate the central point, the way to specify information requirements is for the user first to define the purpose of the information and then to categorize it in accordance with the checklist given above. The designer can then work from these—and with all other inputs to the design process—and establish the feasibility of meeting the requirements exactly as specified. If this can be done within whatever constraints exist, all well and good; if not, further discussions will be needed, either to relax the constraints or to persuade the users to accept some compromise.

There is one further point of considerable importance. Even using the method described above, it is still no easy matter for any manager to think of everything he needs by way of information. It is a common phenomenon that information provokes a requirement for further information. In the past this has been particularly awkward, since users only got to see such information once the system had gone live. This of course is the worst point at which to request changes. More recently, users have been able to get an early indication of what system outputs

80

will be like through the technique of *prototyping*. This is the use of a programming language to create simulated outputs during the specification phase.

The newer 'fourth-generation' languages are increasingly used in this role. In a report on these produced by the UK Treasury Central Computer and Telecommunications Agency,[1] particular reference was made to this fact:

> The eventual design of a business system is often determined at an early stage by one or two key assumptions. Frequently it is too expensive to change them once development is underway. Prototyping and modelling techniques provide a method to ensure that the kernel of an application is correctly designed. Correct design helps ensure user satisfaction.

Such techniques are rapidly becoming widespread. They represent a significant step in improving the specification of the new system and also in fostering user involvement.

---

[1] *Application Generation: The rapid development of application systems without conventional programming*. HM Treasury Central Computer and Telecommunications Agency, IT Series no. 3, HMSO, 1983.

# 10. Problem analysis

*I keep six honest serving-men*
*(They taught me all I know)*
*Their names are what and why and when*
*And how and where and who.*

Rudyard Kipling

Two weeks have passed. During this time Stan has talked to various managers, supervisors, clerical, and warehouse staff. Generally, he has had a good reception and people have reacted positively to the survey. Mr Chichester remains sceptical about whether a computer can ever know enough about the various wines to send out acceptable substitutes when they are out of stock of a particular year.

Stan has arranged an informal meeting with George Wynne to review progress.

GW    Well, Stan, you've had a chance to look at the system now. What do you think are the main problems?

SB    Well, the main problems are those that you yourself pointed out—delays and excessive costs. What I've been looking at is what's causing the problems.

GW    And what have you come up with?

SB    I think there are two major causes. First, there is the volume or order lines being processed manually by the system. It has coped in the past, but your expansion over the last few years means that the current method of working is operating at full stretch. Since you are planning to open two new retail outlets in the coming 12 months, it's obvious that something has to be done before then.

GW    Well that's certainly what Mr Chichester has been telling me for some time now. He seems to think a couple more staff would go a long way towards solving it. Is that your view?

SB    Personally I doubt it. You've reached a point of diminishing returns, where increasing staff by 20 per cent would not necessarily lead to a corresponding increase in throughput.

GW    I'm sure that's right. But you said there were two main causes. What is the second?

SB    Basically, you have a bottleneck in your stock records section. Since you tend to get more orders coming in at the end of the week than the beginning, this leads to a backlog in stock recording at certain times.

Having now established exactly how the current system works, the next step is to examine in what respects, and why, the system is deficient. It never ceases to surprise me how loosely defined is this fundamental activity of systems analysis. Many systems analysts are so titled because that is the next job grade up from programmer; in fact, they spend their time writing file layouts and program specifications, an activity manifestly in the design area. If we consult the dictionary for the definition of the word 'analysis' we find:

> Breaking down a complex thing into its component parts or elements; the study of individual phenomena to discover their underlying principle or cause. (*Chambers 20th Century Dictionary*, revised edition)

Immediately we see that there are two separate definitions. If you ask a layman (or a systems analyst) for a definition, he will invariably give you an approximation of the first. An obvious example is chemical analysis, which tells us that nitric acid is composed of three molecules of oxygen to one each of nitrogen and hydrogen. We may note in passing that 12 chemists, given the same colourless fluid to analyse, will come up with the same answer. That is because it is a scientific activity. If we compare this with *psycho*-analysis, we see that the latter is far more subjective. No two psychoanalysts are likely to come up with identical diagnoses.

Systems analysis lies somewhere between these two—less scientific than chemistry, more predictable than psychiatry. Psychoanalysts, of course, also employ the second type of analysis—in classifying the raw data of large numbers of individual illnesses into general categories such as depressive, masochistic, etc. This grouping process is the way in which human beings in all disciplines make sense of a vast mass of data, and it applies equally in the field of systems analysis.

Reverting to the first definition—breaking down into parts—how do we go about analysing a system such as that of World's Wines? The first thing to realize is that *any set of data can be analysed in many different ways*. If we gave our chemists a dozen test tubes of unidentified liquids, they could analyse them into groups by colour, by taste (though the latter might lead to an unacceptable attrition rate among those carrying out the tests), or by any other criteria they thought meaningful.

83

Two points can be made about this:

1. It is meaningless to talk of analysing a system or a set of data without saying what is the determining characteristic by which it is being analysed.
2. The corollary of this is that we need a clear idea of what we are looking for before we start. Otherwise we run the danger of collecting a large number of unrelated observations and then trying to make sense of them.

Both these statements are usually implicit in a systems investigation, but as always it helps to bring them out. By what are we analysing World's Wines? We have seen that any data processing system breaks down into data and processes. Our analysis of the current system has so far reflected this. We have documented how things are done without making any qualitative judgements about whether any particular process is being done efficiently or whether it needs doing at all.

However, in the progress meeting between George Wynne and Stan Breagan, attention was not centred on how the system worked or even what it was doing: the user's concern was 'Where are the problems?' To answer this question, and its follow-up, 'What is causing them?', we first need to know what problems are at issue. This is why our investigation started at the top of the organization.

The project request defines the problems that were of concern to management. It *directs* the investigation and analysis. That is not to say that Stan Breagan has closed his eyes to anything outside the strictest interpretation of the request, but merely that the latter has dictated the primary line of investigation. If he discovered that large stock losses through pilfering were going undetected, he would not disregard this on the grounds that it was not included in the original terms of reference.

The first step in any problem analysis is to understand the existing system. Our investigation may reveal that management's worries are unfounded and that the system is working satisfactorily. Accurate analysis can only come from accurate data, so first we endeavour to establish the facts and figures on order delays. Time is a continuous function, so we may choose to represent our findings in the form of a cumulative histogram (Fig. 10.1). This will give a more meaningful picture than a bald average figure, which could conceal wild fluctuations.

Once we have quantified order turn-round, we can analyse the figures by time to discover where the delays are occurring. The simplest way,

84

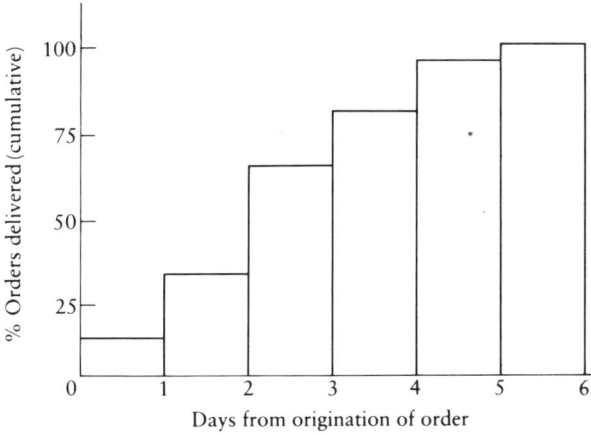

**Figure 10.1**   Order delivery time

working on average delays, could be represented by a straight line showing the respective times taken up by the various processes in the system (Fig. 10.2). Quite clearly, our solution to the problem will be considerably different depending on which of the three situations shown below is actually the true one:

(a)   Delay in post

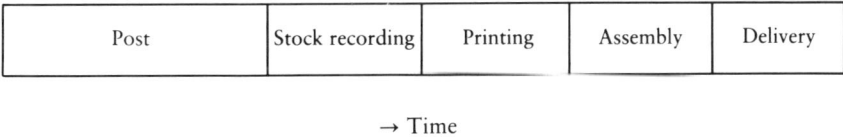

| Post | Stock recording | Printing | Assembly | Delivery |
|------|------|------|------|------|

→ Time

(b)   Delay in stock recording

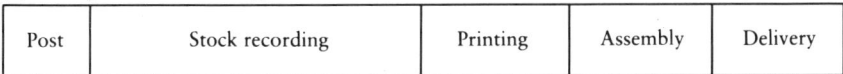

| Post | Stock recording | Printing | Assembly | Delivery |
|------|------|------|------|------|

(c)   Delay in warehouse

| Post | Stock recording | Printing | Assembly | Delivery |
|------|------|------|------|------|

**Figure 10.2**   Analysis of delays, by process/time

85

Both the above analyses can be established by empirical research. That is not to say that this will be accomplished without difficulty; we may decide that we do not need to go into this level of detail at this stage. Both analyses extend our knowledge of World's Wines. They confirm (or refute) management's description of operational problems. We have 'quantified' the problem. We have taken management's broad statement, 'Deliveries are taking too long', and established precisely how long they are taking, and where the delays are occurring.

What we have not yet done is to ask 'Why?' What is *causing* the problems? This is probably the commonest form of analysis. Let us term it 'cause and effect analysis' and apply it to another problem in World's Wines: discrepancies between book stock and physical stock. This results in a typical hierarchy (Fig. 10.3).

Here we have not only identified the causes of a particular problem, we have also tried to assign relative weights to these. Clearly, such an exercise is useful in identifying where to concentrate one's efforts when redesigning the system.

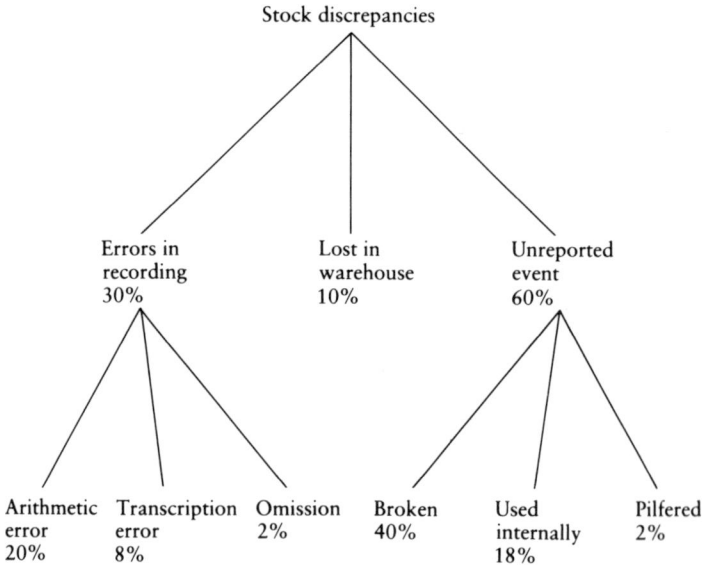

**Figure 10.3** Cause and effect analysis

A complementary approach is a detailed examination of each process, establishing how it is carried out, whether it is necessary, and whether it is being done by the right person at the right time. For our investigative method we need look no further than the Kipling poem quoted at the start of this chapter (see Table 10.1 overleaf).

Although in this chapter I have only sketched in a sample analysis of part of the order processing system, what stands out is that *this skill is not computer-related*. A consultant such as Stan Breagan has experience of a diversity of systems, and may act as a catalyst, but the activity is totally within the competence of the user and is one where he is the repository of knowledge with respect to the current system.

To carry out such an analysis demands a close knowledge and understanding of all aspects of the current system. It also directs our thinking towards many different types of solution. This is particularly true of 'Why' and 'When' questions. These are often overlooked in the rush to solve the 'How' problems by introducing a computer at the earliest opportunity.

Time for another checkpoint. Our investigation and analysis of World's Wines has resulted in a description of the order processing system in terms of what it currently does. On top of that is a set of analyses which explores the problems from different standpoints. We are now confident, having checked them out with the various people in the company, of the following things:

1. what the current system sets out to do and how it attempts to do it;
2. its success or failure in achieving its objectives;
3. the causes of any shortcomings in the current system;
4. the clear requirements for improvement and additional facilities to be incorporated in the proposed system.

This is where it starts to get fun (which is why people never spend enough time over the preceding stages). We can now look at various solutions to the problems we have identified.

## Table 10.1  Process analysis

| What? | Credit checking | Stock recording |
|---|---|---|
| Why? | To prevent bad debts | To initiate stock replenishment<br>To price the orders<br>To record stock availability |
| When? | Immediately on receipt of order<br><br>Why then?  Must always precede ledger-posting and order assembly | After credit-check, before Xerox<br><br>Why then?  To give buyers early warning of low stock<br><br>To avoid searching for non-existent stock<br><br>When else could?  In parallel with, or after, order assembly |
| Who? | Order Processing Manager<br><br>Why that person?  Personal decision based on importance of this function plus need for experience<br><br>Who else could?  Accounts Department | Stock clerks<br><br>Why them?  Requires some product knowledge and clerical ability<br><br>Who else could?  By pickers as they assemble the order but not pricing |
| Where? | Order Processing Department<br><br>Why there?  See 'Who?'<br><br>Where else could?  Sales ledger cards are physically located in the Invoicing section and access to these is necessary | Stock Records section<br><br>Why there?  Section is dedicated to that function<br><br>Where else could?  Possibly in warehouse |
| How? | Estimating value of incoming order; checking with sales ledger to see whether sufficient credit exists<br><br>Problems<br>- Orders not priced<br>- Sales ledger does not reflect work in progress<br>- Back orders not checked | Manual posting of order lines to stock cards.  Orders have to be passed between clerks as each looks after his own set of records<br><br>Problems<br>- Peaking of orders causes backlog<br>- Multiple handling of forms<br>- Discrepancies between book and physical stock<br>- High level of back orders |
| | Exceptions<br>- Orders from large companies bypass the check | Exceptions<br>- Rush orders<br>- Substitutions<br>- Not allocating items with low stock |

# 11. Solving problems

*Managers spend far too much time evaluating ideas and not enough originating them.*

Edward De Bono

Analysis is the best possible precursor to problem-solving. It is a necessary condition of coming up with the right answer, though not, unfortunately, a sufficient one. Those problems which most afflict our society—inflation and unemployment—are ones where there is a lack of unanimity on the analysis of the problem (and the constraints on the solution). Apostles of monetarism offer solutions involving strict control of the money supply, on the theory that excess money is the prime cause. Keynesians put greater emphasis on demand management and incomes control, based on a different analysis of the causes.

Mercifully, the problems that confront systems analysts are less global and, hopefully, less political. It is usually possible to arrive at an analysis of a problem that is agreed by the parties involved. Even though it may not be subject to statistical proof, as for instance the connection between smoking and lung cancer, it is vital that a correct analysis is agreed upon. *Without it, we run the risk of designing an elegant solution to the wrong problem.*

The effect of a well-defined project request is to narrow down the area of search for a solution. This process is taken further by the feasibility study as the overall systems requirements are developed and refined. We learn that credit checking is an integral part of the order processing. We establish the detail of management's requirement for figures on stocks and sales. We note that customers may return goods that have been delivered to them and that credit notes then have to be raised. Our identification of the effects of the problems, and our analysis of their causes, will point us in the direction of a solution.

Exactly the same process can be seen at work in other spheres. We take our medical problems to doctors much as we may take our business problems to a consultant. A bad doctor will hurriedly prescribe a pet nostrum without an adequate diagnosis, just as some systems people have a predetermined solution up their sleeve and fail to analyse the precise cause of the problem. The good doctor carries out a physical examination (investigation), in order to diagnose (analyse) the problem, and then prescribes the appropriate remedy (solution).

The same problem-oriented approach lies behind much advertising. It is no surprise to find that manufacturers advertising male deodorants choose to use men with an aggressively masculine image. It is the obvious solution to the problem of consumer resistance among men to the idea of splashing themselves with perfume. Investigation of the problem—known as market research—quickly identifies the cause: that it is considered effeminate to smell of violets. If this is the cause of the problem, the solution is simple: advertise the product with men about whose sexual proclivities there is not a scintilla of doubt. In fact, the whole advertising industry can be viewed as an exercise in accurate analysis followed by creative thinking.

I shall revert to the analytical approach, but it is important to realize that, when it comes to devising solutions to problems, this is not the only way. Analytical thinking involves deductive reasoning. It works from a given or established set of premises to a conclusion. It is logically correct that, if a company has a problem of delays in delivering goods, one establishes where the delays are occurring in order to speed up those parts. If the delays are caused by the slowness of manual stock recording procedures, and a computer can perform the same task many times faster, the substitution of a computer-based system for a manual one will solve the immediate problem. Ignoring for the moment any new problems that the computer may introduce, the above progression from problem to solution is logically sound. But it is not necessarily the only solution. To use the terminology of Edward de Bono, analytical or vertical thinking is about the 'rightness' of the solution. This is contrasted by de Bono with lateral thinking, which is about the 'richness' of solutions, i.e., maximizing the number of different solutions one can dream up for a given problem (see Fig. 11.1).

We are now at a crucial stage, the stage at which we make the transition from examining the current system to designing a new one. This is a *creative* step. If designing a system requires 1 per cent inspiration and 99 per cent perspiration, this is where the 1 per cent comes in. Before returning to the inspirational element, let us analyse the design or creative process itself. In the vast majority of disciplines this follows a similar pattern. We can identify these, once the problem has been studied, as:

Drafting:    The initial formulation of an idea, and its acceptance as the basis of the final design

Refining:    Taking the original, imperfect, idea and improving it

*Creative thinking*

o Right brain

o Many possible solutions

o Lateral

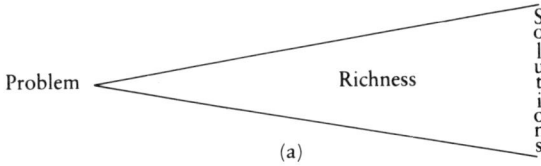

(a)

*Analytical thinking*

o Left brain

o Unique/few solutions

o Vertical

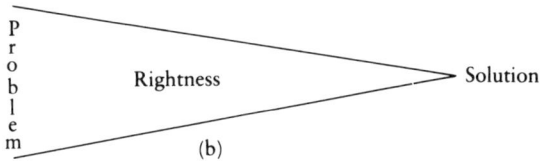

(b)

**Figure 11.1** Analytical *v.* creative thinking. (a) Creative thinking: applicable to major company problems, business system design, and the overall flow of information. (b) Analytical thinking: applicable to detailed or technical system design.

Consulting:  Checking the design with affected parties for their comments and suggestions

Validation:  Checking the final design against the systems objectives and constraints; making sure that the new system has not created new problems

This process has been characterized by Karl Popper[1] in the formula:

$$P \rightarrow TS \rightarrow EE \rightarrow S$$

where P is the initial problem, TS the trial solution, EE the process of

[1] Karl Popper, *Objective Knowledge: An Evolutionary Approach*, Oxford University Press, 1972.

error elimination applied to the trial solution, and S the resultant situation with its own new problems.

This series of steps can be seen at work in a creative process such as the writing of a speech or book. As I draft this book, I know that the ideas are not presented in their best order; that I shall want to review how the case study is integrated with the chapters. I shall certainly send the initial draft to colleagues wiser and more experienced than I for their comments. Possibly by the sixth attempt I shall have something that I am willing to show my publisher. (The analogy between writing a book and designing a system holds good in many other respects, not least that highly optimistic promises are given to the publisher about delivery of the product.)


### Drafting a solution

How then do we arrive at the first draft? In the many years in which I have been working in the field of system design I have constantly searched for an answer to this question, a quest for the philosopher's stone of systems work which will turn base systems into gold. In so doing I have gone out of my way to talk to the designers of what I deemed to be particularly good systems. The quest has been remarkably unproductive, if one is seeking a set of golden rules that can be applied to any problem in order to come up with a brilliant idea. All answers I have found can be grouped into four categories:

1. *See what other people are doing*   There are no new problems: only old problems in a slightly new environment, or to which techno-logical advances have opened up new solutions. The first obvious tack therefore is to see how other people have coped with similar problems.
2. *Use multi-disciplinary teams*   People from different backgrounds look at problems in different ways. There is ample evidence to show that the formation of a multi-disciplinary team is of significant value in coming up with new ideas.
3. *Ensure good problem analysis*   This is the technique to which the previous chapter was devoted. It is worth recording just how many times designers of good systems have replied to my questions by saying, 'Well, really, it just came down to a clear definition of what one was trying to solve.'
4. *Think creatively*   Within this general approach come all those solutions that appear to come as 'a flash of inspiration'.

Let us make the (questionable) assumption that there is one *right*, i.e. pre-eminently superior, solution to World's Wines' problems. This is not the same as saying that there is a perfect solution: the presence of constraints precludes a perfect solution. The right solution will be a compromise, and possibly will not even be recognizable as the best available solution. However, the converse is almost true—one can usually recognize bad solutions. Indeed, I have already remarked on the commonly held view that goodness in systems consists in, or is recognizable only by, absence of badness. This I hold to be a general truth about systems involving people this side of Utopia (which would itself be a very boring system). I shall therefore subsequently concern myself with refining our initial design in order to eliminate its most obvious weaknesses.

The hypothesis, examined earlier, that there is some 'best' solution to systems problems, be they legal, tax, government, or business, with a divine arbiter able to adjudge, may appear academic, but in systems work it is constructive, because identifying the best system involves several necessary steps.

Some of these we have already undertaken. We have rigorously identified the characteristics of that solution in a 'model' composed of the relevant variables: it must reduce stocks by a given percentage; it must be implemented within 12 months; it must cost less than £60 000 to install. (We can similarly define the requirements of a democratic system of representation: that it reflects the will of the majority while preserving the rights of the minority.) We have also endeavoured to predict the future environment within which the solution has to work.

The necessary conditions of then arriving at the 'best' solution are two-fold: *first, it has to occur to you; second, it has then to be recognized as being the best.*

Of the four categories listed above, problem analysis is most important in refining and recognizing the solution, while other people's ideas, multi-disciplinary teams, and creative thinking are most valuable in originating solutions. This is the distinction between the rightness and the richness of solutions. Accurate analysis should lead one to a workable solution: this does not necessarily mean that it will lead one to the best solution. Taking World's Wines as our example, an obvious answer to delays in the processing of orders is to speed up the process (presumably by substituting a computer for clerical effort). But tunnel vision of this sort, to which many computer people are prone, may ignore entirely different classes of solution, such as reducing the number of lines sold, or instituting standard orders.

Creative thinking is a subject that merits, and has received, many books in its own right.[1] In this book therefore I shall only touch on the best-known techniques and demonstrate their relevance to business systems design.

(a) REVERSAL THINKING

Reversal thinking invites you to stand a problem on its head. If we define World's Wines' problem as one of getting the goods to the customers, we might suggest solving it by getting the customers to come to the goods, i.e., by turning the organization into a cash-and-carry, or at least offering a discount for any individual customer willing to pick up his own order.

(b) ANALOGY THINKING

Arthur Koestler defined creativity as 'bisociation'—the putting together of two ideas to form a third. The borrowing or adaptation of ideas from one source to utilize elsewhere is one of the most fundamental methods of invention. This is not restricted to seeing what other people in the same business do; the solution may be drawn from totally different disciplines. A large bookmaking company with whom I had a credit account informed me recently that bets for less than £5 would no longer be accepted by telephone, though I could still of course place them at a betting shop. The systems rationale for this is obvious: the cost of processing a £5 bet is the same as for a £5000 bet, but the return commensurately less; the customer is therefore channelled in a certain direction. For World's Wines, the equivalent would clearly be to impose a minimum order quantity.[2]

---

[1] Most obviously, Edward de Bono's *Lateral Thinking*, Penguin, Harmondsworth, 1977.

[2] Analogy thinking is of course used not only to invent new concepts but to explain old ones. The use of words such as 'memory' in computers stems from an early analogy with the human brain. The function of the heart in human physiology was properly understood only after the independent invention of the pump. Prior to this, the conventional explanation of the heart's function was by analogy to a furnace (a readily understandable misconception in view of the coldness of the body which rapidly follows upon the heart stopping beating).

(c) BRAINSTORMING

The most widespread manifestation of creative thinking is brainstorming. Again, this is merely the formalization of a technique utilized for centuries. According to Herodotus, the Persians used to take all decisions twice: once at night, when full of mead to encourage originality, then again the following morning, to engender discretion. To bring this up from the centuries before Christ to the present day, this process is explained physiologically by the differences between the left and right hemispheres of the brain. The latter is the creative side; the former, the analytical. A sufficient quantity of alcohol serves to deaden the left brain, leaving the right free to come up with bright new ideas. This explains the flashes of brilliance which come to us at late parties, only to seem less inspired the next morning when the left brain is firmly back in command.

Whether one appeals to the classics or to neurological research, the underlying principle is clear: first, originate as many ideas as possible, repressing the analytical process as being fundamentally anti-creative; then, subject the ideas thus aroused to critical evaluation. This fits perfectly with the procedure described above for finding the 'best' solution. The 'best' solution has to be thought of in the first place; i.e., it has to be among the 'candidate' solutions (or at least developed from them), and it has then to be evaluated as superior to all others. This evaluation can, of course, be done only on the basis of a set of agreed criteria, which is the exact function of our project request.

Let us apply the technique of brainstorming to a traffic problem such as Sydney Harbour bridge. The main commercial and industrial area of Sydney is located on the south side of the harbour and a heavily populated residential area on the north. As a result traffic jams build up at the northern end during the morning rush hour and at the southern end during the evening. An investigation reveals that the queues build up at the toll booths, and that traffic moves smoothly once through the booths and on to the bridge. (If traffic were held up on the bridge, our cause and effect analysis would yield a different answer and point to a different solution.)

Having correctly defined the problem and conducted an investigation to determine its cause, we can now begin to look for potential solutions. Employing the first rule of thumb proposed earlier, we recognize that this is a common problem and investigate how other cities with such a problem deal with it. Immediately, a number of different solutions present themselves:

1. Hong Kong has a Harbour Tunnel.
2. The Auckland Bridge in New Zealand has a one-way toll.
3. The George Washington Bridge in New York City has a second level.
4. The Nigerian government instituted a system whereby drivers could use their cars only on alternate days.

Not all solutions will be applicable to our own problem (particularly the latter!), but the process of evaluating the different ideas comes later. At this stage we are merely coming up with possible solutions.

Applying the technique of brainstorming to the Harbour Bridge problem results in an expanded list of possible solutions:

5. Build a second bridge.
6. Abolish tolls completely.
7. Stagger working hours in Sydney.
8. Encourage people to use public transport.
9. Move Sydney to the other side of the bridge.
10. Fill in the harbour.
11. Issue season tickets for toll payment.
12. Quadruple the toll charges.
13. Install automatic tolls.
14. Get people to share cars.

Brainstorming is useful in maximizing the list of candidate solutions, typically 30 or more. Having done this, we can now analyse the list by grouping them into like sets. Our first grouping of the suggested solutions shows two broad classes:

– Speed up the flow of traffic, for example by widening the bridge.
– Reduce the volume of traffic over the bridge, either by providing alternative routes or by persuading people to leave their cars at home.

The first class of solutions treats the volume of traffic over the bridge as a fixed element and concentrates on improving its flow; the second treats the bridge capacity as fixed and looks at ways of having fewer cars use it. Note that, although we have arrived analytically at this division, this does not mean that we cannot combine both approaches in solving the problem: they are not mutually exclusive.

A third class of solutions is implicit in our statement of the problem (but only if the problem is clearly defined): this is to smooth out the morning and evening peaks. An examination of our 14 suggestions shows that they all fit within one of these classes and that therefore our analysis is correct. For simplicity, let us represent this first category of solutions as four separate classes (Fig. 11.2).

What we have arrived at is a number of candidate solutions. We now need to evaluate them. We can only do this by reference to the initial project request. This should describe not only the objectives of the new system but also the constraints. The latter are important if we are not to waste a great deal of time refining unacceptable solutions. An overall constraint on any solution is that it has to be within the power of the user to implement. For the Harbour Bridge problem this eliminates solutions 4, 7, 9, and 10. This does not mean that they were not worth consideration—at governmental level, dispersing commercial activity away from a metropolis is a feasible solution. Indeed, in the mid-sixties the British government set up a body called the Location of Offices Bureau specifically charged with this duty. (The fact that ten years later they started to encourage businesses back to London because of inner-city depopulation is merely another example of the perversity of systems.) But it is an interesting commentary on the brainstorming technique that what is at first glance the most ludicrous idea contains the germ of a possible solution.

A second constraint, that of cost, eliminates solutions 1, 3, 5, and 6. The NSW Traffic Commission can afford neither a new, large capital project, nor the loss of operating revenue from the present tolls.

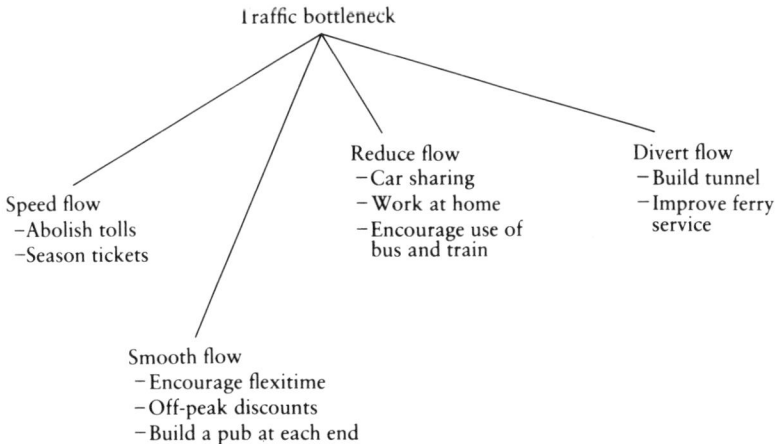

Traffic bottleneck

Speed flow
 −Abolish tolls
 −Season tickets

Reduce flow
 −Car sharing
 − Work at home
 −Encourage use of
 bus and train

Divert flow
 −Build tunnel
 −Improve ferry
 service

Smooth flow
 − Encourage flexitime
 −Off-peak discounts
 −Build a pub at each end

**Figure 11.2** Analysis of solutions to traffic bottlenecks

97

Elimination of eight solutions leaves us with six to consider in greater detail. This consideration will typically involve us in consultation with the user. He advises us that prohibitively increased toll charges are not acceptable, although they are technically within the Commission's competence, and that the use of season tickets is inferior to another of our solutions—that of automated tolls. Our final recommended system is therefore a composite of four individual ideas (all of which have been implemented in Sydney):

- Collect tolls in the north–south direction only, doubling the toll to avoid loss of revenue.
- Install automatic tolls which operate on detection of the correct toll (with an 'exception' manned booth for drivers without change).
- Reduce fares on public transport in order to shift traffic to different carriers.
- Modify existing bus lanes to allow their use by private cars carrying three or more people.

There is a multiplicity of useful lessons about systems work to be drawn from this example. First, there is the recommendation of four different but complementary innovations. We can state it as an inviolable rule that, in the complex world of modern business organizations, there exist no panaceas—least of all the application of a computer. What we will invariably find is that there will be a range of contributory improvements, perhaps including the use of automation, which together will add up to a new system.

Second, in designing a system to be used by our employees, our customers, or the general public, we frequently have to take a view about their reaction to the new system. Can they find an alternative south-bound route into Sydney while still returning in the free direction? What reduction in public transport fare is necessary to make a significant impact on car usage?

Third, and related to the above, the system has to be monitored once it is installed. If there is a significant drop in toll revenue caused by people circumventing the south-bound trip, what is the level at which this becomes unacceptable?

However, the vital point about the above example is that it is pure problem-solving. Once taken out of the field of data processing, with its jargon of databases, on-line access modes, and priority interrupts, it becomes manifestly clear that the analysis of business problems, as opposed to the strictly technical function of file design, is an activity that the non-computer expert is as well equipped to perform as the systems analyst himself.

The Sydney Harbour Bridge problem was given as an example of creative thinking through brainstorming. However, it is also a perfect example of analogy thinking. Sydney Harbour Bridge has a peak-hour traffic jam caused by too many cars using too narrow a channel; World's Wines have a backlog caused by too many orders trying to get through too slow a department.

Let us examine the similarities. For the Harbour Bridge problem we sketched a simple breakdown (Fig. 11.2) which represented the classes of solution to the problem. If we apply a similar analysis to the problem of World's Wines' backlog of orders, we can draw up an equivalent list of candidate solutions (Fig. 11.3). This is an example of the analytical approach to systems design, but notice too that the two other

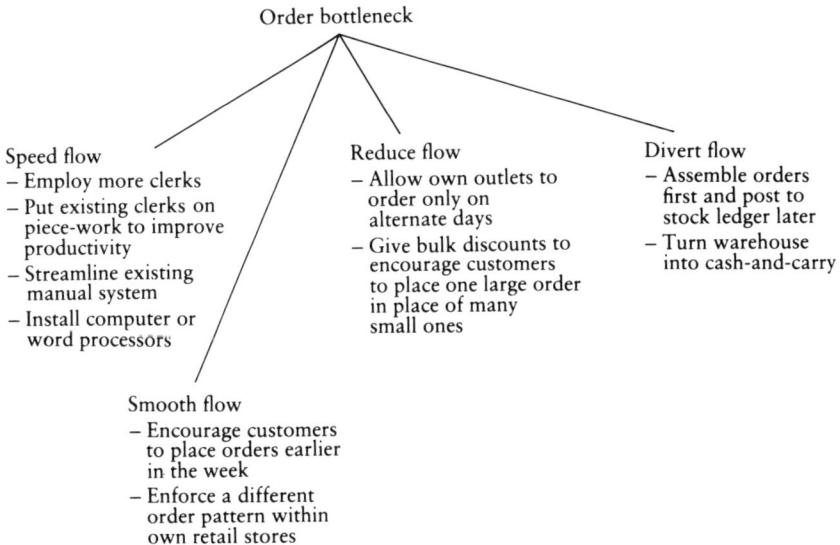

Order bottleneck

Speed flow
– Employ more clerks
– Put existing clerks on piece-work to improve productivity
– Streamline existing manual system
– Install computer or word processors

Reduce flow
– Allow own outlets to order only on alternate days
– Give bulk discounts to encourage customers to place one large order in place of many small ones

Divert flow
– Assemble orders first and post to stock ledger later
– Turn warehouse into cash-and-carry

Smooth flow
– Encourage customers to place orders earlier in the week
– Enforce a different order pattern within own retail stores

Figure 11.3  Analysis of solutions to World's Wines' backlog problem

approaches mentioned earlier—'What are other companies doing?' and multi-disciplinary thinking—also assist us in the task of devising candidate solutions.

Peaking is one of the most common of business problems, and the techniques of differential pricing are well known.[1] Looking at the same

[1] See Appendix A.

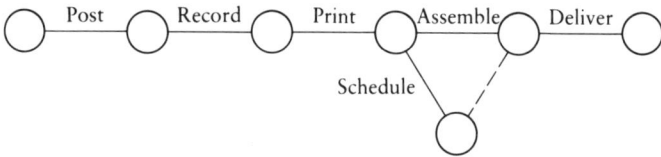

**Figure 11.4** World's Wines current system: critical path analysis

problem through the eyes of someone of a different discipline, it is a critical path problem with an earliest finish date which is unacceptable to the user (Fig. 11.4).

Critical path analysis tells us that to bring the earliest finish date forward we must either shorten some of the activities on the critical path—e.g., add more clerks—or take one of the activities—e.g., ledger posting—off the critical path. As an added bonus from the use of this discipline, our network planner knows that, if he does succeed in expediting an activity, or removing it from the critical path, a new critical path may appear and our saving in time will not be as great as anticipated. Alternative networks therefore suggest themselves (Fig. 11.5). Or we could operate in parallel rather than in series (Fig. 11.6).

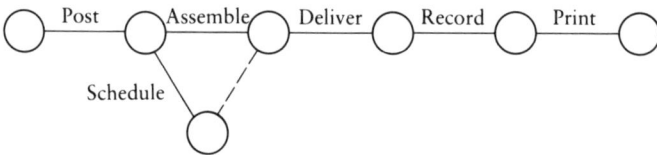

**Figure 11.5** Assemble and record serially

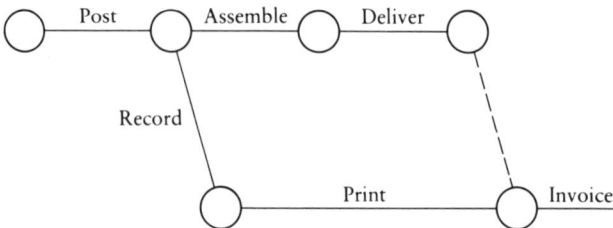

**Figure 11.6** Assemble and record concurrently

Again, once the problem is formulated in this way, it is clear that users can play an essential and active role in designing new solutions. Installing a computer is only one of the solutions within the set SPEED FLOW. This is not to rule it out: these days it would be unlikely if the new system did not use some form of automated data processing. But it is equally probable that, among the many other solutions considered, there will be other improvements which can be implemented in conjunction with a computer-based solution, and which will increase the effectiveness of that solution.

# 12. Logical systems design

*The golden rule is that there are no golden rules.*

George Bernard Shaw

Stan has been thinking about the various possible solutions. In fact, he has been analysing them by a different approach. This analysis divides the possible solutions into two groups: those that, being either trivial or sufficiently technical, he will not bother at this stage to put forward, and those that are sufficiently far-reaching in terms of changes in working practices to require immediate discussion. In the second category is any new system which changes the sequence of processes within the company. He goes to see George Wynne.

GW    Stan, you said you wanted to clarify a couple of points. Tell me, how are things going?

SB    Well, you'll remember in our last conversation I said I thought the main problem was the bottleneck in stock recording. In fact, we both agreed on that.

GW    Sure.

SB    Since then I've been looking at various ways in which we could solve that problem and the others that we have defined. A lot of ideas are just for small improvements. Others depend upon what decision we come to about a computer. However, the reason I wanted to get back to you was to get a *business* decision—a policy decision, if you like, about stock control.

GW    What's that?

SB    It's this. The company, as you know, is currently running a 'free stock' system. That is, you examine your records to determine availability before sending orders to the warehouse—as opposed to a physical stock system, where you assemble orders first and then simply record what was sent.

GW    That's right. We've always done it that way.

SB    Why?

GW    What do you mean, 'Why?' It's been done that way as long as I can remember.

It is to be hoped that George Wynne is not quite as blinkered as his last remark makes out. Nevertheless, it is a fact that a high proportion of business practices are carried out the way they are because 'it's always been done that way'.

Before any radical change is recommended, it clearly must be agreed by senior management. A new system which sent orders straight to the warehouse would necessitate a major change in working practice. Our most significant analysis of World's Wines can therefore be seen as having nothing to do with computers. Either system can work with or without a computer. This can very simply be represented in Fig. 12.1.

To come up with a reasoned answer to the question of why World's Wines do it one way and not the other, we could perform an analysis of the various strategies for stock control. Stan Breagan has performed his own analysis as a result of his investigation, and his conclusions form the remainder of this chapter. But one could argue that he was re-inventing the wheel. The pros and cons of what he terms 'pick first' and 'record first' are well documented.[1]

The previous chapter ended with a number of ideas for solutions to World's Wines' order processing problem. Some are mutually exclusive, others not. Some are at a high level, necessitating major policy decisions; others are minor improvements to existing procedures.

After the creative stage of formulating candidate solutions comes the evaluative stage of determining which are worth pursuing. This is first done by reference to the original project request, examining each solution to see whether it meets the objectives, without breaching any of the constraints. Additionally, we determine whether a given solution is

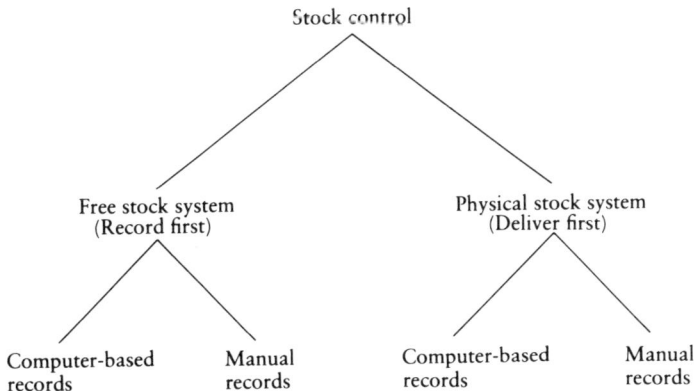

**Figure 12.1** Free stock *v.* physical stock system

[1] Stan would have been well-advised to read R. G. Breadmore's *Organisation and Methods*, Teach Yourself Books, 1971.

workable. For example, if we cannot get more clerks, or if the introduction of double-shift work is ruled out, these ideas are rejected. We consult with interested parties, such as the storemen, to find out whether our idea of sending orders to the warehouse first poses problems for them. If it does, say because of legibility difficulties, do we reject this approach, or can we get round this?

The conclusions we reach after carrying out this exercise on World's Wines are that the solutions aimed at smoothing the flow contribute, but only marginally; the same applies to the introduction of bulk discounts. Either of these may be implemented in conjunction with a wider solution. Outlets ordering only on alternate days, or turning the warehouse into a cash-and-carry, are policy matters needing referral to senior management.

But the high-level strategic decision concerns the flow of the system. Is it better to assemble orders first, leaving the stock recording until later, or should we update our stock records before order assembly? This is the most important decision that management has to make. We can represent these alternatives diagrammatically.

*Solution 1: Deliver first*
Figure 12.2 shows orders being passed to the scheduling function immediately after credit checking. From here they are assembled and delivered prior to updating the stock records. Goods are delivered, and any adjustments—returns or breakages—are fed back into the system, updating the stock records and customer billing.

Were this considered the best sequence of operations, we could foresee various physical means of accomplishing it, ranging from a completely manual system involving multi-part order sets to a computer system with data being captured after the goods had been picked.

*Solution 2: Record first*
This flow is the same as that of the current system (see Fig. 12.3). Orders update the stock records before going into the warehouse. Again, we can identify variants of this overall solution. For example, if the number of breakages or returns is low, invoices can be produced at the same time as dispatch documentation rather than waiting for the signed delivery note to return. The answer to the question, 'Why then?' On our problem analysis of the current system (i.e., 'Why do they wait for the delivery note to return before invoicing?') is that customers withhold payment if there are discrepancies between what is delivered and what is
104

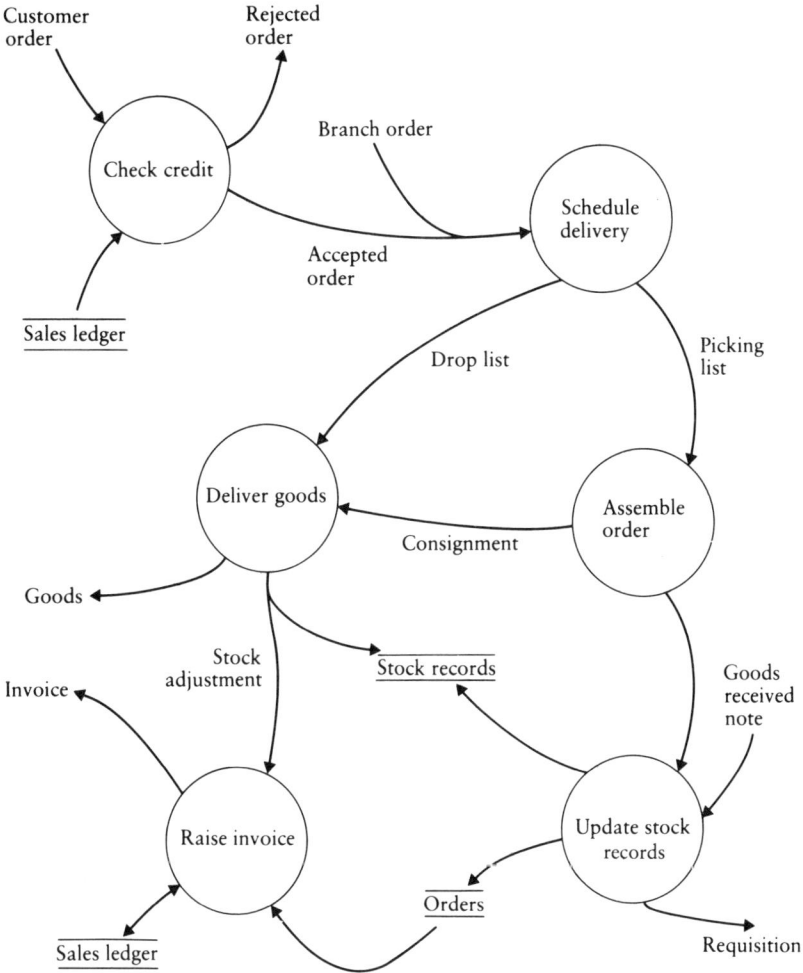

**Figure 12.2** Solution 1: Deliver first. Consignment = goods + delivery note; Goods =
Physical goods + customer advice note

invoiced. We must be careful not to accidentally worsen our cash flow
when we think we are helping it (see Chapter 14 below).

Having identified the alternatives, we need to examine them to see if
they meet the objectives. This can only be done by assigning tentative
*physical* solutions. In determining a physical solution, the requirement
to produce regular, current management information is crucial. Given
the volumes of data involved, there is no realistic way of doing this

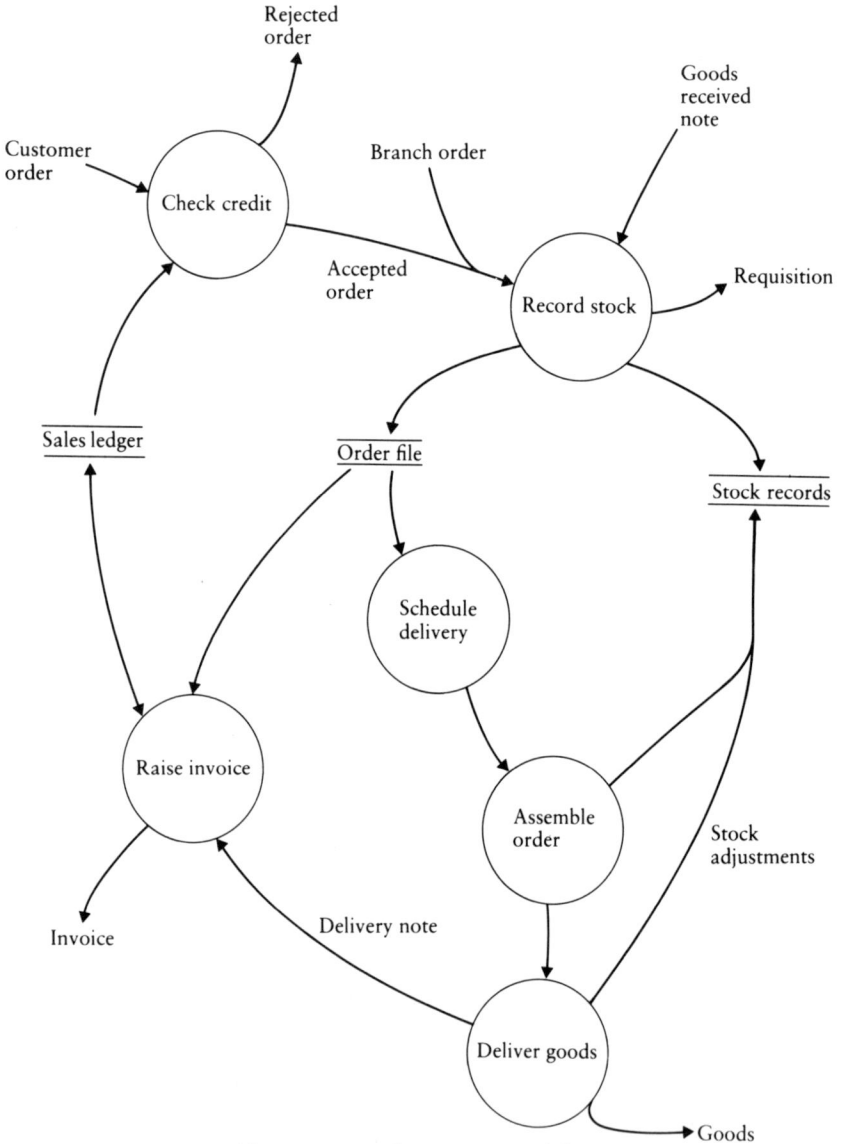

**Figure 12.3** Solution 2: Record first

without using a computer. But note that this decision results from specifying certain business objectives, which brought a requirement for improved management information. The computer is the means, not the end.

106

We can now evaluate the alternative solutions. Both can meet all three primary objectives set by management. Whether they can meet the cost constraint we shall determine only by doing a preliminary costing. Let us look at the advantages of Solution 1, picking the orders first.

1. This is probably the cheapest solution. Taking the computer function of stock recording off the critical path means that we can contemplate a system which does not require the company to purchase its own computer—it can use that of a commercial bureau to maintain its stock records and produce invoices.
2. It can be more speedily implemented. For one reason, the computer system is likely to be simpler. But also, it appears possible to implement Solution 1 as an interim measure before the computer system is ready.
3. It has the attraction of going straight to the heart of the problem. If the objective is to get the goods on the road, let us do that and worry about recording things afterwards.

What, then, are the disadvantages?

1. Picking first, recording second, will mean that we lose our advance warning of low stock. This will now become known to us after, not before, the items are picked. Recording stock concurrent with picking will largely overcome this, but we may still have to be prepared to raise re-order levels slightly.
2. Our analysis of why the current system records orders before picking gave the following user responses:
   - Not all orders are on standard stationery. It is better for us to prepare standardized picking documents than to rely on the warehouse picking from non-standard ones.
   - We can control the substitution of one product for another. We would not trust the storemen to do that.
   - We can use our judgement and hold back fast-moving stock that is in short supply. Again, we could not expect the storemen to do that.
   - We can more efficiently deal with back orders.

   These are all difficulties for a solution involving picking first. They can possibly be overcome by expedients such as a two-bin system in the warehouse, or transferring a couple of stock clerks to the warehouse, but they reduce the initial attraction of this solution.
3. In talking to the stores manager, we discovered that it would be of

considerable help to him if orders arrived in the warehouse with the lines on each order sequenced to match the physical layout of the warehouse. A computer will do this easily; a 'pick first' solution cannot, other than by using pre-printed order forms.

This type of analysis can be repeated for Solution 2. I shall not do so here because in general the advantages and disadvantages are the converse of those for Solution 1. What is required is for someone to choose between them. The rule here is: *analysts clarify decisions; managers take them.* The major influences on the free stock *v.* physical stock decision are business-oriented—level of customer service, standard orders, call-offs. But the introduction of a computer itself changes the business environment. Possibly the greater speed and accuracy of their computer will allow us to operate a 'free stock' system while still meeting management's objectives for faster turn-round of orders. We can only answer this by coming up with 'trial' physical solutions.

Working at the logical level is a marvellous way of throwing ideas around without getting bogged down in technical matters. But if you want to know whether a given logical system will work within such constraints as processing time, cost, and security, we are forced to 'go physical'.

# 13. Physical systems design

*The executive exists to make sensible exceptions to general rules.*
Elting Morison

George does not think much of sending the orders straight to the warehouse. The Chairman would have a fit. The people there would be sending out Pouilly Fuissé instead of Pouilly Fumé. Mr Chichester may not be part of the white heat of the technological revolution, but he does know the wines and, most of all, the important customers. Better to leave things to go through him first.

GW  Well, Stan, my immediate reaction to your question about our method of stock control is to leave things the way they are—particularly if a computer system is fast enough to get the orders into the warehouse in time to fit in with our load planning.

SB  One of the people I've spent a fair bit of time talking to is Bob Griffiths, your Transport Supervisor. He's obviously keen to get a sight of orders as soon as possible, but reckons that, provided a new system can guarantee to have them to him by early afternoon, that'll be OK.

GW  But how can we be sure of that? We don't really know what the new system will do. Your diagrams are very good at showing what's going on, but they don't appear to show anything about *when* things happen and how fast.

SB  That's absolutely right. To do that we shall need to examine different physical solutions.

GW  What do you mean by that?

SB  I mean that we shall have to take our diagrams and make some assumptions about what they will look like in terms of actual files, inputs, and outputs in a computer system, and how the programs will link them together.

GW  Well that's where I'll just have to hope you know what you're up to. My daughter has got one of these home computers, but it's all beyond me.

SB  Hold on a bit. No one is suggesting you are going to have to sit down and write programs. But the new system is critical to your company's success. You need to check any design decisions. Don't worry. Let me teach you a bit about how computer systems work—enough at least for you to know what's going on and enable you to ask the right questions.

There are two basic methods by which computers process data:

- *batch processing*, where data is collected over a period of time and then all processed together; banks process cheques in this way;
- *transaction processing*, where each transaction is entered and processed separately. This is usually done via a screen, as airlines do when they book seats.

We can represent the batch processing approach to World's Wines in Fig. 13.1. This, which is broadly typical of all batch solutions in the sequence of processes, captures all data concerning orders and receipts together. The input medium may be diskettes where data is captured *off-line*, i.e., away from the computer, or it may be input through screens directly on to a disk, though without immediate updating of files. Either way, this confers the advantage of speed, as we may assume that this activity is done at an average speed of 10 000 key depressions per hour, giving a total time to capture the data of about 18 person-hours. The data then goes through the system in one batch and is processed according to the rules written into the individual programs. This of course necessitates that such rules are sufficiently clear-cut to be followed by a machine.

The significance of this last observation becomes clear when we consider the alternative system, which transacts orders (or order lines) as they come, rather than in a batch. As each order line is input, so the stock file is updated there and then (see Fig. 13.2). Entering data in this way will be slower, but you gain a crucial advantage. This method allows the user to *interact* with the computer system. If there is an error or a stock-out he is immediately made aware of this on his screen; he himself can decide what action to take when this arises.

Let us consider one of the exceptions that we identified in our investigation—substitutions. This is where a stock clerk, finding a stock-out of Nuits St Georges 1980, supplies a case of 1979, or even a Maçon.

What concerns us are the rules for such procedures. Are the clerks dedicated wine buffs who use their years of experience to exercise fine judgements about the merits of different vintages, or are there simple

110

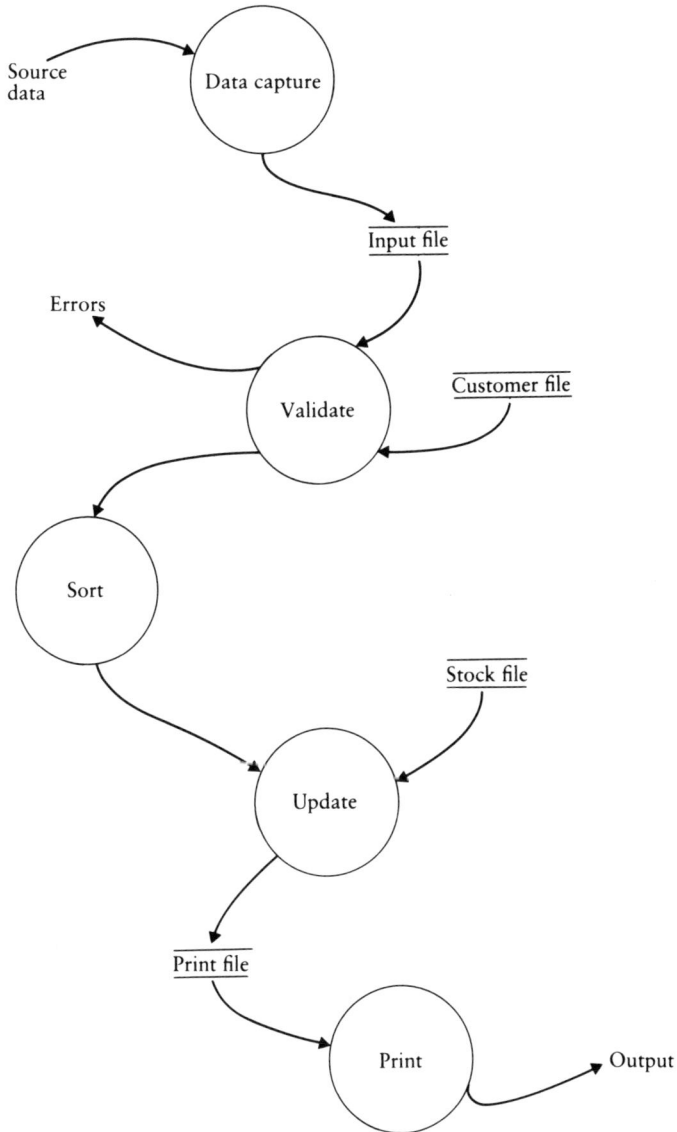

**Figure 13.1** Batch processing

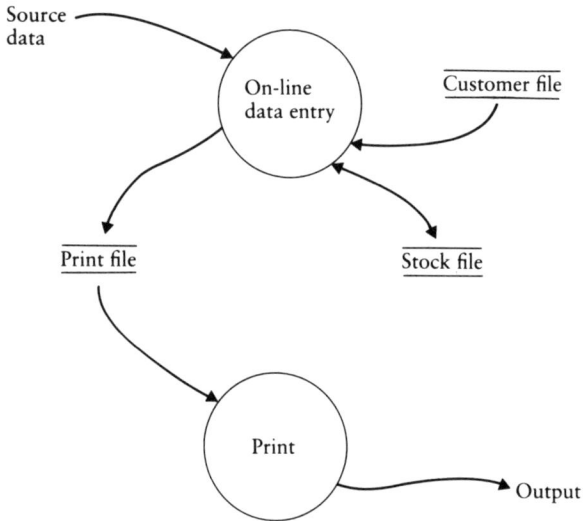

**Figure 13.2**  Transaction processing

rules that lay down that Côtes du Vivarais is always a substitute for Côtes du Rhône and vice versa?

*This distinction—between clearly formulated procedures and those that rely on judgement, experience, and 'feel'—is fundamental to designing good computer systems.* Computers are ideal for the first type but still have great difficulty with the second (that is, until the advent of 'expert systems' in the wine trade).

Our batch processing solution can work really efficiently only if the rules are clearly formulated, because all the 'intelligence' of the system is contained in the file-update program, which is not interactive. This program can easily handle substitutions if they are merely the automatic replacement of one line by another. But if the stock clerks really do apply 'local knowledge' then they can do this only by means of a system which allows them to make the decision at a terminal.

I have dwelt on this exception to the World's Wines' system because it typifies a critical design decision. Another procedure our investigation identified—that of 'holding back' certain fast-moving lines rather than working on a strict 'first-come, first-served' basis—would have served equally well as an example. What these two procedures illustrate is the key dilemma that comes up in every computer-based system:

What shall we do about exceptions?

Manual systems are good at exceptions, because people can make their own decisions (or refer them up); computer systems are bad at them, because they can only deal with things that have been completely thought out in advance. Since the problem of exceptions is universal, we should be able to formulate guidelines for dealing with them. My analysis of this problem dictates that the designer has three broad options open to him:

– program the procedure into the new system;
– leave as a manual procedure;
– abolish the procedure.

As an intellectual discovery, this falls some way short of the theory of relativity. Nevertheless, in terms of saving you money, it is invaluable. One of the commonest complaints levelled against computer systems is that they are complicated, inflexible, and difficult to maintain. What causes the complexity? Almost certainly, the multiplicity of exception conditions that have been included in the system. *The easiest way to simplify a computer system is to leave out as many of the exceptions as is feasible.*

Obviously, this is not always practicable. What I am advocating is not that we refuse to include exceptions in a system—that is totally unrealistic. What I do say is that the second and third options are usually given insufficient consideration in the rush to computerize everything in sight. And often this is the result of systems design being seen as the sole domain of the computer technician.

The key to the effective use of computers is to understand that there are many systems problems which are much better addressed by humans than by computers. For too long the balance has been struck in the computer's favour; it is time to redress it. Once the mystique has gone out of computers, they can be treated as a management tool, extending people's abilities rather than usurping them.

Let us apply two simple observations to World's Wines:

1. Computers are best suited to high-volume, repetitive tasks.
2. Exceptions and decision-making are much better handled by humans.

The first suggests that, since the vast majority of order lines behave in a precisely similar fashion, it is sensible to use the computer to batch-process these as speedily as possible. The second suggests that the minority of exceptions—substitutions, rush orders—are best either abolished or subject to some form of manual override. The latter implies some form of transaction processing so that clerks have access to an up-to-date stock file as they process the orders.

The initial physical design decision therefore revolves around the trade-off between batch and on-line. In some cases it is easy. It is no good having a batch-processing airline reservation system; it will tell you that you have available seats when the plane is half-way to Bahrain. Batch-processing is often necessitated by the mode of data capture. Transactions captured at point-of-sale terminals arrive already batched; so do large numbers of, say, electricity meter readings.

With World's Wines, the decision is more evenly weighted. Can we gain the benefit of batch processing by abolishing such exceptions as substitutions and working on a strict first-come, first-served basis for stock allocation? Do we prefer to settle for slower data entry as the price to be paid for a system that allows our experienced clerks to exercise their decision-making function?

At this point the user needs technical advice. How much faster is it to process data in a batch than to update the stock file with each transaction? Do the added security considerations of immediate updating make the system more vulnerable or more expensive? Indeed, do we need to decide this at this point, or should we start looking for a package and leave the decision as part of our evaluation of packages?

The answer to this last question is as follows: If we are to cost the proposed system, and see whether the business objectives are being met, we need at least an outline physical system; e.g., we need to know how many screens and operators there will be. We are not irrevocably committing ourselves to this exact design, but we do need some basis for a cost–benefit analysis.

Significantly, the choice between different physical systems has forced user management into making decisions of business policy on issues such as substitutions, stock priority, back orders, and so on. My guess— and therefore our working presumption for what follows—is that World's Wines would opt for a transaction-processing system, updating the stock file with receipts as well as orders as they arrive.

Another checkpoint. We have now arrived at a provisional physical design for World's Wines' new order processing system. How closely the final system will resemble this is difficult to foretell. For a start, we intend to look for a packaged system, and there is no certainty that the one we choose will exactly match our own physical solution. However, even if this turns out to be the case, the work we have done so far is not wasted. Close investigation and careful analysis are totally necessary. Without them, we would have no basis on which to decide between a purpose-built system and a package, or between rival packages which purport to fit our needs.

# 14. The law of unintended effect

*Real skill lies not in finding a solution to your problem but problems in your solution.*

Antony Jay

In the 1970s, three pieces of legislation were enacted designed respectively to protect employment (the Protection of Employment Act), to increase the rights of tenants against rapacious landlords (Fair Rents Acts), and to abolish government subsidies to direct-grant schools, thereby forcing them back into the public sector. It is arguable that all three had the reverse effect to that intended. The Employee Protection Act so entrenched employees' rights that companies often feared to take them on in the first place, preferring to sub-contract work; the Rents legislation caused a drying-up of furnished accommodation to let while thousands remained homeless; and most direct-grant schools went completely independent.

In New South Wales, the introduction of random breath tests for motorists caused an increase in the work of the social services in dealing with cases of wife battering—as a result of a switch to home-drinking.

Devon County Council contemplated removing litter bins from Exmoor on the grounds that they attracted litter and overflowed, thereby making the place more, rather than less, unsightly.

To avid collectors of systems anomalies, these are all prize examples of the Law of Unintended Effect, whereby a new system has results unexpected by its designers and, in the extreme case, opposite to their intentions.

What causes this is *people*. People are perverse. They look for ways round systems, for means of bending the rules to their advantage. This is why the system called communism is such a total failure. *It suffers from the oldest constraint—original sin.*

It is this characteristic, amplified by Murphy's Law, that makes design validation so necessary. I meet few users who complain that their computer system failed to cure the problems of the previous manual system. What I do meet is users who complain that the new system brought new problems. Our modest but best hope in implementing new systems is that the new problems are less onerous than those they replace.

How can we hope to spot such problems? It helps if we divide them into two classes: those that are *generic* to all computer systems, and those that are *specific* to the system we are proposing. By virtue of being generic, we can devise a checklist of those problems that computer systems are heir to. First and foremost among them is:

What happens if the computer breaks down?

It is no easier to answer just because it is an old chestnut. Computers tend to centralize data. Companies quickly become dependent on them. In extreme cases, such as airline systems, companies go to the expense of duplicating computers to guard against machine malfunction. Actually, the question is more properly expressed as:

What happens if we lose our processing capability?

This formulation of the problem then embraces industrial action by operations staff as well as power failures and other misfortunes. As computer-dependency increases—in organizations such as the Inland Revenue or Customs and Excise—so does the temptation for unions to pull out a small number of key computer operations personnel. The government is currently contemplating decentralizing systems in these areas for just that reason.

Centralization of data, combined with user access through remote terminals, gives rise to legitimate concerns about security and privacy of data. This is another manifestation of the Fallacy of the Notional Ideal, in that few *manual* systems are all that secure, but users are naturally, and rightly, anxious. We have seen that, when specifying information requirements, security and privacy are key elements. There have been many instances of computer fraud on a large scale, of 'hackers' penetrating companies' security procedures, and of accidental errors leading to multi-million-pound losses.

In this chapter I want only to indicate the principles of increasing the security of systems. Appendix B contains checklists for computer audit which centre on the integrity of data and control of access.

The simplest approach to the security problem is to identify four essential elements:

prevention;
detection;

recovery;
insurance.

Most auditors work on the basis of two types of reviews, organizational and applications. The former will embrace an overall review of the organization of data processing within a company, the management controls, and installation standards; the latter examines individual applications, looking at the initial specifications, documentation, file controls, audit trails, and test data.

## Prevention

Guarding against accidental corruption of data consists mainly in, first, training users well enough to stop the occurrence in the first place, and then devising controls on input data—range checks, format checks, etc.—which reject errors before they are accepted into the system.

Prevention of deliberate breaches of security is considerably more difficult. Among the multiplicity of techniques aimed at this are the following.

### Passwords
User access can be controlled at many levels. The most fundamental is to deny access to the system at all. This can be by hardware lockout (otherwise known as a key to the terminal), or by password.

Passwords can be employed in many different ways:

- to control access to a specific file;
- to control access to specific records within a file;
- to control access to specific items of data within a record;
- to allow the user to read data but not to update it.

### Terminal controls
Another simple method is to restrict access to given files to specific terminals. Thus, only terminals located in the personnel department can be used to access the employee database.

### Data encryption
It is possible to 'scramble' the data held on a file. This will require a special program, which will amend data as it is added to a file in such a way that it becomes unreadable to an unauthorized 'browser'. Auth-

orized users possess a 'decrypt' password which causes the data to be converted back to its original format.

The essential principle behind any preventive measures is the multiplication of controls. If any one control mechanism gives you a 50:1 chance of avoiding a breach, then two separate controls make the figure 2500:1, and three lift it to 125 000:1. Of course, these odds are hypothetical, and the level of security has to be related to what is at risk.

### Detection

If security is breached—accidentally or deliberately—the next safeguard is to detect the breach. If an error occurs in allocating cash against a debtors' file, the system should detect this by a recalculation between the total of debits and credits input against the respective brought-forward and carried-forward totals on file. Most systems automatically close down on people who make multiple (therefore, presumed illicit) attempts to put in a password. The same principle causes Cashpoint dispensers to swallow bank cards. An on-line system should automatically log all transactions input through terminals so that random checks can be carried out to detect unauthorized use. Auditors will routinely carry out inspections of random accounts with a view to discovering any discrepancies.

### Recovery

Although computer frauds make the best newspaper stories, the commonest problem is with accidental loss of data. This may range from corruption of one file caused by a program error to loss of the installation's complete data as a result of fire, flood, or Act of God. This is where back-up comes in. Any computer operations department will copy all major files daily, together with the transactions necessary to reinstate them. Such procedures form part of any installation's standards and are done routinely. One problem with users' installing and operating their own micros is that, if proper standards are not enforced, such good 'housekeeping' tends to be neglected—with disastrous results.

### Insurance

Where the potential damage caused by a security breach is large, then the remedy is insurance. Hardware insurance may well be covered by the contract with the supplier, but the greater problem, requiring separate cover, is consequential loss resulting from the inability, for example, to invoice customers. The latter has a deleterious effect on cash-flow.

Responsibility for systems security rests in the first instance with its designers. The latter, however, may not possess expertise in such matters as audit trails. It is therefore essential that the company's auditors—internal or external—review any system *at the initial design stage* so that proper controls become part of the specification model.

Other questions on the general design validation checklist are:

- Can end-users cope with the new procedures—in particular, the loss of visible records?
- Does the system comply with legislation such as the Data Protection Act?
- Can the system adapt to changes in company policy or in the business environment?
- Is the system itself likely to change the behaviour of the users or the characteristics of the business?

The last one is where particularly the Law of Unintended Effect comes into its own. Our new order processing system could be so successful in improving customer service that customers respond by placing smaller orders more frequently, thereby increasing the volume of transactions in the system.

The first step in design validation is therefore to subject the proposed system to these questions. Once satisfactory answers have been obtained, we can move on to the search for potential problems specific to World's Wines.

By this stage in the proceedings, we should be reasonably confident that the proposed system is sound. What we are spotting are potential problems or combinations of circumstances which we have not considered. This activity therefore mirrors the systems investigation carried out on the existing system; specifically in that one is asking 'What if . . .?' questions:

- What happens if a substituted product is on a special offer?
- What happens if a customer rings up to amend a back order?

In the World's Wines example, one of the easiest things is accidentally to increase the number of deliveries. (This could happen if, for instance, the computer rejected one line on an order through an erroneous product code but let the remainder of the order through. The current system corrects such errors as they are met without destroying the integrity of the order.) Another would be if all that our system succeeds in doing is to shift the bottleneck from the stock recording department to the warehouse.

Very few people sit down and, as a deliberate process, try to spot such problems; yet it is one of the most important activities in the whole of a project.

# 15. Cost–benefit analysis

*If you require sophisticated calculations to justify an action, it is probably wrong.*

Robert Heller

Q.  When do you get cost figures for a project that you can believe?
A.  When the project is finished (if then).
Q.  When do you actually need such figures?
A.  Before the project starts.

When lecturing about topics such as project control and cost–benefit analysis, I would frequently feel a twinge of embarrassment that I had been flown vast distances to lecture to experienced managers on what was really only the application of common sense. The embarrassment was never so great as to cause me to turn down the trip, but it persisted—until I came across a quote from Will Rogers:

The trouble with common sense is that it ain't so common.

Cheered up by this, let us try applying common sense to the problem of costing computer systems.

My first observation is this: *you will not get the figures right.* Costing computer projects is about minimizing the miscalculations on which decisions are based.

My second observation is: *the earlier in any project that you estimate, the less accurate your predictions are likely to be.* We can represent this graphically (Fig. 15.1). The line is like a learning curve, rising quite steeply at first before flattening out. The kink near the end represents the unexpected cost increases caused by amendments to rectify the bugs found during systems testing. Note also that the line never reaches 100 per cent. Once the project is completed, the cover-up begins.

The problem with costing is that the usefulness of the prediction is an almost precise mirror-image of the accuracy line (Fig. 15.2). The line flattens out as soon as the project passes the point where the investment of money and management ego is such as to make its cancellation impossible. Normally there is a tacit agreement to stop counting at this stage.

The line does not reach zero usefulness provided we record the figures to assist in future project estimating. If the two lines are superimposed,

122

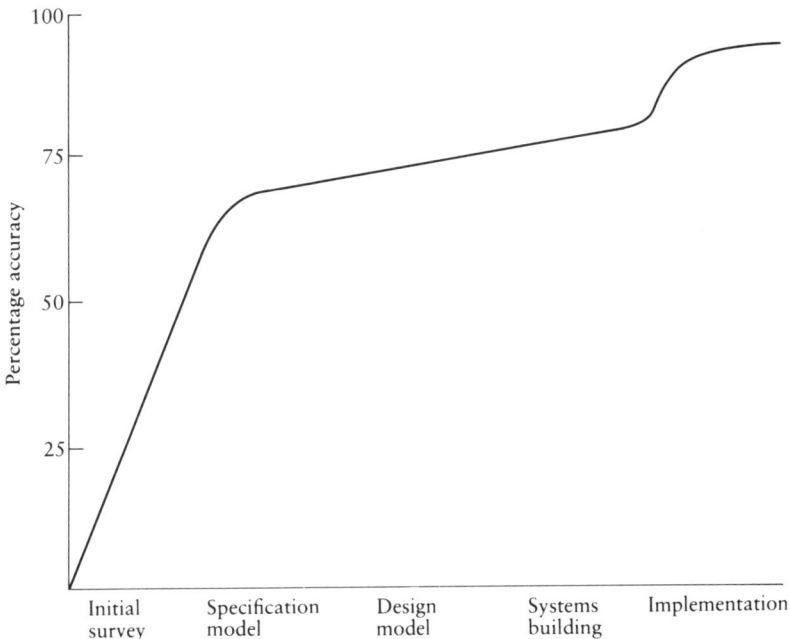

**Figure 15.1** Accuracy of estimates as a function of project phase

the intersection would show the point which optimizes the trade-off between accuracy and usefulness.

With World's Wines, this point is reached when we make our decision about which specific computer, with which particular software, will form the basis of our new system. We have not yet reached this point, but it is nevertheless an appropriate time to make our first quantified estimate of costs and benefits. The adjective 'quantified' is chosen deliberately to imply that there has already been an earlier 'gut feel' estimate. The 'gut feel' was sufficient for World's Wines to spend the initial £5000 for our initial survey. Before spending any more, it is sensible to get some indication of total project cost. Our most important analysis will come during the next phase when we make the expensive decision to go ahead and implement a new system. That decision is likely to involve hundreds of thousands of pounds in lifetime costs.

It is important to establish the principle of conducting the exercise more than once. Getting cost–benefit estimates right is as much an iterative process as getting systems designs right. Typically, however, companies look once, and once only, at a project, give the go-ahead on

123

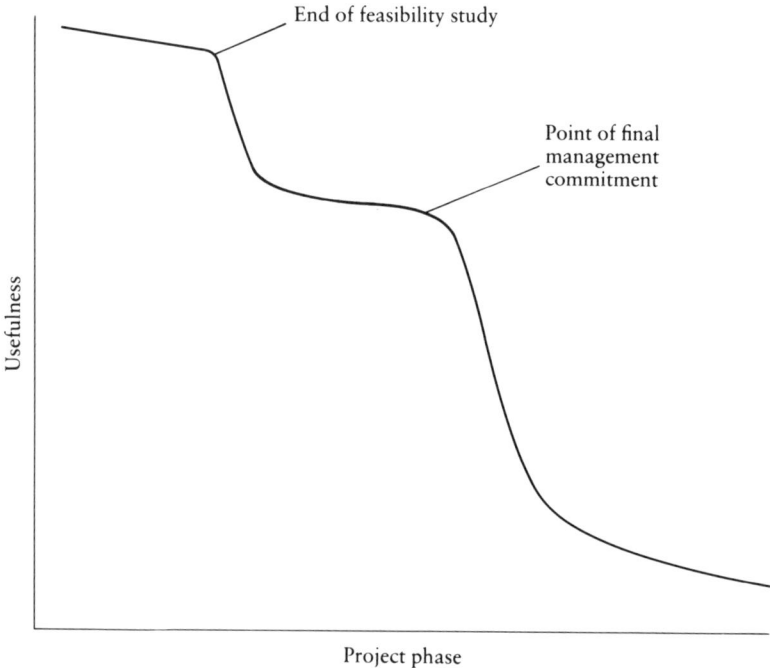

**Figure 15.2**   Usefulness of estimates as a function of project phase

optimistic figures arrived at in order to support a decision already made in principle, and then resist all temptation to review the figures— because revising estimates is seen (correctly) as a euphemism for increasing them, and no one wants to be caught doing that. With this caveat, let us examine the procedure for performing a cost–benefit analysis of a computer project.

The decision to implement a computer system is an investment decision. It is a decision to commit resources to a project so that the resultant system will improve efficiency and thereby reduce future operating costs. In this it differs little, if at all, from innumerable similar decisions that managers have to take.

Therefore, the feasibility study, having identified possible solutions, must evaluate them to see:

1. whether any or all are cost-effective in terms of return on the investment;
2. if more than one can be justified, which one is the preferred solution.

In order to ensure that one is comparing like with like, the normal practice is to reduce all choices to the same common denominator, viz. money. Those things that we cannot express in money terms—commonly known as 'intangible benefits'—will have to be treated separately.

This gives the following procedure:

1. Calculate development (one-time) cost.
2. Calculate operational savings (old system costs − new system costs).
3. Identify any non-quantifiable benefits.

The resultant figures can then be presented in whatever form is desired by the decision-maker, depending on which method of investment appraisal is used.

### One-time costs

#### The Thames Barrier

The Thames Barrier rose in all its glory for the first time yesterday three years later than planned and at a cost unthinkable at conception.

London's unique movable flood defence gates, spanning the Thames at Woolwich, stand 52 feet above the river-bed when fully operative. Ten gates, lying horizontally in concrete sills, turn 90 degrees to provide the capital with a solid wall against high waters.

It is, said Mr Iltyd Harrington, deputy leader of the GLC, 'A unique project which has taken away the fear of over one million Londoners. It is not the Kraken but Aphrodite.' The city's 'Aphrodite' has cost the Government and the Greater London Council more than £435 million to build. When the idea was first mooted in 1974 costs were estimated at £55 million and the work, which took eight years, was expected to last only five.

Mr Ray Horner, chief consultant for the flood defence system, said yesterday that problems were greatly underestimated because the project was the first of its kind. (*Guardian* report on construction of London's flood barrier)

The comment that problems were underestimated is so universal that the news story almost comes within the newspaper's category of 'Dog bites Man'. Sydney can quote two—the Eastern Suburbs Railway and the Opera House—and I recall once reading that the average ratio of final cost to initial estimate in US defence projects was 7:1. Perhaps more instructive would be stories of the 'Man bites Dog' variety, i.e., of large-scale projects which were delivered on time and within budget, such as the Hong Kong Mass Transit Railway.

What lessons can we draw from this? If one were cynical, one would remark that most such projects appear to be financed by central or local government. It is a great encouragement to lousy estimating that you do not bear the consequences of the over-run.

The more constructive lesson to be learned is that we need to identify those characteristics of a project that maximize the risk. If we can identify the latter for computer projects we can achieve two things:

1. better estimating in the future;
2. an actual reduction of risk on a given project by our ability to concentrate our attention on changes to a specification (e.g., reduction in project size) that will positively reduce risk.

A high-level analysis of cost over-runs gives us three reasons:

1. The system expands beyond the original specification.
2. Activities are overlooked in estimating resources needed.
3. The cost of individual activities is underestimated.

The first of these is about control of the development of the system. A specification must set the boundaries carefully, and they should then be adhered to. The contingency factor should be built into our estimates to allow for the small changes that are inevitable in any system. If during the project we need to increase its scope by a non-trivial amount, then the decision to do so should be the subject of a separate cost–benefit analysis and estimates should be revised.

The other reasons for cost over-runs are to do with the estimating activity itself. Can a user hope to do his own estimating, or is he reliant on technical expertise? The answer to this is that estimating calls for experience more than technical expertise. *People are bad at estimating because they lack practice.* As has been pointed out elsewhere,[1] this same reason explains why most people are bad at playing the zither. It is not much use asking me to estimate the time and cost of building a 15 mile section of motorway; however, an estimator employed by a construction company should become pretty good at it. Indeed he would have to, since the company's continued profitability depends largely on his expertise. His skill would be greater than mine because of

[1] Tom DeMarco, *Controlling Software Projects*, Yourdon Press, 1983.

his knowledge of the variables—not only the easily quantifiable ones, like the time taken to lay 100 cubic metres of concrete, but less predictable ones, such as weather and the influence of the terrain.

What are the equivalent variables that affect computer projects? Specifically, what are the factors that involve the greatest risk of project over-run? The many studies that have been carried out indicate that the major factors are:

- project size (the larger the project, the greater the risk);
- user commitment;
- number of systems interfaces.

We can refer to these as *strategic* risk factors.[1] It assumes that we have already done our cost estimates for project investment and time-scales and are able to make judgements about issues such as functional complexity. The single most important—and most difficult—estimate, that of software development, will be dealt with in the following chapter.

In some instances a management (or accounting) decision is necessary to define what items are to be included in project costs. Do we include management time at presentations? Do we cost the interviewee's time in a systems investigation? The same body will also have to decree the rate at which people's time is to be charged (components are recorded as person-hours).

Let us suppose that a cost estimate has been drawn up for World's Wines (see Table 15.1). Since World's Wines has no prior experience of computer projects, it will have relied heavily on Stan for these figures. One service he will perform for them in his role as project manager will be to ensure that actual costs are collected. This will be the start of World's Wines' own estimating database.

### Operational savings

Whether the one-time cost turns out to be £50 000 or £250 000, it will need to be justified in terms of increased profit to the company.

The first question we need to answer is, Over what period do we perform the analysis? Five years is a reasonable time to adopt for the life of the system. So we will use this as our base, starting from the anticipated date on which the system will go live. (If the figures do not look too good we can always go back and re-do them over seven years!)

---

[1] For a more detailed treatment of this important topic, and a weighting method to cater for risk, see Appendix D.

**Table 15.1** Project cost estimate

| | |
|---|---|
| Hardware* | £26 000 |
| Software† | £9 000 (£20 000) |
| Site preparation + installation | £8 000 |
| File set-up‡ | £3 000 |
| Training | £5 000 |
| Implementation | £4 000 |
| Consumables | £2 000 |
| Project management (Stan) | £5 000 |
| Redundancy payments | £8 000 |
| | £70 000 |

\* Based on minicomputer with five screens as advised by Stan.
† Lower estimate assumes purchase of package; higher estimate assumes development by outside software house.
‡ Based on data capture from existing manual files including physical stock-take.

There is a choice of two approaches to calculating operational savings. We can either extrapolate the full running costs of the current system and subtract from these the full estimated costs of our new system; or, because there will be a fair degree of costs common to both, we can concentrate on the *differences* between the systems. Adopting the latter method in World's Wines, we arrive at the figures given in Table 15.2.

Having now estimated both one-time cost and running costs, we can use our chosen investment appraisal method to complete this part of the analysis. World's Wines use a net present value approach, as is shown in Table 15.3. Because this is merely an illustration, there are some qualifications that must be added.

– World's Wines' current system is labour-intensive, so we would expect a computer-based system to show operational savings. In systems in which the main function is to produce management information, it is likely that the new system will cost more to run than the old and the cost justification has to be based on the use of this new information.
– The example is over-simplified. To undertake such an exercise for real requires a checklist from which to work to ensure that no obvious cost categories are forgotten.[1]

[1] An excellent book for checklists such as these is M. J. Turner's *Buying a Business Computer*, First Computer Handbook, 1980.

**Table 15.2** Operational costs and savings
($£'000s$ p.a.)

| | | | Year | | |
|---|---|---|---|---|---|
| | *1* | *2* | *3* | *4* | *5* |
| *Costs* | | | | | |
| Computer hardware | | | | | |
|    Site | 2 | 2 | 2 | 3 | 3 |
|    Maintenance | 3 | 3 | 3 | 4 | 4 |
|    Consumables | 6 | 7 | 8 | 9 | 10 |
| Systems supervisor | 15 | 16 | 18 | 20 | 22 |
| Order entry staff | 28 | 30 | 32 | 34 | 36 |
| Stan Breagan retainer (!) | 4 | – | – | – | – |
| | 58 | 58 | 63 | 70 | 75 |
| *Savings* (net) | | | | | |
| Stock clerks | 30 | 34 | 38 | 43 | 48 |
| Typists | 15 | 17 | 19 | 22 | 26 |
| Invoice clerks | 15 | 17 | 19 | 22 | 26 |
| Transport | 8 | 8 | 8 | 10 | 10 |
| Order assembly | 6 | 6 | 6 | 8 | 8 |
| | 74 | 82 | 90 | 105 | 118 |

*Notes:*
– Assumes that some existing clerical staff are retrained as order entry clerks.
– Savings in transport and order assembly based on estimates given by user management in these areas.

– In our example, *any* computer-based system is likely to show impressive savings; hence the necessity for considering more than one solution. Going ahead with a system with an NPV of £15 000 is a good business proposition—but not if a different solution shows an NPV of £30 000.

However, the primitive nature of our costing, and the scepticism with which I trust the reader has viewed it, is educative. Cost–benefit analysis is *not* a precise science. Indeed, there is the suspicion that some people adjust figures retrospectively in order to arrive at a predetermined result. The responsibility of management is to set up a system for estimating, and then tracking, both costs and benefits which cannot easily be manipulated. A prerequisite of this is the charging out of costs

**Table 15.3** Investment appraisal

| Yr | One-time costs | Operational costs | Operational savings | Net cash flow | DCF factor | Discounted net cash flow |
|---|---|---|---|---|---|---|
| | (£'000s) | (£'000s) | (£'000s) | (£'000s) | | (£) |
| 0 | 70 | — | — | −70 | 1.00 | −70 000 |
| 1 | | 58 | 74 | 16 | 0.87 | 13 920 |
| 2 | | 58 | 82 | 24 | 0.756 | 18 144 |
| 3 | | 63 | 90 | 27 | 0.658 | 17 766 |
| 4 | | 70 | 105 | 35 | 0.572 | 20 020 |
| 5 | | 75 | 118 | 43 | 0.497 | 21 371 |
| | | | Net present value (NPV) | | | 21 221 |
| | | | Risk-adjusted NPV* | | | 15 916 |

* Applying our risk adjustment factor of 0.75: see Appendix D.

to the users whose project it is. This may be dismissed as 'funny money', but inter-company it is the only type there is. All inter-company transfers are notional in this sense, but that does not make them any less real on a user's budget. Without the discipline that this provides, there is little incentive on a user to trade-off his full requirements against the cost of providing them.

### Intangible benefits

Much nonsense is talked and written about intangible benefits. Most of it partakes of the Fallacy of the Notional Ideal, i.e., the belief that, outside of computer projects, the world is full of projects the benefits of which are all tangible and easily quantifiable. The reverse is true. *In the real world, tangible benefits are the exception rather than the rule.* If you take a decision to educate your children privately, you can reasonably accurately quantify the costs of so doing, but the benefits . . .? What if you decide to go abroad for a holiday rather than stay at home and work on the house? If government legislates in favour of smoke-free fuel, it does not try to put a cash value on the additional hours of sunlight thus gained.

Should management therefore give up the attempt to put cash values on benefits such as 'improved management information'? Let us revert to the point that assigning money values is the only way of reducing disparate projects to a common denominator, and thereby the only rational method of choice. Management is not normally faced with the decision of whether to spend money on a computer system or not spend it at all: the decision is whether to spend the money on a new computer system or on a new switchboard, re-equipping the paint shop, or a host of other competing projects.

The only way to compare unlikes is by reducing them to a common denominator. In the absence of some agreed unit of Generalized Human Happiness—the maximizing of which would be the common end of all projects—money will have to do. Therefore one assigns cash values as best one can. The practical problem is that there is a continuum, ranging from the relatively easy to the near impossible, of the difficulty of assigning such values. This relates closely to the hierarchy of systems, from record-keeping, through control and enquiry, to management information (see Fig. 15.3).

To compound the problem, the higher up the difficulty scale one goes, the larger are the potential benefits. Saving four clerical jobs can be relatively easily estimated at £40 000 per annum. Reducing inventory of £3 million by 10 per cent at a stockholding cost of 20 per cent saves £60 000 per annum. Increasing direct sales by 3 per cent may yield an additional profit of £100 000. Providing your Research and Development staff with an information retrieval system which may result in

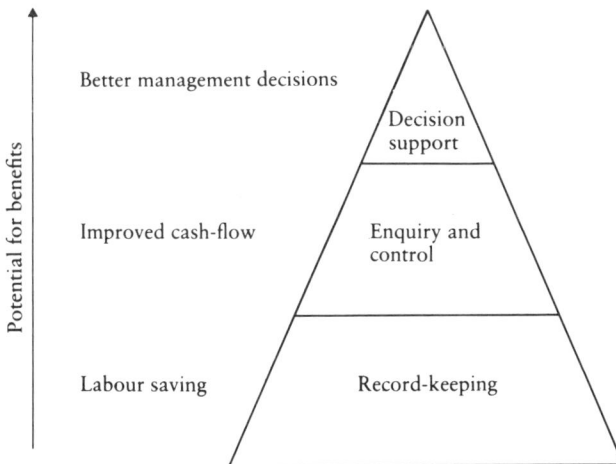

**Figure 15.3**   The systems hierarchy

131

much faster product improvement: £?. Giving senior management a financial model enabling them to improve strategic planning: £??.

Let us take two examples from different fields. A local government authority has to determine how to apportion its limited road improvement budget most efficiently. The criterion it uses is minimizing personal injuries through traffic accidents. To come to its decision, it compiles statistics about the incidence of accidents at various black spots in the area under its control. For this purpose accidents—or, to be precise, casualties—come in three categories: slight, serious, and fatal. We assume that the cost of effecting any improvement is known. We can now draw up a league table (Table 15.4).

Given that the sum of all possible schemes is £10 million and your budget is £5 million, which do you choose? Of course, the choice may be arrived at by the 'he who shouts loudest' method—a common method of decision-making in both business and government. But this is not guaranteed to deploy the budget in the most cost-effective manner. To do this clearly requires a scientific prioritization of the possible locations. The only means of doing this is by assigning respective cash values to slight, serious, and fatal accidents. Indeed, such figures are available. Multiplying them out enables you 'scientifically' to decide which location should have priority.

Or does it? I have a lurking suspicion that any such personal injury figures are *averages*. They draw together in one value fatalities of 25-year-old college graduates, in whom the community has invested thousands of pounds and who are about to become net creators of

Table 15.4   Evaluation of accident blackspots

| Location | No. of accidents last year | | | Cost of improvement (£) |
| | Slight | Serious | Fatal | |
| --- | --- | --- | --- | --- |
| 1. Intersection, A1/B276 | 14 | 6 | 3 | 800 000 |
| 2. Roundabout, A27/B14 | 10 | 5 | 2 | 400 000 |
| 3. Stretch, A271, 200 yards north of Five-ways Corner | 6 | 2 | 0 | 100 000 |
| 4. S-bend on B376 south of Townsville | 8 | 4 | 1 | 200 000 |
| 5.          (etc.) | | | | |

wealth, and those of elderly people, who are net recipients of community funds.

Does one then draw the conclusion that the scheme to put a pedestrian overpass next to the Old People's Home should be downgraded, as its cash value to the community is negative?

Finally, a story from school. At the end of term a schoolmaster of mine used to play a game to discover our relative preferences for detention, caning, and money. The question would be posed: 'You have been caught committing a misdemeanour [smoking behind the cycle sheds was his favourite in those days of innocence]: which punishment do you elect to undergo—60 minutes' detention after school, six strokes of the cane, or a 50p fine?' Votes were then recorded, values adjusted, and voting continued until equilibrium was reached, i.e., until the class votes were equal for each punishment. The end result was a notional class cash value for time spent in detention and corporal punishment.

This is in fact the only way of putting a value on non-cash benefits or dis-benefits. It is extremely difficult to answer the question, What value do you put on having this information available to you instantaneously? On the other hand, if you *first* quantify the cost of providing information immediately as opposed to having a report on your desk in 24 hours, the question can be rephrased in a much more intelligible manner:

'A system to provide you with the information you require the next day will cost £5000; one to provide it within 10 seconds will cost £20 000. Is the faster response worth the extra cost?'

For George Wynne, the major system objective is to improve order turn-round. What would be really useful to him would be a similar menu of options, such as:

| | | |
|---|---|---|
| System to reduce turn-round time to 2 days | | £40 000 |
| | 1 day | £70 000 |
| System to provide overnight turn-round | | £120 000 |

A prerequisite of true cost–benefit analysis is that the recipient of the benefit and bearers of the costs are one and the same. Often this is not the case. The beneficiaries of a third London Airport are travellers; the dis-beneficiaries (if this word does not exist, it is necessary to invent it) are those unfortunate enough to live under the flight path.

Thus far I have spent most of this chapter showing how difficult cost–

133

benefit analysis is. Is there a solution? I believe so—along the following lines:

1. Establish the basic method of investment appraisal—payout period, nett present value, discounted rate of return, management inspiration.
2. Decide which items are included as attributable project costs as opposed to being regarded as a general business overhead.
3. Quantify those things that are quantifiable, both costs and benefits.
4. Maintain historical data comparing actuals with estimates so as to develop skill in estimating. Analyse carefully the reasons for variance and compensate next time. If practice in estimating does not make perfect, it at least makes you a lot less bad.
5. Pay particular attention to the key assumptions, especially those that affect the benefits side. Do we really expect to reduce inventory by 15 per cent, or has that figure been arrived at retrospectively to bolster a rather thin case?
6. Regard estimating and costing as an *on-going* activity. Keep all assumptions, components, and estimates under review.

But the overall key to the original investment decision is this. No one is ever short of places to invest money. Your £50 000 could in complete safety earn 12 per cent on the money market. If that is too dull and you like a run for your money, buy gold or tin, or—if you insist on a computer-related project—buy shares in 'hi-tech' companies. The stock exchange exists as a mechanism for balancing return against risk.

On the spectrum of investment opportunities, which ranges from 'totally safe' to 'mad risk', computer projects are still well towards the risky end. Your basic approach to the decision on developing a new computer system should be:

- Estimate the costs.
- Estimate the benefits (tangible and intangible).
- Discount for risk factor.
- *Insist on a high rate of return.*

My final word. Remember Corder's Law of Costing:

Any system costs more than you think it will—even after making allowance for Corder's Law of Costing.

# 16. The estimating problem

*An estimate is the most optimistic prediction that has a non-zero probability of coming true.*

Tom DeMarco

I drive from my home north of London to Gatwick Airport, south of London, about ten times a year. If you ask me to estimate how long my next journey to Gatwick will take I am reasonably confident (depending upon time of day) that I will do it in 1 hour 40 minutes plus or minus ten minutes. I have sufficient data to work out not only my average time but also the standard deviation. I also know which variables—time of day, weather, etc.—most affect my time.

Impressed by this display of estimating skill, you now ask me to estimate how long I would need to drive from my home to the north of Scotland. Of what use to me is the data I have collected about my frequent trips in the opposite direction? The answer is that its usefulness to me is precisely a function of the degree of similarity between the two journeys. If I decide to go to Scotland by train or air, clearly, my Gatwick trips have no relevance. If I go by car, I must look for common factors between the two trips. If I analyse my Gatwick trips I discover that I average 60 mph on motorways, 45 mph on A roads and 20 mph in conurbations. To this extent, my previous data will help in estimating my trip to Inverness.

You now ask me to estimate an overland trip to Australia. I would have to reply that my prior experience makes me sufficiently confident to estimate the time to reach Yugoslavia as three days, but that thereafter I am in uncharted waters (metaphorically, I hope). I could continue to make good progress and be on schedule only to be held up for weeks by political or mechanical problems which I could not have foreseen when I set out. I may even be forced to retrace part of the journey.

What my journey estimating makes clear is what estimators in industries other than computers have long known. To estimate Project F on the basis of our experience of projects A–E demands some degree of commonality between the projects. The common element favoured by a software house where I once worked was the weight of the specification.

This had a good track record until customers started using lighter-weight paper.

We can categorize the above method as 'high-level commonality'. Another example is the advice, 'Take the initial estimate, double the costs and halve the benefits.' This, however, begs the question of how you arrived at the first estimate. High-level commonality really exists only at what may be termed the 'cynical' level of 'everything costs more than you think it will.' It is certainly no use as a basis for controlling the progress of the project during systems development.

If we revert to my London-to-Gatwick example, the commonality between that and other journeys is at a lower level. When we break down our estimate by examining the critical variables, we find that much of what I have learned from my Gatwick trip is immediately applicable to a drive to Scotland. The components have much in common.

Let me invent a measure: the Component Commonality Index (CCI). As the name suggests, this is a measure of the degree of similarity between elements of systems under comparison. A CCI of 0 would indicate totally dissimilar projects, e.g., estimating how long it will take to build a Channel Tunnel based on the time taken to build a model aeroplane. A score of 1 could only mean that one was undertaking an identical project with identical resources. Clearly, the higher the value of CCI the better equipped one is to estimate a given project. London to Inverness compared against London to Gatwick has a high CCI; compared with London to Sydney, a low one.

The usefulness of CCI is that it overcomes the standard objection, 'We haven't done anything like this before.' It *is* difficult to estimate the time to design and install a multi-user, on-line system involving data transmission from remote offices if all you have done before is implement a packaged payroll. The difficulty is reflected in a low CCI. But the value is not zero. Secondly, and just as important, your *next* project estimate is likely to have a higher CCI, provided that you identify the critical components and record values for them.

Expressed in this way, the key to estimating is the search for common components, followed by recording of actuals (time, cost) for each. These then become your database for future projects. This is easily illustrated by the journey example; the components (or variables) would be such things as:

- distance,
- type of road,

- time of year,
- day of week,
- time of day,
- weather conditions,
- knowledge of route.

Having identified these, and collected data, one could then estimate that the same journey would take you twice as long during a wet rush hour than in good conditions in the middle of the night.

The key element, therefore, in estimating computer projects is to choose your components. One that is frequently bandied about is lines of programming code. The reason for this is that it is easy to record, and people often do what is easy but useless in preference to what is hard but relevant. Lines of code are manifestly useless since you do not know this figure until the project is virtually finished and the complexity of code can vary greatly.

The components that are chosen must perforce reflect the way in which a given company goes about developing systems. The methods outlined in this book are based on data flow diagrams. Stan Breagan has used these not only to represent the order processing system being developed but also to represent *how he is going about the project itself.* If you initially draw up a project model and during the project produce lower-level models, then your components are very similar even if the high-level view is dissimilar.

The components of the data flow diagrams tend to be logical and deliverables-oriented. However, as with our specification model for the system itself, they need to be amplified by physical constraints. In practice, this means that the time taken to write a given deliverable, e.g., the common component 'current logical system', will be influenced by such physical factors as whether the people to be interviewed are dispersed or all in one building. When we come to the components that comprise the 'new physical system', factors such as technological innovation and experience of staff are bound to be important components.

In summary, the correct way to estimate is:

1. Use a standardized approach to the development of systems.
2. Use the tools of this approach to develop the components at various levels.
3. Record actual resources used at the component level.
4. In so doing, validate the components and establish standard timings.

137

The better the quality and coverage of these, the higher the likely CCI for any new project.

5. When estimating new projects, use previous experience to model the project, and standard timings to estimate it.

One of the most significant benefits of this approach is that the project model becomes increasingly more detailed, and therefore your estimates more precise, *pari passu with the systems development activity*. Thus you have the technique and data to give an outline estimate of the outline design stage and a detailed estimate of the detailed design stage.

Because World's Wines is a first-time user, the CCI for this project is very low. However, by recording the actual time spent against their project models, they can build up the database necessary to improve their estimating of future projects.

# 17. Specifying the system

Conclusion of presentation given by Stan Breagan to the Board of World's Wines on his survey into their proposed new order processing system

SB    And so finally, gentlemen, I would just like to reiterate the main conclusions I have come to, and which are embodied in detail in the report which you have before you.

1. *Cost justification*    The cost–benefit analysis shows a net present value for the project of £16 000. This figure takes account of 'operational savings', mainly arising from a reduction in staff. Any benefits accruing from an enhanced level of customer service, which is indeed the main justification for the new system, have not been quantified in money terms, and are therefore not included in this figure.

2. *Free stock* v. *physical stock*    In terms of how the new order processing system will function, I examined two basic strategies: that of sending orders immediately to the warehouse and using the computer to update the stock records retrospectively, and (the current sequence) that of processing and allocating stock to orders prior to sending them through to the warehouse. In consultation with you, I decided that the speed of the computer would enable us to update the stock records first while still meeting the deadlines necessary to ensure the specified 36-hour turn-round of orders.

3. *Processing method*    Within this overall systems strategy, the new computer system is a combination of what is referred to as batch and transaction processing. Orders and receipts of stock will be entered into the computer by stock clerks working at visual displays. Your stock records, which henceforth will be held on the computer, will be immediately updated by these transactions. The clerks will, then and there, make any decisions about stock allocation, back orders, and so on. The orders will then be printed in batches and sent to the warehouse for order assembly.

The timings of the various operations are laid out in my report, from which you will see that a complete day's orders should be printed and available to the warehouse early in the afternoon. This allows ample time to meet the primary systems objective of a 36-hour turn-round to your own branches and 48 hours to your external customers.

GW   Thank you, Stan. Obviously my colleagues and I will want more time to consider the implications of the new system and to look in detail at both the costings and the implementation plan that you have drawn up. However, since we actually have you here at the moment, this is obviously an opportune time for us to clarify some points. For instance, I see from your report that the figure of £16 000 NPV is based on the assumption that we will find a package system which will fit our needs and save us writing our own. However, what if we can't find one that is suitable? Obviously, this wouldn't just affect the return on our investment—it would also delay things.

SB   I'm sure you'll recall, George, that at the outset of this project we agreed that we would take it a step at a time—'festina lente', was I believe your way of putting it. What that means is that the ball is now in your court to decide two things: first, that the system outlined in my report meets your requirements and is acceptable both to you and your staff; second, that the cost–benefit analysis shows that it is worth proceeding to the next stage, which involves the drawing up of a formal invitation to tender. Only after that will we be in a position to decide the 'package v. bespoke' question.

GW   What form does the invitation to tender take?

SB   Essentially, it is a logical specification of your requirements incorporating all the essential business processes which we have already agreed but leaving the companies that are submitting proposals free to put forward their own best physical method for achieving the desired solution. These may of course include packaged systems. In this way we do not pre-empt technical decisions which only people with a close knowledge of the particular hardware and software are competent to make.

The preceding chapter saw us doing our first formal cost–benefit analysis of the proposed system. To enable us to put any sort of figures on the initial cost of the system, we had to make some assumptions about the size, and therefore cost, of any computer on which a new system would be implemented. For example, we estimated that five screens would be necessary for inputting data. This was sufficiently accurate to enable us to get within £3000 or £4000 of the hardware costs. We then further estimated the cost of developing the systems software or of acquiring a package.

Because our appraisal, even using the higher figure, for specially written software still gave a satisfactory return on investment, management is willing to go on to the next stage, which is that of writing the invitation to tender. Notice that this, and only this, is the decision which management is being asked to take at this juncture. It is a commitment of probably another £5000. If the quotations in response to the tender indicate that the one-time costs of the system have been vastly underestimated, there is still time for management to abort the project before more significant costs have been incurred.

The heart of the invitation to tender will be the *specification model*. This is our description of the required system based upon the decisions, such as those concerning free stock versus physical stock recording, made during the preceding survey. The specification also identifies the man/machine boundary (i.e., what the computer does, and what people do) and indicates which processes should be handling batch or transaction data. It is thus more detailed than a pure functional specification, which merely instructs the tenderer in the major inputs, processes, and outputs of the new system without any indication of how, or in what sequence, these are to be performed.

However, the specification is still mainly logical; it makes no presumption whatsoever about the particular computer on which the system will be implemented. The cardinal principle is that business decisions, such as what to do about substitutions, should be taken by businessmen, and technical decisions, such as the most convenient file structures to meet a particular enquiry, should be made by technical people. This principle always holds true but particularly so where a first-time user is concerned. A first-time user, by definition, does not have a computer and is therefore free to implement his system on whichever is the most suitable computer. This means that the invitation to tender will go out to a number of different computer houses. Each of these, expert in the particular facilities of its own hardware and software, can formulate a proposal which utilizes its particular equipment to its fullest capacity.

In addition to the original project request, the specification will utilize

141

the four tools described in Chapter 8 to describe the requirements as they have been agreed:

Data flow diagrams: to indicate the flow of data through the system
Data dictionary:     to describe the data
Data model:           to show the relationships between the different types of file data in the system
Process descriptions: to lay down the processing rules

The relationship between these four tools can be shown diagrammatically (Fig. 17.1). The advantages of this as a description of the required system are many:

- It is graphic, clear, and concise.
- It is intelligible to the layman, who has therefore been able to contribute to its content.
- It is rigorous for the designer.
- It shows what the system has to do but leaves the designer free to decide how to do it.
- It is easily maintainable.

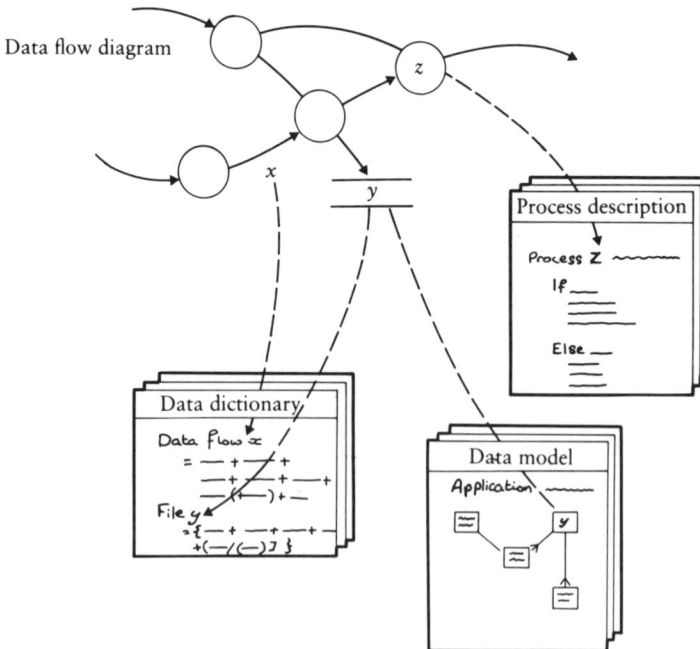

**Figure 17.1** Structured specification

In addition to this logical model of the described system, the specification will include physical constraints, such as:

- speed of response of the system,
- security aspects,
- audit requirements,
- volumes and timings.

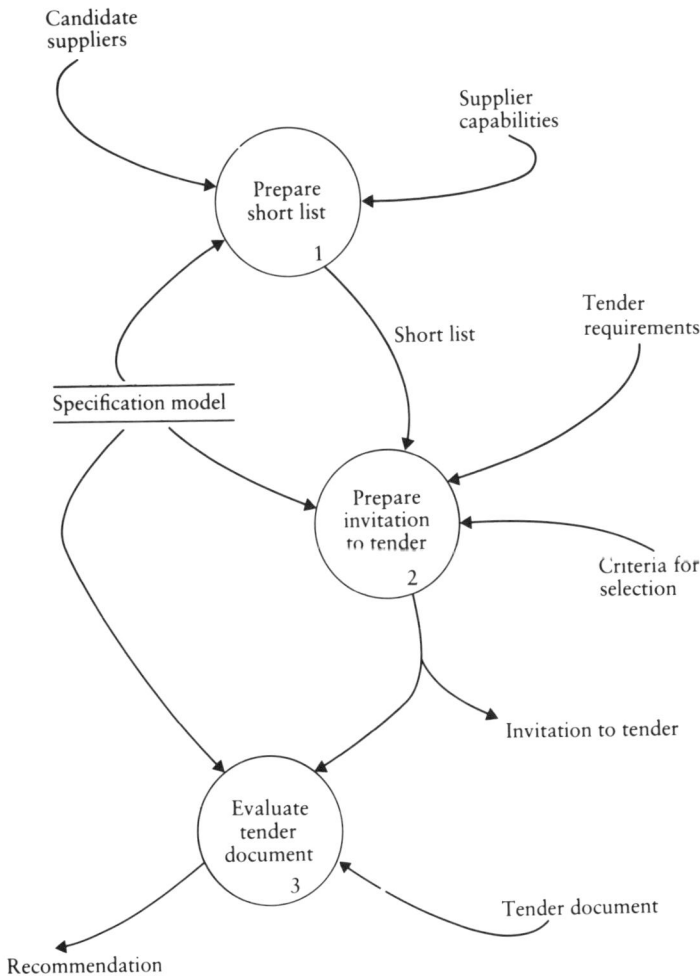

**Figure 17.2**  The tendering process

Working from this, a systems designer can construct the physical files necessary, getting their content from the data dictionary and their access paths from the data model. Inputs and outputs are also specified in the data dictionary; and program specifications can be derived from the process descriptions.

Turning the specification model into an invitation to tender simply requires additional information about what is expected from the successful company in terms of such things as:

- prices for hardware and software,
- implementation assistance,
- post-sales support,
- training,
- engineering call-out.

One item that it is important to include in such a document is a section headed 'Criteria for Selection'. This lists those items on which the user places most importance—e.g., availability of support locally—and thereby informs the tendering companies what they have to do to win the contract. As before, we shall ourselves use a data flow diagram to clarify the process (Fig. 17.2).

We shall rely on Stan to draw up the short-list of companies who will be invited to tender and to assist in the evaluation of the submitted proposals.

# 18. Building the system

*Be not the first by whom the new is tried,*
*Nor yet the last to cast the old aside.*

Alexander Pope

George Wynne is getting nervous. Despite retaining Stan Breagan to ward off unwanted sales approaches, he has been the recipient of unsolicited advice from a computer expert.

GW    Stan, I got a dreadful ear-bashing at my golf club the other day. There wasn't much I could do about it. It was an invitation event and this bloke was in the four that I was playing in. He kept going on about fourth-generation languages and how everybody should be using them these days. . . . I said I thought that all we needed was to find a package and bang it in as soon as possible. I mean, surely that's the answer for a company like ours.

SB    Well, George, basically I tend to agree. When I first started in computing, virtually all systems had to be written from scratch. There were packages around, but most of them were so unreliable and badly documented that you wouldn't touch them with a barge-pole. If you did, you were liable to spend as much money modifying the package as you would have done to have written your own system from the start. Obviously things have changed a lot since then. You can get packages these days for everything from archaeology to zoo-keeping.

GW    Why the big change?

SB    Well, packages were getting better throughout the seventies as development methods improved and documentation got better. But obviously the major impetus was the advent of cheaper computers. To pay out £50 000 for a system to be written for a computer that cost you £250 000 sounds reasonable; but it doesn't sound so good if the computer has only cost £5000. Consequently there are virtually no 'bespoke' systems written for micros.

GW    So why doesn't everybody just use packages? You said you could get them for anything.

SB    The whole point about packages is that they work best where there is a high degree of similarity between the same application in different companies. That's why you hear expressions like 'bespoke' and 'off-the-peg'—or 'tailoring' a system to meet your requirements. Look at it this way, George. You're a pretty standard build. If you feel like it, you can go into a shop and come out with a suit that fits. But if you were 6 ft 7 in. tall, weighed 10 stone, and had one shoulder six inches lower than the other, you'd have problems finding one that fitted.

GW    Yes, but order processing's pretty universal, isn't it?

SB    Certainly the process is. What differs are the particular products. You sell wines in cases of a dozen—so that an order for 18 bottles is written as $1\frac{6}{12}$. This is different from when you are selling other products such as cigarettes. Also, I notice that the rules for valuing stock contain quite a few differences depending upon the particular product. Not all that many companies have stock that appreciates in value as it gets older. We might have some difficulty in locating a package which has sufficient flexibility to cope with all the various procedures we use here.

GW    Well, surely that's just a case of modifying the package?

SB    I suppose so; but my basic rule is—never modify a package. It's a bit like fitting a non-standard carburettor on to a Mercedes. They let you do it, but they won't take the responsibility for the consequences. If you find a package that does 98 per cent of what you want, it's usually better to modify your system to the package, rather than vice versa.

GW    But we can't do that—we can't suddenly start recording wines as single bottles where they've always been recorded by the dozen. And the stock clerks must still be free to use their own discretion in filling individual orders.

SB    Well, there is a sort of halfway house between a package and bespoke system. These days many packages are *parameter-driven*; that is to say, the central system is already written but you can modify inputs and outputs—for example, to reflect the fact that you may use a 14-character product code where somebody else uses an 8-character code. As well as this, the software should also be flexible enough for the company supplying it to tailor it to your particular requirements in World's Wines.

GW    What if we don't find that sort of thing? What about all these things this bloke was bending my ear about at the golf club?

SB    Well, in the final analysis, of course, we would have to write a system especially designed for you. In fact, we have gone quite a way down that road in writing our specification. After all, all large companies have their own computer departments. Nobody that I know has yet claimed that user-friendliness is making data processing people redundant (or even keeping up with the growing shortage). The things your golfing partner was talking about were various new programming languages, some of which are usable by non-data processing staff, others of which are really just improved development aids for use by experienced computer people.

Users of computer systems come in all shapes and sizes, from the owner/manager of a company employing 20 people to the sales manager, production manager, or chief accountant of a large corporation or senior executive officer in a government department. Thus far, this diversity has not been a problem. No matter what size of organization, or what type of application, the principles of specifying clearly what you want, analysing current methods and data, and developing a generalized solution sufficient to perform a cost–benefit analysis are applicable across the board. The activities may take half a morning and be sketched on the back of an envelope or may occupy two man-years, but the principles are the same.

At this point things begin to diverge. Building a world-wide foreign exchange and currency dealing system for a multinational bank is likely to involve a little more effort than installing a package for your local newsagent. The differences are not merely a matter of scale; they invite a different approach.

The tools and techniques used to build computer systems give the appearance of changing so rapidly that anyone actually installing a system (rather than talking or writing about it) runs the risk of feeling passé at the end of it. You congratulate yourself on the decision to introduce 'structured design' only to learn—too late—that these are third-generation methods which only the most benighted are still clinging to: to hold your head high at the local Rotary or British Computer Society meeting, you should be using a 'fourth-generation language' (4GL) with the appropriate methodology—say, Mantis with EVIM (Evolutionary Incremental Methodology (sic)).

The speed of technological change can lead to a state of 'project paralysis'. You dare not start a project because you know that, the moment you are irrevocably committed, some new product will come on to the market which is exactly what you should be using (or such will be its claims). With hardware prices still falling, new users are reluctant to buy,

147

feeling instinctively that by waiting they will get better value for money. The problem with any approach which delays getting 'stuck in' is that the obviously right time never arrives. If you plump for the latest fourth-generation language hot off the presses, you will open your morning paper to see that someone has released a fifth-generation language.

Relax. Alexander Pope sorted this out over 200 years ago. In the language beloved of football commentators, the quotation that heads this chapter 'says it all'. To reinforce the wisdom of the couplet, you should know that with most computer-related products—hardware and software—there is something like a *ten-year* technology gap between drawing board and general use. This is not least occasioned by such products being extravagantly marketed while still on the drawing board. Microprocessors were invented in the early seventies and widely installed in the early eighties. The techniques of structured analysis and design were originated in the mid-seventies and only now are in wide use. Fourth-generation languages are an early eighties tool, just gaining acceptance.

What the intelligent manager requires is an appreciation of the various strategies for acquiring software, with an overview of the pros and cons of each. Let us examine Fig. 18.1. The best way to view the available choices is to divide them into ready-written software that one buys off the shelf, and software that is purpose-built—either by computer experts, in an internal data processing department or external software house, or by users themselves.

### Ready-written software

From the earliest days of computing, some software has always been supplied with the computer. Typically, this is the computer's operating system, together with many essential utilities such as sort programs, disk copying routines, and so on. Within the heading of generalized ready-written software we can now include word processing and spreadsheets. Any computer acquired by World's Wines would have these facilities. They are so widespread as not to require further comment in this book, other than saying that, as spreadsheets become more powerful, they take on the characteristics of fourth-generation languages in enabling the user to build his own system. This emphasizes the fact that these are instances of *generalized* software. George Wynne's immediate search, however, is for something that is *application-specific*.

'Application packages' seek to address a specific application such as

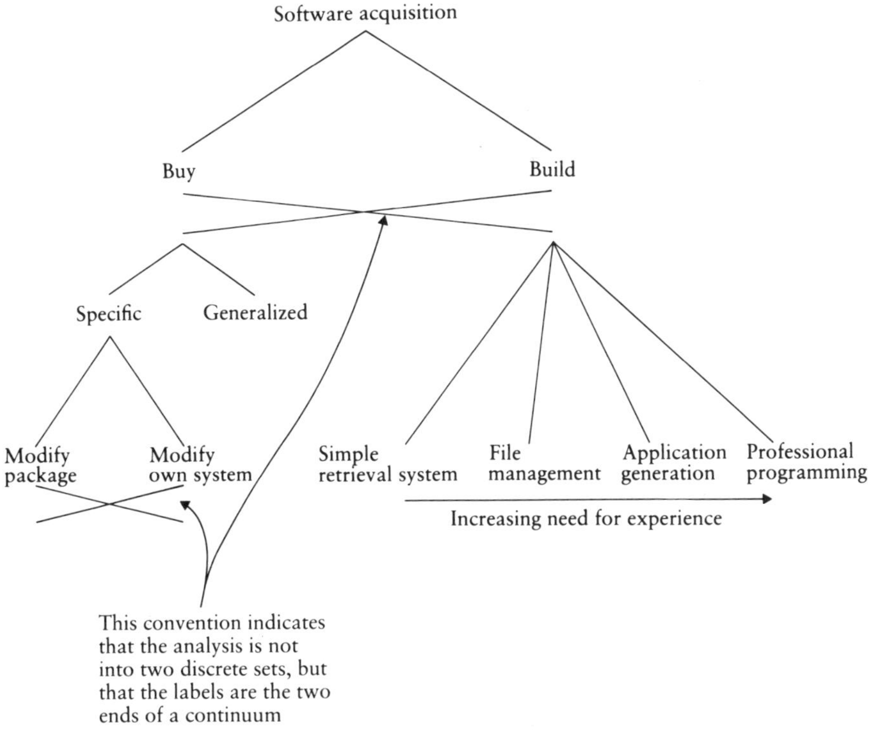

Figure 18.1    The build/buy choice

payroll or stock accounting. They may have been developed by the computer manufacturers, as was mostly the case in the early days, or more usually nowadays by software companies keen to sell products as well as services.

The secret to packaged computer systems lies in how closely your application resembles other people's and, to a lesser extent, in how flexible a given package is in being able to accommodate your idiosyncracies without the need for extensive re-writing. It is for this reason, as Stan Breagan said, that packages abound where there is a high level of homogeneity across different companies' systems. Payroll, general ledger, sales, and purchase ledgers exhibit this tendency, which is why such packages are both common and successful; production control systems do not (since what *differentiates* Ford from Shell is what they produce).

Packages confer significant benefits. They are almost certainly cheaper than writing your own system. They will be quicker to install.

149

They ought to be better written. Enhancements and modifications necessitated by changes in government legislation will (hopefully) be written by the package company. They should be well documented and free of errors. There is a certain feeling of security in being the five hundredth user of a particular system.

Against this must be set the fact that they are never *exactly* what you want. You may have to make some concessions by way of fitting your system to their solution. As a general rule, it is safer to modify your procedures to fit in with what is available than to tinker with the package. As soon as your modifications to a package pass beyond the most simple, you rapidly reach the point where you wish you had written your own system from scratch.

In the case of World's Wines, the areas of difference that might invalidate the package approach are, as always, the exceptions—rush orders, splitting of packs or cases, substitution, and the holding back of stock in short supply. Nevertheless, it is by no means out of the question that a suitable package should be found.

However, 'having your own system' is nowadays not exactly the same as 'designing your own system from scratch'. The package *v.* bespoke decision is not a black/white choice: they are opposite ends of a continuum. Many systems houses have developed order processing systems for a number of different clients. In so doing, they will have built up modules of re-usable programming code which they can then configure to suit a new client's requirements. Frequently these will be companies specializing in one particular make of computer and able to supply a complete 'turnkey' system embracing both the hardware and software. This halfway house can potentially give you the best of both worlds—a company-specific system at a cost half that of building it yourself.

As an example of what is available in package software at the bottom end of the market, the document illustrated in Fig. 18.2 was produced by a package which included invoicing, stock recording, sales ledger, purchase ledger, general ledger, and payroll for a combined price of under £1000.

Were World's Wines processing 300 order lines a day instead of 3000 then a microcomputer with this software package might well do that job. However, the facilities of the software (with some justification, at the price!) are very restricted, so that it is ruled out not only on grounds of volumes, but also for its inability to cope with exceptions. However, a more expensive package, written in such a way as to minimize the

INVOICE

World's Wines
9 Station Road
Neashill
London NW10
01-123 4567

| Page | : 1 of 1 |
| Date | : 15/10/85 |
| Account No. | : BO 21 |
| Your order no. | : QUOTE |
| Order date | : 14/10/85 |

*Invoice to:* Banks Booze Stores
Empire Way
Wembley
Middx

VAT Reg'n No.: 317 214 6902

| CODE | DESCRIPTION | QUANTITY | UNIT PRICE | DISCT % | GOODS VALUE | VAT CODE |
|------|-------------|----------|------------|---------|-------------|----------|
| 20761 | Beaujolais Villages 1982 | 2 | 24.00 | 0.0 | 48.00 | 2 |
| 21219 | Côtes Du Rhône 1983 | 4 | 22.00 | 0.0 | 88.00 | 2 |
| 26140 | Bordeaux Blanc 1980 | 1 | 20.00 | 0.0 | 20.00 | 2 |
| 27211 | Anjou Rosé 1983 | 2 | 22.00 | 0.0 | 44.00 | 2 |

Total Goods Value: 200.00

VAT ANALYSIS

| Code | Rate (%) | Taxable | VAT |
|------|----------|---------|-----|
| 2 | 15.000 | 200.00 | 30.00 |

Total VAT : 30.00

TOTAL : 230.00

**Figure 18.2**   World's Wines: sample invoice

difficulties of modification, remains the most likely solution. In order to show how extensive such a system can be, I include, in Appendix C, a description of a typical application package which would cover all operating aspects of World's Wines' requirements plus an enquiry facility. This description is taken, without editing, from a series of fact sheets available from the company marketing the software. It does not imply any recommendations on the part of the author, who is, nevertheless, grateful for their permission to use these as an illustration.

## Purpose-built software

The 'package' solution is attractive to World's Wines partly because they do not have extensive data processing ambitions. An approach which avoids the necessity for employing full-time computer people has obvious merits. However, there remain many situations in which no suitable package is available. We are then forced to build a new system to the user's specification. There are two good reasons why users should have an appreciation of the different ways in which systems are built:

1. because the methods used dictate the deliverables and therefore the system of project control (*not* the other way round);
2. because users may wish to build their own systems independent of computer people.

In the context of reason 2, I should make it clear that I am not restricting the term 'building' solely to the development of complete new systems: it can cover enhancements to existing systems, including those as trivial as the user formatting a new report.

I assume as starting point a clear specification of what the new system, or sub-system, is required to do. There is then a diversity of ways in which systems are built, and these are constantly changing. The major causes of the different approaches are as follows.

1. Systems builders usually have to work within the constraints of their company's existing hardware and software. Large organizations have long-established databases, and any new system would need to fit in with these.
2. Existing data processing departments have developed internal standards dictating how the development activity is carried out. They will not immediately shelve all the procedures, training, and staff experience to jump headlong into the latest 'flavour of the month'.
3. Projects vary tremendously in size and complexity. An enthusiastic and intelligent user could well set up his own system for cataloguing books and papers: a materials requisition and planning system estimated at 20 man-years' development effort will call for different methods.

To categorize simply the tremendous range of options for systems building has been the most difficult aspect in writing this book. As pointed out in Chapter 8, one can only analyse a set of data by some particular characteristic. In the end, as illustrated in Fig. 18.1, I have represented the choice as a continuum based on the level of expertise required. This, for example, rules out, for users, the use of third-generation languages such as COBOL; using these requires more training and experience than the average user possesses. The layman needs user-friendly, high-level languages. However, the latter are just as useful to systems analysts and programmers as they are to users, so Fig. 18.1 should not be read as implying that such tools are the monopoly of users—they achieve considerable productivity gains in the hands of 'professionals', also.

Let us start at the simplest end—those tools which enable a user to write some procedures for himself, independent of computer experts. We can then trace the added facilities offered as one moves along the scale, with the concomitant need for more training and experience.

QUERY LANGUAGES/REPORT WRITERS

In the early days of computing, management's information requirements had to be defined in complete detail as part of the systems specification, which was then frozen. The management reporting aspects of an operational system such as order processing were delivered as a part of the total system, and little flexibility was available to produce new reports. Even if the data needed for such a report was held within the system (a big 'if'), the user had no means of getting at it himself. If you wanted a new report, you would have to contact the computer department and ask a programmer to write a small retrieval program.

Clearly, this was a most inconvenient state of affairs for both sides. The user wanted independence as much as the programmers wanted him to stop asking them for one-off programs. The answer lay in recognizing that most requests were for simple selections from the existing data, possibly re-sequenced and with some calculations thrown in. Recognizing this, it became relatively easy to write generalized report generators, allowing the user to specify those characteristics of the records in which he was interested and the way in which he wanted the information presented back to him. He could be given a standard form on which to enter the selection criteria which was then processed in batch mode. Increasingly, such enquiries are now formatted interactively with the response back on the screen for simple enquiries or printed out for more extensive reports. The instruction below would result in details of all pre-1982 French red wines being displayed:

DISPLAY ALL FOR (FRANCE $COUNTRY and RED $COLOUR
AND AGE < 1982)

153

The principle that the user can now access his own data and format his own reports is good news both for the user and for the computer department, which normally has more pressing tasks than responding to *ad hoc* requests of this nature. Of course, the Law of Unintended Effect can apply here—users could take up so much of the machine's resources to process these requests that the overall service level could begin to decline.

The above example concerned the retrieval of information. The file being interrogated may be part of a larger system set up by a centralized data processing department and maintained by them, or it could have been created by the user.

FILE MANAGEMENT SYSTEMS

The next level of complexity therefore is software that enables its user not only to retrieve records but also to create and modify them. All microcomputers nowadays have such systems available. The illustration in Fig. 18.3 is from one such—CARDBOX. It shows one of 24 records retrieved as a result of a search. This is a powerful search, as six criteria have been selected.

As the name implies, the software simulates a file of cards. Typically, such systems allow users:

1. to specify their own file(s) by naming and describing items to be recorded on each record;
2. to index those items—e.g., product code, supplier—on which they wish to search the file;
3. to then set up the file by inputting details for each record;
4. to modify information held on any particular record;
5. to select records according to given criteria, e.g., Product Code 37614, or all products available from Supplier 72;
6. to sort records and print out the results.

At the level illustrated, the system does not provide facilities for maintaining and updating that information, such as stock balances or customer accounts, which is the result of calculations. This is the next step along the continuum. It is a significant step, because it brings in complex rules and conditions that characterize such processes. Once the user is able to specify calculations which update values, as opposed to manually updating them himself, the software is having to generate program code to accomplish this. For his part, the user has to be considerably more experienced in order to specify the updating rules

154

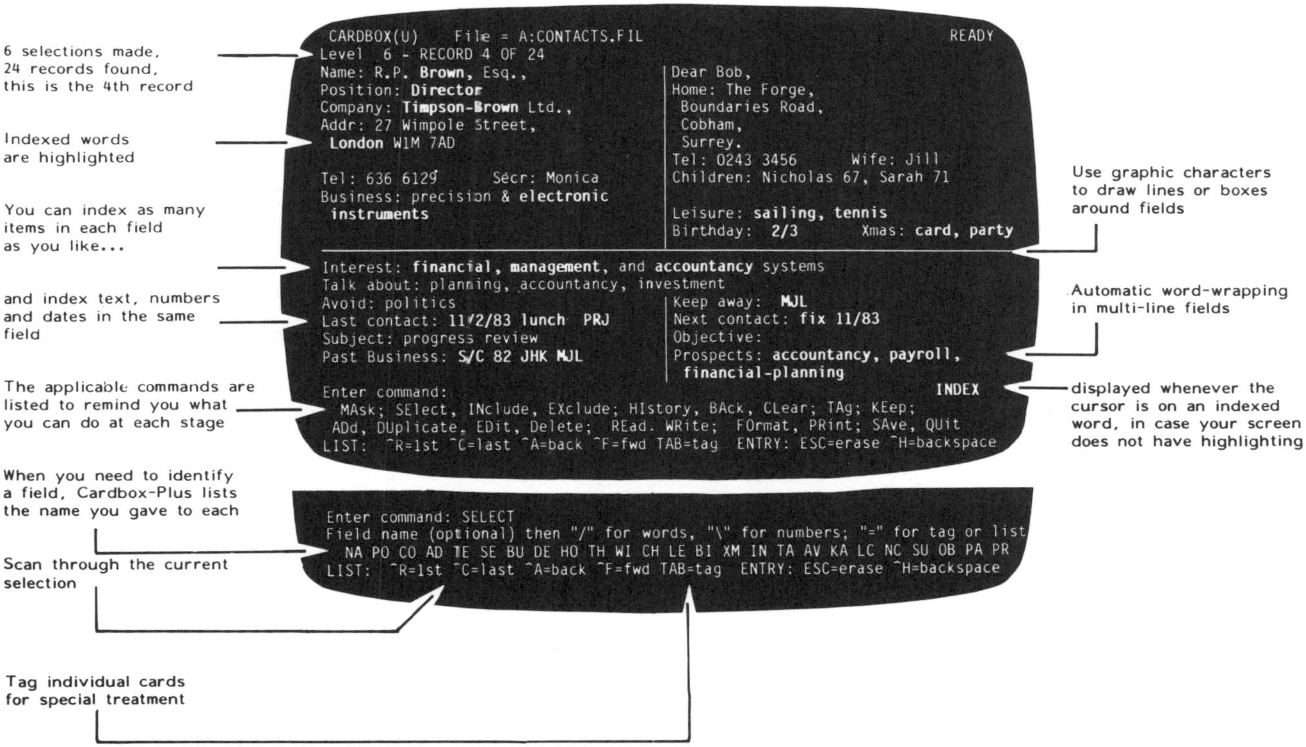

Use graphic characters
to draw lines or boxes
around fields

Automatic word-wrapping
in multi-line fields

displayed whenever the
cursor is on an indexed
word, in case your screen
does not have highlighting

```
CARDBOX(U)    File = A:CONTACTS.FIL                      READY
Level 6 - RECORD 4 OF 24
Name: R.P. Brown, Esq.
Position: Director
Company: Timpson-Brown Ltd.,
Addr: 27 Wimpole Street,
      London W1M 7AD        Secr: Monica

Tel: 636 6129
Business: precision & electronic
instruments

Dear Bob,
Home: The Forge,
      Boundaries Road,
      Cobham,
      Surrey.
Tel: 0243 3456    Wife: Jill
Children: Nicholas 67, Sarah 71

Leisure: sailing, tennis
Birthday: 2/3    Xmas: card, party

Interest: financial, management, and accountancy systems
Talk about: planning, accountancy, investment
Avoid: politics            Keep away: MJL
Last contact: 11/2/83 lunch PRJ    Next contact: fix 11/83
Subject: progress review            Objective:
Past Business: S/C 82 JHK MJL       Prospects: accountancy, payroll,
                                              financial-planning    INDEX

Enter command:
  MAsk; Select; INclude; EXclude; HIstory; BAck; CLear; TAg; KEep;
  ADd; DUplicate; EDit, Delete; REad; WRite; FOrmat; PRint; SAve, QUit
LIST: ^R=list ^C=last ^A=back ^F=fwd TAB=tag  ENTRY: ESC=erase ^H=backspace

Enter command: SELECT
Field name (optional) then "/" for words, "\" for numbers; "=" for tag or list
  NA PO CO AD TE SE BU DE HO TH WI CH LE BI XM IN TA AV KA LC NC SU OB PA PR
LIST: ^R=list ^C=last ^A=back ^F=fwd TAB=tag  ENTRY: ESC=erase ^H=backspace
```

**Figure 18.3** Information retrieval system

6 selections made.
24 records found.
this is the 4th record

Indexed words
are highlighted

You can index as many
items in each field
as you like...

and index text, numbers
and dates in the same
field

The applicable commands are
listed to remind you what
you can do at each stage

When you need to identify
a field, Cardbox-Plus lists
the name you gave to each

Scan through the current
selection

Tag individual cards
for special treatment

comprehensively and unambiguously. Such software exists. They are called—unoriginally but accurately—*program generators*. They 'prompt' the user to describe processing rules—e.g., line value = quantity times unit price—and turn these into program code.

APPLICATION GENERATORS

Where a program generator enables a user to describe a set of processing rules and turns these descriptions into a program, an application generator allows the user to describe a complete system. It generates not only programs but files, inputs, and outputs. It is therefore a most powerful tool. Some programs are compatible with a variety of hardware and software; others, such as Burroughs' LINC or Sperry's MAPPER, are specific to the manufacturer's own computers. As my pen dries on the last word, so Sperry announces an IBM PC-compatible version of MAPPER. An indication of the manufacturers' own claims for these is given in the advertisement depicted in Fig. 18.4. To my knowledge, nobody has seen fit to report this to the Advertising Standards Authority, so presumably artistic licence is within bounds and, indeed, experience of using such software has been generally favourable. The CCTA report quoted earlier concluded:

> There can be no doubt that application generator products exist which:
>
> 1. can achieve very significant savings in program development and maintenance time and cost;
> 2. can achieve those savings without the use of highly trained personnel;
>
> ... good application generation software can significantly increase the possibility of a system's successful implementation.

Many qualifications are needed before one can conclude that 'traditional' systems development methods are outmoded. Users in the survey included systems personnel. In many cases the software was being used primarily for prototyping or as a query language rather than for the generation of complete systems.

In the World's Wines' situation, their status as a first-time user, allied to the complexity of their requirements, makes it improbable that Stan Breagan would recommend that they attempt to build their own system. However, it is perfectly possible that the companies invited to tender will be making use of some form of application generator or fourth-

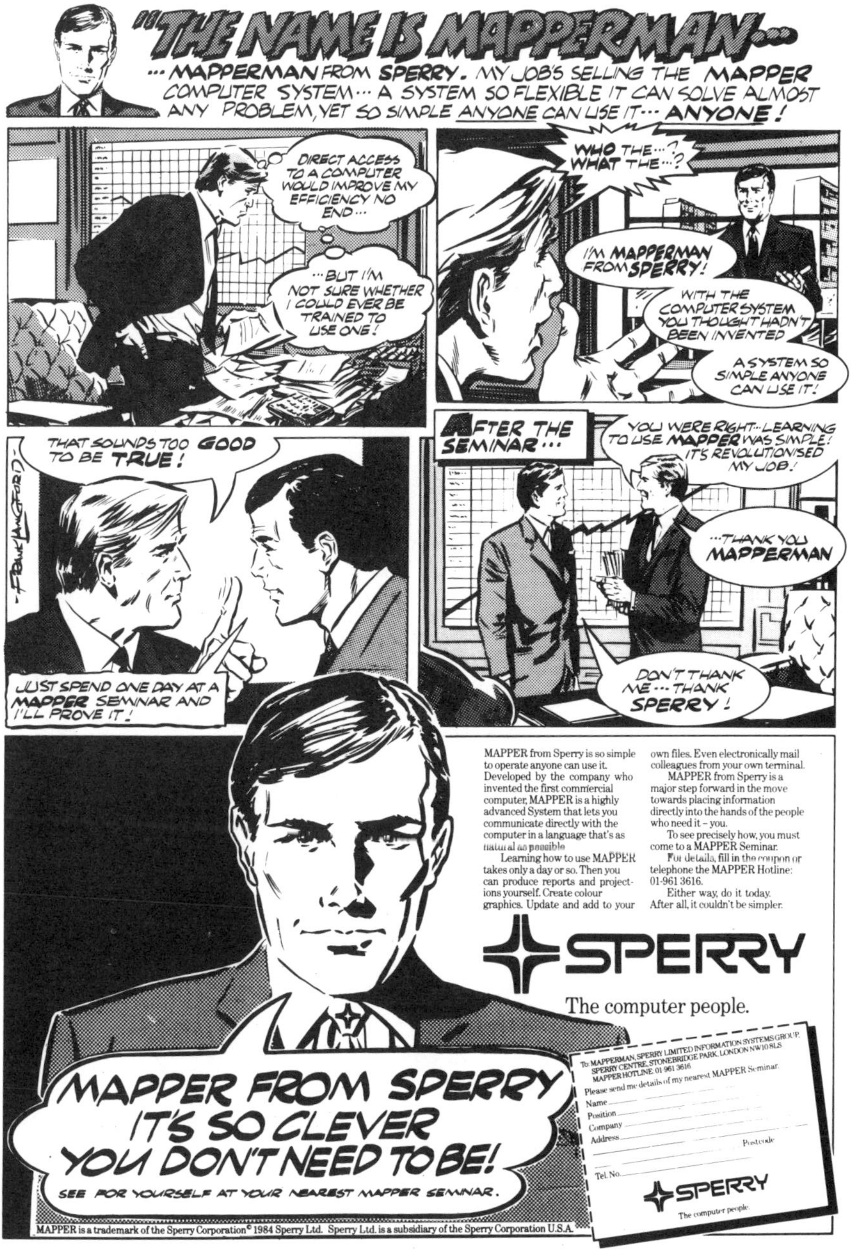


**Figure 18.4** User-friendly software

generation language to write or produce programs. One expert[1] foresees data processing professionals writing complete application systems in one-fifth to one-tenth of the time it would take using a third-generation language.

PROFESSIONAL PROGRAMMING

We have now arrived at the end of the continuum, i.e. development by experienced computer staff. To see an example of this, let us examine the process of stock requisitioning as defined by one of the data flow diagrams in our specification model (Fig. 18.5). This shows an individual line of an order updating the stock records. If the quantity-on-hand falls below the re-order level, the system issues a requisition for replenishment stock. Our data dictionary shows us the constituents of the named data flows:

ORDER-LINE = PRODUCT-CODE + PACK-SIZE + QUANTITY-ORDERED

PRODUCT-CATALOGUE = {PRODUCT-CODE + DESCRIPTION + PRODUCT SUPPLIER CODE}

SUPPLIER = {SUPPLIER-CODE + SUPPLIER-NAME}

STOCK-RECORD = PRODUCT-CODE + PACK-SIZE + UNIT-QUANTITY + REORDER-LEVEL + SALES-PRICE + COST-PRICE + QUANTITY-ON-HAND + (DATE-REQUISITIONED)

REQUISITION = SUPPLIER NAME + PRODUCT-CODE + PRODUCT-DESCRIPTION + UNIT-QUANTITY + REORDER-LEVEL + QUANTITY-ON-HAND + DATE REQUISITIONED

If we want to know the procedure for requisitioning new supplies of stock, we can consult our mini-spec:

---

[1] Roger Sisson, 'Solutions Systems and MIS', *Proceedings of the Twelfth Annual Conference of the Society of Management Information Systems*, Columbia University Press, 1981.

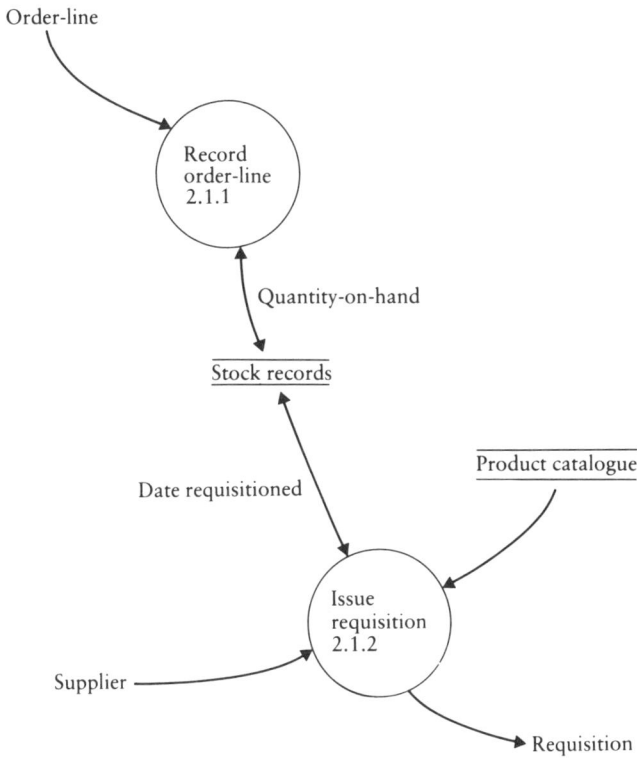

**Figure 18.5**    DFD: Requisitioning stock

If QUANTITY-ON-HAND is less than REORDER-LEVEL and

    if DATE-REQUISITIONED is not present, then

        issue REQUISITION and record DATE-REQUISITIONED as "today"

    otherwise (DATE-REQUISITIONED present)

        do nothing

Otherwise (QUANTITY-ON-HAND equal or greater than REORDER-LEVEL)

    do nothing

The essence of the transition from logical to physical is that the builder is free to take decisions on the most efficient way of implementing the desired system. What type of decisions does he take?

## 1. *Physical stock file*

In the current system the stock records are held on cards. There is one card for each product. Where a product has a number of different pack-sizes, these are recorded on the same card, together with the different prices, etc. This is a convenient procedure because the pack-sizes all share the same product description.

However, it will not necessarily be the most convenient way of organizing our stock file in a computer system. The fact that products have varying numbers of pack-sizes would result in different-length records. Although this is manageable by the computer, it makes things more complicated. Consequently the analyst, in preparing the logical view of the data, will always break down long and complex records into shorter, simpler ones. In this instance it would treat the stock records as two sets of data—one containing all the data at the product level, e.g., the description and supplier, and one containing the data that pertains to an individual pack-size, e.g., price, re-order level, quantity-on-hand. The process, known as 'normalization', is shown in the results of the data dictionary above under 'Product-catalogue' and 'Stock record'. The link between the two is the product-code which is present on both.

In doing this the analyst has identified the lowest-level 'building blocks' for any physical files that the designer may now specify. The designer may in fact merge the two logical files into one physical file, or he may keep them separate. This decision is machine-dependent. Specifically, it will be dictated by the particular database software he is working with.

## 2. *Program specifications*

Having decided upon the structure and contents of the physical files, the designer will next need to write program specifications. Our logical specification has made explicit what processes need to be performed on the data and under what circumstances.

The designer will now group, split, or, if necessary, re-sequence these operations to turn them into program specifications. The general principle which he will observe is that of keeping individual programs small. How this principle is applied in practice will depend on technical considerations of memory size, manufacturer's software, internal standards, and convenience of processing for the operations department when the system is live.

In the current system, fresh supplies of any product are requisitioned at the time when quantity on hand falls below its re-order level. Within the confines of the manual system, this is the most convenient time, as the stock clerk has in front of him all the information he needs to write out a requisition. It would obviously be less efficient for the stock clerk to leave this process until the end of the day and then have to go back and examine each stock card individually. However, a computer system, with its ability to examine all stock records at great speed, may find the latter method the best way of doing things. This could be true if we found another requirement—e.g., for daily stock valuation—which already necessitated an examination of all stock records on a regular basis.

Since the stock file has to be read completely each day, the program designer may decide to keep requisitioning out of the file update program and incorporate it instead into the stock valuation run. This simplifies what is probably the most complex program in the system— that of the stock file update. However, it does so only at the expense of complicating another one, thereby reducing the maintainability of the total system. What happens if World's Wines later decide to run the stock valuation weekly rather than daily? We have an immediate program amendment (since requisitioning will still need to be done daily), which we would not have had if from the start we had specified requisitioning as a separate program. This is how simplicity rather than smartness makes systems more flexible.

Having made this, and other similar decisions, the designer now writes a series of specifications for individual programs. These draw heavily on the mini-specs contained in our specification model for the processing rules.

These processes—of splitting or combining files, of deciding which programs perform which functions—together with other physical design decisions, such as the precise layout of source documents and printouts and the design of the man–machine dialogue for inputting data through screens, are the essence of physical systems construction. At no point is there anything so esoteric or complex that an intelligent user cannot monitor what is going on by using the techniques described in the following chapter.

# 19. Project control

*Everything has been thought of before, but the problem is to think of it again.*

Goethe

Stan has participated in the evaluation of proposals for World's Wines' system and has helped in narrowing the choice down to two suppliers. He manages to avoid committing himself to a specific recommendation, leaving the final decision to World's Wines' senior management.

GW    Well, Stan, we've gone for Universal Structured Automation. But before I sign anything tell me this: how do we tie them down? Everything sounded fine in their presentation, but how can I be sure we don't finish up with one of these disasters I keep hearing about?

SB    That comes down to project control. How do you control other projects you get involved with?

GW    Well, we know something about those. First, we make sure both sides are clear about what is required, when it is required by, and how much it is going to cost. Then we try not to make any changes because I know they'll screw me on those; otherwise I just keep a close eye on things to see they are on target and the work up to scratch.

SB    Fine. You've just described how you're going to control the new computer system.

GW    Huh! it's easy to say that, but if we're building a new depot I can actually see that going up. I can't see a computer system in the same way. . . .

SB    Stop worrying. You may have noticed that the cost–benefit analysis included a derisory retainer for me to look after your interests and make sure things are delivered as promised. . . .

Throughout this book I have used data flow diagrams to model both World's Wines' system and the way in which we are tackling the system—what was termed in Chapter 8 the 'development framework'. The development framework and its derivatives model the activity of *doing* the work. Figure 19.1 is a generalized representation of how the doing is controlled.

In planning the project, we take as our input our terms of reference

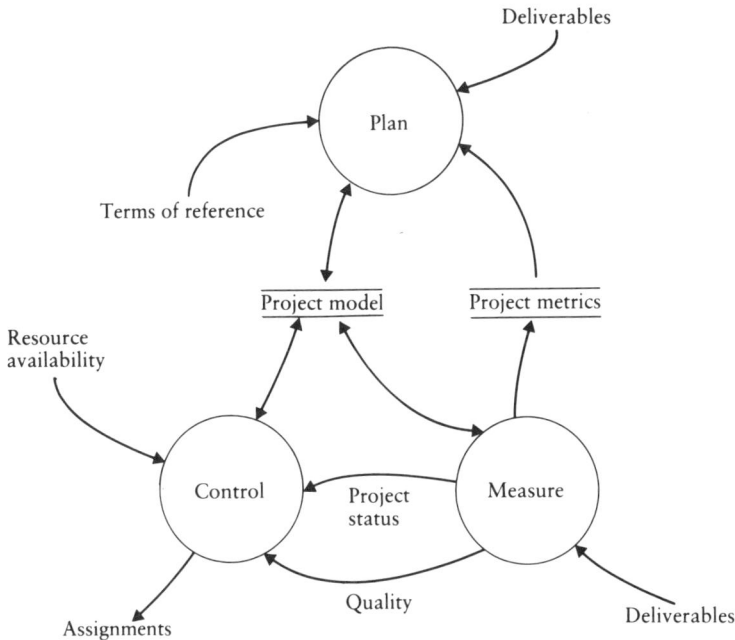

**Figure 19.1** The management framework

and those deliverables that have already been produced. It is an obvious prerequisite of planning any work that the end-product is clearly specified. The specification drawn up by Stan meets this test, and the software house has based its proposal on it.[1]

Working from these inputs, we will draw up a project model. This will break the computer project into activities and deliverables. Once the work is underway we measure, and thereby control, two aspects: quality of work done, and progress made. We also retain information on actual resources used to help us in planning future projects.

The framework helps by identifying activities and deliverables that are common to all projects. Within this, there are significant differences for any individual project dependent upon its size and the nature of the end-product.

## Project control methods

The simplest type of project control is what I term 'control by end-product'. If I want a builder to do a small extension to one of the rooms

---

[1] In accepting the contract, Universal Structured Automation have entered into a legally enforceable agreement. Attempts to enforce this will succeed only in enriching the legal profession.

in my house I might use this method. It consists of agreeing the requirements, fixing a time for it to be done ('when I'm on holiday so that we won't get in your way'), and agreeing the price. This is a technique I have recently used (successfully) to have part of my roof re-tiled. The characteristics of a project which make it suitable for this minimal type of control are:

1. a clear specification of the job,
2. a small project,
3. non-critical time-scale,
4. *complete confidence in the person doing the work.*

It is seldom that all these characteristics—particularly the last—apply to computer projects. Nevertheless, in the past the users' control over projects amounted to little more than this, owing to their inability to understand what was going on.

If users and computer people do not understand each other and systems are so difficult to modify that everything has to be got right first time, it is indeed difficult to control projects. The user signs a systems specification, closes his eyes and keeps his fingers crossed as it disappears from view. Nervous enquiries as to progress are met with bland assurances. No tangible signs of progress are evident except perhaps for an incomprehensible 'module completion chart', which rapidly gets to 90 per cent and then stays there. No evidence as to the quality of the work done is available until the system is live.

However, computer projects are no longer like that. It is possible to break them down into clearly defined stages with visible deliverables quality-checked at each stage. In examining the general question of project control, let us identify two different types of projects. We can differentiate them as:

– those that deliver a product which is of use only when everything is completed;
– those in which the product is usable in some form before the project is completely finished.

*Product completion*
An example of this type of project is the building and launching of a space rocket. It is no good saying to the astronauts, 'We have finished the part of the product which will get you into space. We have still got some work to do on the re-entry module, but don't let that stop you.' Similarly, a new stretch of motorway is not usually opened until

everything has been completed, though an extreme gradualist such as I might point out the theoretical possibility of opening the motorway for daytime driving before the lighting system is complete.[1]

With this sort of project, the project plan first identifies the final product. It then identifies milestones along the way, the activities between the milestones, and the key dependencies. The result is to establish the earliest possible completion date, i.e., availability of the end product, and the critical path leading to this. Both of these are of vital interest to the project team, who can focus attention on key activities and schedule around them those not on the critical path.

*Incremental development*

There is greater flexibility in planning a project if the product can be delivered in versions. In real life this may happen in unplanned fashion when a user is forced to go live with a part-completed system simply because it is late. However, what interests us is the possibility of making controlled use of this characteristic to assist in planning the project.

We could regard the building of a sports stadium as a possible example of such a project. One would then argue that the stadium is ready for use once the playing surface has been laid down. An enhanced version would include terraces for people to stand on and watch the sport before the seating was installed. (Presumably, the owners of the stadium would like to see turnstiles built early in the project as a means of extracting payment!)

It is important not to regard the second type of project as an excuse for sloppy planning. A project plan which foresees the end-product being available incrementally must be subject to the same stringent process of progress and quality control as the first type. The essential difference however is this: if a project of the first type is late, the user gets nothing; if a project of the second type is late, the user has the possibility of using part of the product while waiting for the late work to be completed.

Developing computer systems has always been viewed as the first type. The user got nothing until he got everything. This stemmed historically from the restrictions placed on the systems builders by the primitive state of the software tools and techniques which were in use. The latter were not sufficiently flexible to allow the concept of building

---

[1] It can be quite a diverting exercise to brainstorm how a project such as this could be developed incrementally. Do both sides of a motorway have to be constructed together? How about one side at a time? You could then open it sooner as a one-way system, with the road it is replacing as the temporary reverse route.

165

the 'shell' of a system and then refining it, or of leaving hooks on to which to hang new code.

Nowadays, better design techniques allied to more powerful software confer the opportunity to treat systems development as an incremental activity. This has significant benefits:

- Deliverables can be specified for completion in shorter time; slippage therefore becomes immediately evident.
- Deliverables can be quality-checked as they appear, rather than handing over a large working system and asking the user to accept it.
- The user gains confidence from seeing progress in the form of accepted deliverables.
- By increasing participation, the project becomes less dependent on key staff leaving halfway through.

### Project planning

We can take as our starting point for control of World's Wines project the 'design model'. Stan produced a specification model for the companies that tendered; in the tendering process they each would have converted this logical specification to a technical one in order to arrive at their price quotation. We shall therefore assume that specification of physical files, screen and print layouts, source documents, and programs has already been done. These have been documented in the design model produced by Universal Structured Automation (USA) on the basis of which they were awarded the contract. (I should add that the activity of producing the design model is somewhat more time-consuming than might appear from the above. In order to keep the treatment of project control tolerably concise, I have chosen to restrict myself to the building phase. The principles hold good for all phases.)

Let us look at what is involved in building a system. By excluding the physical installation of World's Wines' computer, we can treat Fig. 19.2 as a generalized representation of how systems are built and installed. The inclusion of 'existing files' and 'existing software' means that it applies both to first-time users and to companies enhancing an existing computer system. In World's Wines' case the existing files are their manual records; existing software is that which USA already has and is partially modifying in writing programs specific to World's Wines.

Going back to my earlier comments about the different types of project—those that are built all at once and those that are delivered incrementally—what type of building project do we consider ours to be?

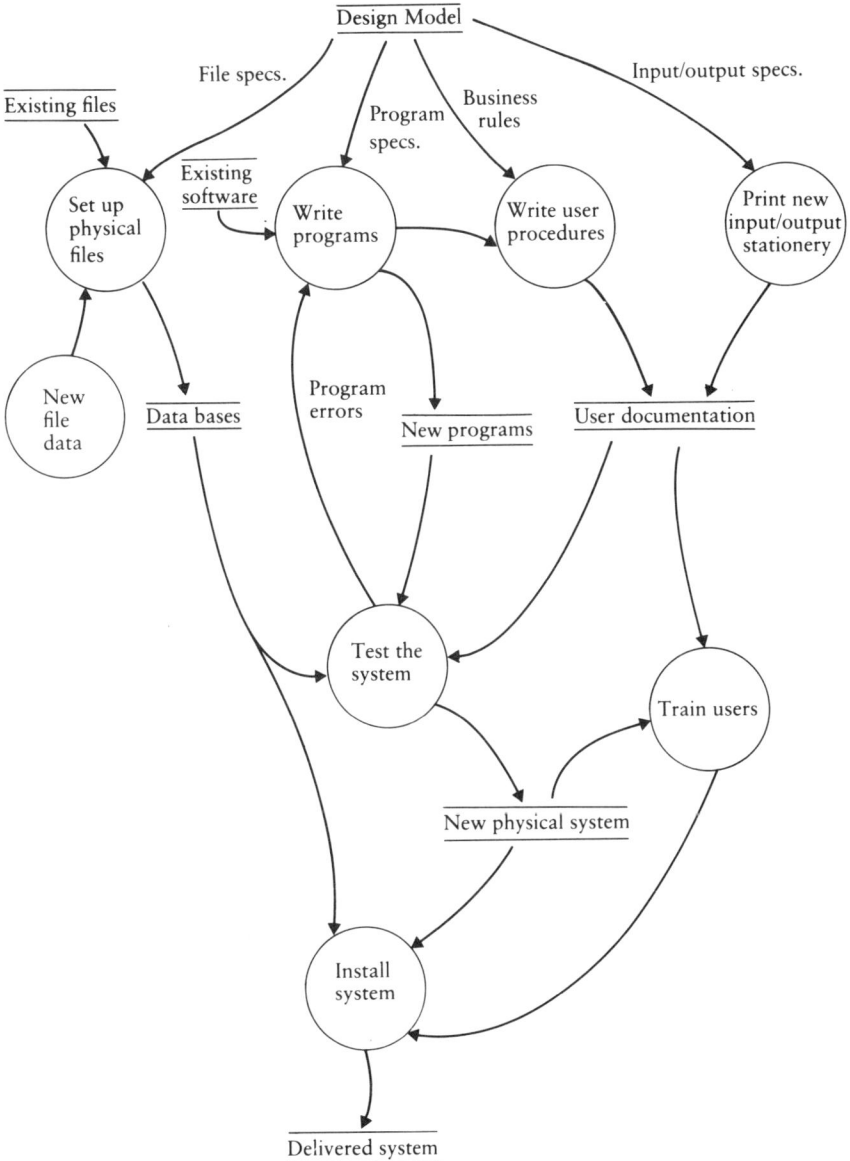

**Figure 19.2** Building and installing the system

Are we implementing the complete specification model or only part of it? Perhaps Stan should ask George Wynne's opinion on this:

SB    George, going back to what you said about controlling the building of the system, and also about seeing things happening as they went along, I thought I'd come back and show you a plan of the main activities involved [Fig. 19.2].

GW    That looks OK. If you're happy with it, then I'm content to go along with you. Just one thing. There's no indication on these as to when the system is actually going to be ready. It would be nice to think that it was in and people had got used to it before we start the Christmas rush.

SB    Well, George, one reason why I wanted to get to you at this stage was to discuss our strategy for building the system. The design model is of the complete system that we specified. We asked people to quote for the whole job. However, we do have the option of adopting a step-by-step approach to actually building the system.

GW    What do you mean by that?

SB    What I mean is this. An army marches at the pace of the slowest. By building and attempting to deliver the system in one go, we incur the risk of missing our scheduled installation date because a couple of relatively unimportant items are late. What I'm suggesting is that we identify different 'versions' of the system, building and installing these one by one, rather than trying to implement the whole system lock, stock, and barrel in one go.

GW    That sounds fine in principle, but I would have thought it is easier said than done. In practice, I would have thought that things are so closely linked to each other as to make that very difficult.

SB    Well, yes and no. A lot depends on the type of system you are building. However, let's take the easiest bit first. Quite a substantial part of our specification concerns the management information you want the system to produce. I've no wish to be rude, but you have gone for a few years without this information so I would have thought that three or four more months would not have made much difference.

GW    OK. But surely that's not going to have any great impact on the development effort.

SB    Well, every little helps, as the old lady said. . . .

GW    Quite.

SB    What about invoicing? The specification calls for the system to hold invoice data on file and match it up against the delivery note before extending it and posting it to the sales ledger. Initially, we could print out the invoice at the same time as the delivery note and then do any subsequent adjustments manually. That would make Version 1 a plain stock recording system. . . .

Let us assume that George Wynne goes along with this.

The activities where most benefit is derived from splitting off in this way are those that are on the critical path. There is no good reason to design and print only some of the documents; nothing is gained by capturing the data for setting up the files in a piecemeal fashion (unless, of course, management information requirements demanded a lengthy collation of product demand history: in this case, file set-up could quickly become the critical path, and leaving this element to a later version would make sense).

The major use of the project model is to identify the deliverables from each activity. The secret to controlling computer projects lies in breaking them down into a series of defined deliverables so that at any checkpoint the question is not, 'How far have you got?' or, even worse, 'How are things going?' but, 'Has document X been agreed?' We replace the analogue question, 'How far?' by a series of binary questions, 'Is it done or not?' Provided the deliverables are carefully defined and the mechanism for signing them off properly constructed, this technique quickly detects any slippage.

Our data flow diagram gives no indication of time, or of the allocation of resources—who does what. We must therefore now incorporate these so that we can put dates on the various activities. Time taken will of course depend—taking program writing as an example—on the quality of the people doing the work and the extent to which existing software can be used. Since USA have quoted a fixed price, the details of their resource utilization are not of immediate concern to World's Wines: what they want to know is when the different activities will be completed. In addition, since some of the activities—e.g., file set-up, user training—will be done by World's Wines, they need to know when to schedule these.

In order to make the diagram of more generalized applicability, the project model shown in Fig. 19.2 left out some activities specific to World's Wines. Let us reinstate these in our next step, the creation of a project plan. This is for the version of the system as agreed between

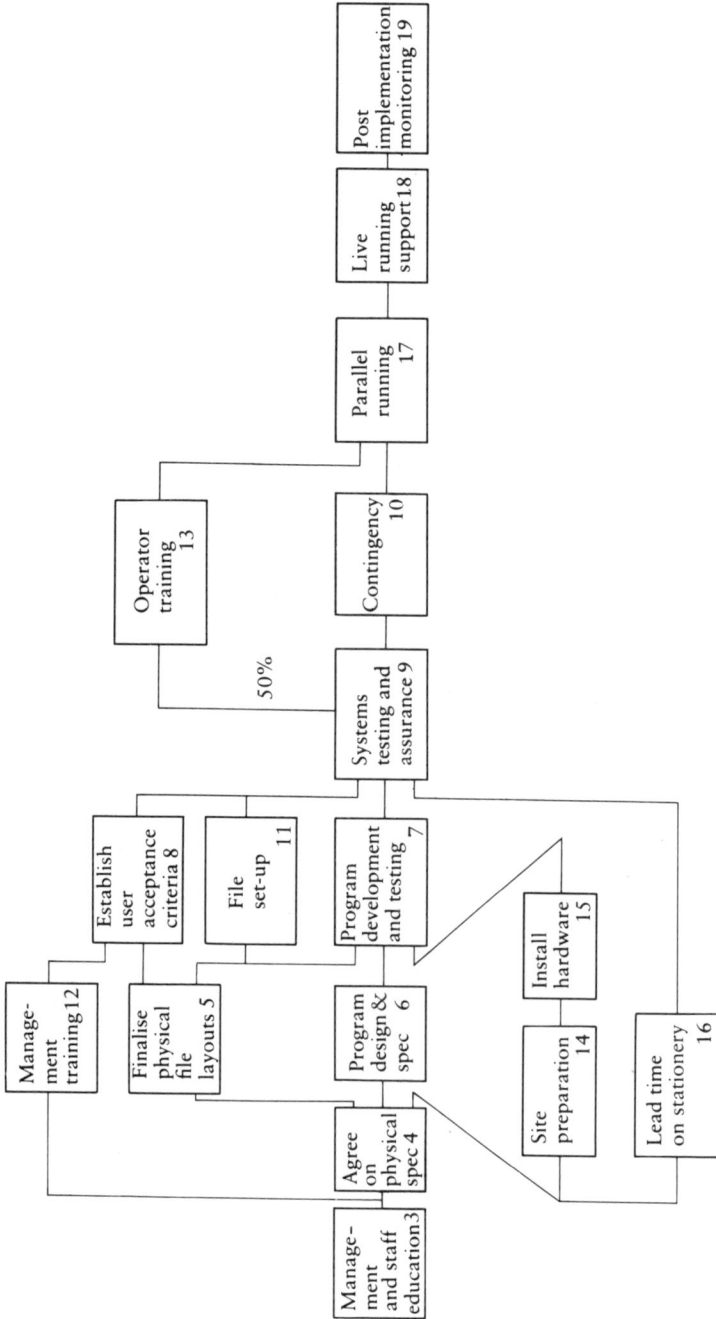

**Figure 19.3** First-draft project network

George Wynne and Stan Breagan. Building the enhanced second version—bringing in management information and complete invoicing—could overlap with some of the later activities, but this is not shown. Our major concern is to get the basic system up and running before Christmas.

We will start by drawing up a network based on:

1. identifying the activities;
2. identifying the dependencies between the activities; e.g., parallel running can start only after both systems testing and operator training have taken place; operator training can start halfway through systems testing.

This gives us a first draft of a project plan (see Fig. 19.3).

We can now incorporate the time element by including:

1. proposed completion date;
2. earliest start date;
3. estimated duration of each activity;
4. any other calendar-related information, such as non-working days or that we do not want the computer to be physically installed before August.

If we use a computer to process this data we can immediately get the information presented to us in various different formats. For control, the most obviously useful purpose is to know the critical path. We therefore specify a printout listing activities in sequence by their criticality (Fig. 19.4). This shows that, given an earliest start date of 31 March, the system can go live on 2 October, assuming that slippage does not exceed the ten days' 'contingency time' built in as activity 10. By

```
Worlds Line                               Overall Project Plan                          Plan Author GPQ
      REPORT TYPE :STANDARD LISTING                          PRINTING SEQUENCE :Most Critical Activities First
                                                             SELECTION CRITERIA :ALL
      PLAN I.D.   :COLIN   VERSION  4                        TIME NOW DATE     :10/FEB/86
=====================================================================================================================
I-J    ACTIVITY DESCRIPTION              EARLIEST    EARLIEST    LATEST      LATEST      DURATION  FLOAT
                                         START       FINISH      START       FINISH
=====================================================================================================================
 3 Management & Staff Education          31/MAR/86   2/APR/86    31/MAR/86   2/APR/86     3         0  *
 4 Agreement on Physical Specification   7/APR/86    2/MAY/86    7/APR/86    2/MAY/86    20         0  *
14 Site Preparation                      6/MAY/86    27/MAY/86   6/NAY/86    27/MAY/86   16         0  *
15 Install Hardware                      28/MAY/86   3/JUN/86    28/MAY/86   3/JUN/86     5         0  *
---------------------------------------------------------------------------------------------------------------------
 7 Program Development & Testing          4/JUN/86   29/JUL/86    4/JUN/86   29/JUL/86   40         0  *
 9 Systems Testing (Assurance)          30/JUL/86   12/AUG/86   30/JUL/86   12/AUG/86   10         0  *
10 Contingency Time                     13/AUG/86   27/AUG/86   13/AUG/86   27/AUG/86   10         0  *
17 Parallel Running                     28/AUG/86    3/SEP/86   28/AUG/86    3/SEP/86    5         0  *
---------------------------------------------------------------------------------------------------------------------
18 Live Running Support                  4/SEP/86   17/SEP/86    4/SEP/86   17/SEP/86   10         0  *
19 Post Implementation Monitoring       18/SEP/86    1/OCT/86   18/SEP/86    1/OCT/86   10         0  *
13 Operator Training                     6/AUG/86   12/AUG/86   20/AUG/86   27/AUG/86    5        10
 5 Finalise Physical File Layouts        6/MAY/86   19/MAY/86   21/MAY/86    3/JUN/86   10        11
---------------------------------------------------------------------------------------------------------------------
 6 Program Design & Specification        6/MAY/86   30/JUN/86   28/MAY/86   29/JUL/86   40        16
11 File Set Up                          27/MAY/86   30/JUN/86   25/JUN/86   29/JUL/86   25        21
16 Lead Time on Stationery Order        20/MAY/86   16/JUN/86    2/JUL/86   29/JUL/86   20        31
 8 Establish User Acceptance Criteria   20/MAY/86   26/MAY/86   23/JUL/86   29/JUL/86    5        46
---------------------------------------------------------------------------------------------------------------------
12 Management Training                    1/MAY/86    2/MAY/86   21/JUL/86   22/JUL/86    2        56
=====================================================================================================================
```

Figure 19.4  Project plan

171

definition, activities on the critical path have zero float, as shown in the last column. According to this plan, the least time-critical activity is Management training, which can be undertaken anytime between 20 May and 29 July.

In addition to this report, we can print activities in other sequences— e.g., earliest activities first—and obtain the information in the form of a project bar chart.

Once the work has begun, we can at any time update our plan by re-running the package, changing the 'time now date', reducing activity durations to 'time still remaining' for those already under way, and making any other changes in estimates, dependencies, or new activities that have cropped up since the last run.

### Project monitoring

Breaking the project into activities gives us the checkpoints at which we can monitor progress. Specifying deliverables resulting from the activities gives us something tangible to check. A proven method of quality assurance is that of the 'walkthrough', so-called because the participants mentally and actively 'walk through' the system to see whether it meets the requirements and 'looks' right in terms of fitting into the organization. These are frequently referred to as 'structured walkthroughs', but you will look for a long time before you find someone admitting to conducting 'unstructured' walkthroughs! The adjective is redundant, used only to enable the activity to partake of the good connotations of the word 'structured' in the computer industry.

A walkthrough is essentially a quality control check of a specified deliverable by a peer group, including users. They confer many advantages:

1. They spot errors or weaknesses which the author has missed.
2. They propagate good design and programming habits.
3. They encourage group participation in, and responsibility for, the product.
4. They disseminate knowledge of the product should someone quit halfway through the project.

The philosophy of walkthroughs is based on the well established fact that the author of a piece of work is not the best person to spot its faults. Having other people examine it is an effective way of eliminating errors before committing oneself to production.

Walkthroughs should be confined to spotting errors or weaknesses, not attempting to cure them. Trying to re-design a file, or re-write code, in a meeting is asking for trouble. Any required revisions are noted, and the author instructed to make them. Depending upon the number and extent of such revisions, the outcome of the scheduled walkthrough can take four forms:

1. product passed;
2. product passed (subject to minor revisions which we trust the author to make);
3. product not passed (author to incorporate revisions and a further walkthrough to be arranged);
4. walkthrough not conducted (a key person failed to turn up).

Such a system of walkthroughs is absolutely essential. No matter what size of project you undertake, walkthroughs should always be based on quality assurance procedures.

With this control mechanism in place, we can sit back and let the designers and programmers build the system. The walkthroughs will not only control progress and quality, they will result in excellent communication between users and technical staff. Given a good systems specification and a timetable that has some inbuilt slack for the inevitable day-to-day problems that occur in any project, we can be reasonably confident that the system will be written on target and will perform to the user's satisfaction.

# 20. Testing the system

*Everything is connected to everything else.*

Lenin

We are now well into the project. A number of deliverables have been produced and accepted by the steering committee that had been set up to monitor progress. This is chaired by George Wynne—who is not always present—and comprises Stan, Don Chichester, and representatives from purchasing, marketing, distribution, and internal audit. At their latest meeting, they have approved the design of screen layouts for subsidiary procedures such as stock adjustments and write-offs. The meeting then turns its attention towards systems testing.

GW  Next item. Procedures for ensuring that the new system works properly before it goes live. Stan, perhaps you'd like to talk us through these.

SB  Certainly. But first of all I'd like to make the point that we've already gone a long way towards ensuring this.

DC  In what way?

SB  What I mean is this. Although systems testing is shown on our project plan as an activity taking place between programming and systems installation, this only refers to one particular aspect of testing. What we've been doing is testing the system as we go along. That's largely what these meetings have been about. It's important to see testing—like documentation, for that matter—as an on-going process, not a last-minute scramble to see if the system works.

GW  So you are saying that we've already checked out a lot.

SB  Of course. Don's people have agreed that the screen layouts are OK. In fact, they've even had a go at entering some orders. That part of the programming has already been done, so we set up a dummy stock file and let them try it. We made a couple of minor adjustments, but there weren't any real problems.

GW  Tremendous. Any other things that you've checked out?

DC  Yes, we've had an initial look to see whether the system is coping OK with things like back orders. As far as we can tell that's all right. What we haven't yet done is to follow things right through to final invoicing.

GW   So what's left to test? What, specifically, are we testing at the systems testing phase shown in our plan?

SB   Well, obviously the main thing we're testing is that the system actually works. What we've been doing up to now is testing separate parts of the system in isolation: we still need to unite all these together to make sure that they work as a system. This type of testing is essentially making sure that there are no bugs left in. This is concerned with establishing that the system is *accurate*— that it comes up with correct answers and doesn't re-order stock at the wrong time or hand out erroneous discounts. After that, we need to establish that it is *acceptable*—that it meets your overall objectives, that response times are reasonable, that users are happy working with it.

GW   Presumably it's up to us to gauge acceptability, but what about this linking things together? Do we do that, or is that included in the contract with USA?

SB   Oh, we're holding them to more than that. Our tender document not only specified that the system must be accurate but also laid down some performance criteria. If you remember, the final payment of 20 per cent of their contract price is withheld until three months after delivery to make sure the system meets its objectives.

DC   Well that's obviously a useful safeguard, but there's going to come a time when they want us to sign on the dotted line that the system works. Is it me that has to give the say-so? In which case, how do we know? After all, none of us knows anything about programming. . . .

Systems testing is always a problem area, with neither users nor technical staff being anxious to take ultimate responsibility. Although it is an unspoken motive, I am sure this results from an innate feeling that they can never be completely certain about accepting a system as fully tested. This is because a system never *is* fully tested. The number of possible permutations of circumstances relating to products, customers, suppliers, and other parties is so high as to be incapable of exhaustive checking. Once this is realized and accepted, we can begin to look sensibly at what depth of testing is required, with specific reference to the final tests which result in the decision to install.

   In order to put this problem into context, let us for once look at the problem 'bottom-up'. In other words, let us examine what is involved in testing—specifically, program testing—and then work back from this to consider how we can define standards to reduce the risk of errors going undetected to an absolute minimum.

### The problem of testing

In 1978, statistics revealed an unexpectedly high increase in the productivity of pharmacists in Australia. An investigation into this revealed an error in a Health Service computer system which reimbursed pharmacists for making up prescriptions.

What was the error, how did it come about, and how did it go unnoticed? I quote from the Public Accounts Committee's report:

> The error occurred in translating a requirements specification—which expressed the task to be done in mathematical notation—into a specification for a computer program. The program designer (a consultant) correctly gave directions for calculating a table of ratios to enable the allocation of total pharmacy dispensary staff costs to be made across sectors and activities in the pharmacy. The designer should then have given directions for calculating a corresponding table of ratios for allocating the costs of retail staff labour by sector and activity. Instead, it was specified that both retail and dispensing staff costs were to be allocated according to the one set of ratios calculated for the dispensing staff only. (*Pharmaceutical Benefits Scheme*, Joint Committee of Public Accounts, Canberra)

*In the years 1973–79, the errors resulted in overpayment by the government to pharmacists of an estimated $A253 million.*

This is a dramatic illustration of the need to ensure that a system is working properly before installation. In running the World's Wines' project, Stan has correctly viewed testing as an on-going activity, not as a last-minute check. His whole approach has revolved around the quality checking of deliverables throughout the project. In this way he has minimized the chance of errors occurring through bad communication. It is inconceivable that a mistake such as that described above could have slipped through a properly conducted walkthrough. Nevertheless, the words 'minimize' and 'inconceivable' (as opposed to 'eliminate' and to 'impossible') were chosen with care. We still need to test the complete system once it has been delivered.

All that the builders have told us is that the individual programs work according to specification (and they won't swear to that). We have yet to prove that the programs work properly when linked together; that data control knows its role; that users understand the input procedures; that people required to fill in new forms know how to do so.

Let us turn our attention first to how program testing is carried out. To illustrate the problem with program testing, and *a fortiori* systems testing, let us examine the objective of testing. What the user wants to hear is 'the system works'—by which is meant that all individual programs have been tested and proved to be error-free and that, when linked together, they produce the correct outputs from a given set of inputs. The problem is, it is not sufficient to hear such a statement: we also need to believe it—particularly if we are talking of a financial system processing millions of pounds worth of transactions per day.

How can we know whether the statement is true or not? This is, in the truest sense, a philosophical question—so let us turn to philosophy for an answer. It is an example of what philosopher's term the 'problem of induction'. How do we attempt to prove the truth of statements made about the real world? Indeed, is it possible to do so? Let us examine two such statements:

1. All swans are white.
2. In all right-angled triangles the square on the hypotenuse is equal to the sum of the squares on the two opposing sides.

One way of attempting to verify the first statement is by prolonged observation of swans. But as philosophers never tire of pointing out, there is no logical way in which this method can prove the correctness of the statement. No matter how many white swans we see, it only takes one black swan to falsify the statement. The nearest we can get to a proof is to say that, 'as far as we are aware, after prolonged study, we believe the statement to be true'. Our endeavours are best directed at looking for black swans, not white.

What about the second statement? Do we attempt to prove the correctness of this statement by drawing innumerable right-angled triangles and measuring them to see whether they adhere to the rule? If so, we would have to draw a lot of triangles; including, presumably, triangles 300 × 400 × 500 miles, in case the statement holds true only for small triangles. That is how a programmer would look at it. After all, the statement 'water boils at 100 °C' appears to hold true in all cases, until you test it out a few thousand feet above sea-level. However, we do not have to prove the second statement by observation. It can be proved *deductively*, and indeed was done some time ago by a certain

177

Pythagoras. There is a theorem to prove it, and at the bottom of the proof you can write QED. (Actually, even here there is an exception— if the triangles are drawn on a sphere, as opposed to the implied flat surface.)

The relevance of these examples to testing computers is this. All testing falls squarely into the first type of proof. You cannot deductively prove the correctness of a computer program.[1] All testing is concerned with *falsifying* the statement, 'this program works'. Systems and program testing is the search for black swans (as opposed to 'bugs', as is commonly supposed).

The difficulty with testing, and therefore the reason that errors or omissions can remain undiscovered for months or possibly years, is that the number of paths that a given set of data—and in particular given combinations of data—can take through a program is extremely high.

Figure 20.1 represents a relatively simple program containing a number of different possible paths through it. (The ellipse represents a decision with two possible outcomes.) Assuming that a program executed the loop from nought to twenty times, the number of unique paths, and therefore the number of tests required, is given by the formula:[2]

$$5^{20} + 5^{19} + 5^{18} + \cdots + 5^{1} = \text{approximately } 10^{14} \text{ or } 100 \text{ trillion}$$

If you could test one path every five minutes, it would take a billion years to test all possible combinations of paths taken by twenty transactions.

To see why this is (and what can be done to minimize the number), let us take the example of World's Wines. Imagine that we are testing the program that updates the stock file with receipts into stock and issues from stock. In terms of the computer program, there are two input transactions: receipt lines and order lines. For any line, the program must first check that the product code is correct, i.e., that there exists a matching record on the stock files. Provided this is true, the program now has to update the quantity-on-hand for the relevant product. Here we have written—and therefore need to test—two different procedures, respectively, for a zero value and a positive value for quantity-on-hand

---

[1] I should add the rider that I frequently see reviews of books or articles on the subject of 'mathematically proving the correctness of programs'. However, since such a proof would immediately make its originator a multi-millionaire, and since I have not yet seen any companies floated based on such a proof, I take leave to doubt that it currently exists.

[2] Glenford Myers, *Art of Software Testing*, John Wiley, 1979.

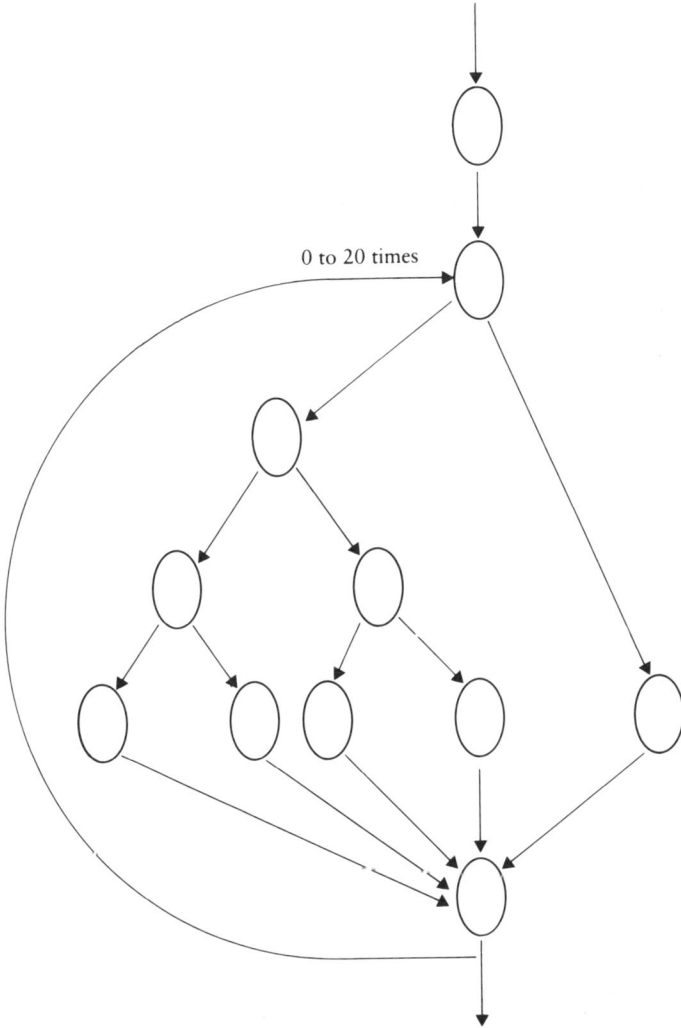

0 to 20 times

Figure 20.1   Program logic paths

(if quantity-on-hand is allowed to go negative, things get even more complicated).

We have now identified:

- two different transaction types (orders and receipts);
- two possibilities regarding the product code (match or non-match);
- two states of stock availability (zero or non-zero quantity-on-hand).

179

Three tests, each with two outcomes, gives you eight possible combinations. Each time we add in other complications—more types of input transactions, procedures triggered off by conditions such as stock reaching re-order level—the number of tests necessary rises exponentially. The essential point to grasp is this: *Each new condition or procedure added to a program does not add to the complications: it multiplies them.*

The solution is to break complex systems down into sub-systems, and to break large programs into small programs or modules. Within this, we should endeavour to make the various components as *independent* of each other as possible, and the connections between them as simple as possible. Good program design accomplishes this. When we designed the program that controls the requisitioning of stock, we ensured that one self-contained module was dedicated to the procedure for stock re-ordering. This brings significant advantages:

- The module is capable of being tested in isolation from the rest of the program. We reduce the number of different combinations of data with which this part of the program has to deal.
- If it is subsequently desired to change the rules for stock re-ordering—for example, to introduce considerations of seasonality into demand prediction—we can re-write the module secure in the knowledge that we will not unwittingly introduce new errors elsewhere in the program.

By breaking the complete system into modules we simplify testing. We can now legitimately ask of the programmer that his program works, or at least that it has passed all reasonable attempts to disprove this. We can legitimately ask of the project leader that the programs link together successfully to form a complete system.

A nagging doubt persists, however. It would be so much more comforting if one could write QED under the system. To this I can only reply that this is how life works. Even at law, proof is only 'beyond reasonable doubt', and men hanged who have subsequently been found innocent.

What we *can* do is get the chances of errors remaining undetected to an irreducible minimum. The vast majority of missed bugs do not actually stem from a totally unforeseen, one-in-a-million, set of circumstances: they come from a failure to build and test programs in accordance with good standards. How can this be? Back to the Australian Public Accounts Committee:

One reason why thorough tests were not applied appears to have been the urgency of completing the 1972–73 Inquiry which caused a number of short-cuts to be taken. (Para 5.12)

If unrealistic deadlines are set for ADP (data processing) staff, the latter should formally communicate to their management any apprehensions they feel about meeting the deadlines and the risk of error that might result from over-hasty work. (Para 5.18)

### On-going testing

The Health Insurance disaster stemmed originally from a highly optimistic time-scale imposed on political grounds which ignored technical considerations. World's Wines steered round this particular problem by concentrating attention on the time-scale in the original project request and by ensuring that it was realistically set at the outset.

A second problem is that systems testing is perceived as the final activity in development rather than one that is on-going throughout the project. Again, this is a relic of the historical separation between user and builder. Walkthroughs as described can be used as testing sessions. As a new part of the system is delivered, so it can be tested independently by those users designated for this role. This removes a large part of the activity from the critical path, encourages close user involvement, and significantly reduces the number of problems encountered in pre-installation testing.

### How to do it

To answer this, let us turn our attention back to pre-installation accuracy testing. This is the critical time when the individual programs are linked together.

There are two basic approaches to this, white box and black box testing. The first of these implies a knowledge of what is going on inside an individual program; it is therefore the programmer's domain. Black box testing implies that the tester has no knowledge of how a program, or series of linked programs, is written; he is concerned with establishing that certain inputs produce certain end results. This is clearly the user's main approach.

All testing necessitates the creation of test data, and of a schedule of anticipated results. Whose job is it to provide these? The systems builders are ruled out because this level of testing is essentially an independent check. Some companies set up a separate testing group whose full-time occupation is checking out systems. One advantage of this approach is that, before such a group can test a system, they must be able to understand it. Therefore their first check is on the quality of the system's documentation. Since this is often a neglected part of the system, it is an extremely useful benefit. Such a group would usually be part of the data processing department. Since World's Wines has no such staff, and Stan Breagan is too expensive for this task, they will call upon their own clerical staff to fulfil this function.

How will they go about it? The first essential is that the people should have the right psychological approach. By this I mean that they should accept the following definition: *A successful test is one that finds an error.* This is the reverse of the way in which most people approach the task (though a Popperian would immediately recognize the principle of falsifiability). If you ask most programmers how a given test turned out, they will answer: 'Fine, we didn't find any mistakes.' The attitude that you are hoping not to find errors is bound to lead to less exhaustive testing than the reverse attitude. The tester's ego is invested in the product under test, not in the testing process itself.

This definition of the process leads easily to the strategy for going about it. The tester will naturally be on the look-out for all the oddities, ambiguities, and exceptions that occur in the current system. Without a great investment of time he can build up, as a by-product of his everyday job, a folder of 'nasties', i.e., orders which cause problems. He can then supplement these with those which he originates himself. I have already itemized some of the conditions to be tested in the World's Wines system. Other types of conditions of general applicability are:

1. *High volume*  The programmer is likely to have spread his tests thinly across a range of different conditions. It may well be that certain paths through a program are only activated by large numbers of transactions. A simple example is page overflow. Unless someone enters an order with over thirty lines, we will not know whether the system successfully prints a two-page delivery note and invoice.

2. *Simultaneous file access*  It is much easier for the programmer to test his program by inputting one transaction at a time and following its path. But in any multi-terminal system there is the certainty that more than one user will want to access the same masterfile record at the same time. Does the system successfully lock one out and queue the other where necessary? Combining acceptability testing with accuracy testing, what is the effect on response times of six clerks all trying to enter a screenful of information simultaneously?

182

3. *Untried conditions*   It is not difficult to think up tests for things that are foreseen as likely to happen—not least because the specification explicitly takes account of these. But are there any possibilities left unmentioned? What of the user who rings up and asks for a repeat of last week's order? The system may implicitly cater for these, but it is as well to try them.

4. *User reaction*   The above leads naturally to the important comment that testing should not be perceived as merely trying to defeat the program code. Do the users know how to work the system? What will they do when the message 'FATAL ERROR' appears on their screen? How will they cope with the system going down?

Putting this together into a coherent testing strategy results in the following set of guidelines:

1. Think testing from the start of the project.
2. Regard testing as a continuing activity.
3. Involve users at all stages.
4. Leave adequate time for pre-installation testing. If the project is running late, this is the first activity to get squeezed.
5. Keep testers and builders independent of each other.
6. Differentiate between accuracy testing and acceptability testing.
7. Be sure to keep the test data—you will need it to check out any subsequent modifications made to the system.
8. Do not call it 'testing'—'systems assurance' is sexier.

# 21. Installing the system

*'It'll be all right on the night. . . .'*

As our project model made clear, there are many activities beyond those of writing the system software. I have made only passing reference to the physical task of installing the computer. An examination of our model will reveal other activities. Specifically, there are three major tasks involved before the tested system goes live. Two of these—file set-up and user training—will have been undertaken in parallel with the computer system development; the third—the cut-over from old to new system—brings all aspects together in the final test.

### File creation

Most computer systems involve the setting up of new master files or the modification or extension of existing ones. Existing files may be computer-based or manual. In either case, this can be a time-consuming task. My first job in data processing was the conversion of an 'accounts receivables' file from a balance-brought-forward system to open-item. Every account balance had to be retrospectively established and reconciled. The task of file set-up is not intellectually stimulating. It requires planning and attention to detail rather than inspiration. Certainly it is less fun than designing systems or writing programs. Hence its problems are easily overlooked.

The starting point is the definition of the contents of any new file, and the information contained on any existing files. Almost all master files contain a mixture of permanent data, or data of low volatility (such as names and addresses) and highly volatile data (such as balances). If the task of file set-up is of any magnitude, then the volatile data can only be collected as a separate final task immediately prior to going live. The less volatile data can be captured earlier, put on file, and checked over a period of time. Within this common strategy there are many pitfalls. None of them is difficult, and an awareness of them should be sufficient to ensure a smooth take-on of information.

Let us take a look at the World's Wines stock file to see what typical difficulties arise. Clearly, the source document which will form the basis of the new stock file is their current stock card (Fig. 21.1).

We can next compare the data on this with that to be held by the new system.

184

| Pack size 70 cl. £42·00 | | | | | Pack size 35 cl. £26·00 | | | | | Pack size | | | | |
|---|---|---|---|---|---|---|---|---|---|---|---|---|---|---|
| Date | Ref. | In | Out | Bal. | Date | Ref. | In | Out | Bal. | Date | Ref. | In | Out | Bal. |
| 11·8·85 | 35216 | 828 10/12 | | 828 10/12 | 11·7·85 | 4269 | 400 | | 460 | | | | | |
| 15·8·85 | 6507 | | 60 | 768 10/12 | 15·7·85 | As per Sav 2/10 Breacage in bond | 4/12 | | 459 8/12 | | | | | |
| 21·8·85 | B.N.C. Oxford | | 24 | 744 10/12 | 19·7·85 | Greene King | | 50 | 409 8/12 | | | | | |
| 1·9·85 | Rug Antiggs | | 20 | 724 10/12 | 20·8·85 | Loose Ends | | 24 | 385 8/12 | | | | | |
| 10·9·85 | Pinner | | 4 | 720 10/12 | 1·9·85 | %P/12 | | 50 | 335 8/12 | | | | | |
| 17·9·85 | Kingston | | 6 | 714 6/12 | 17·9·85 | House of Commons | | 120 | 215 8/12 | | | | | |
| 18·9·85 | French Embassy | | 40 | 674 10/12 | 24·9·85 | 764/2 | | 30 | 185 9/12 | | | | | |
| 21·9·85 | T.H.F. | | 120 | 554 10/12 | | | | | | | | | | |
| 24·9·85 | St. James Palace | | 10 | 544 10/12 | | | | | | | | | | |
| 27·9·85 | S.O.P. Cowley St. | | 60 | 484 10/12 | | | | | | | | | | |
| | | | | | | | | | | | | | | |
| | | | | | | | | | | | | | | |
| | | | | | | | | | | | | | | |
| | | | | | | | | | | | | | | |
| | | | | | | | | | | | | | | |
| Re-order level: 180 | | | | | Re-order level: 100 | | | | | Re-order level: | | | | |
| Description: St. Emilion 1981 | | | | | | | | | Product code: FR 20781 | | | | | |

**Figure 21.1**  World's Wines: stock card

$$
\begin{aligned}
\text{PRODUCT-CATALOGUE} = \{ &\text{PRODUCT-CODE} \\
&+ \text{PRODUCT-DESCRIPTION} \\
&+ \text{SUPPLIER-CODE}\} \\
\text{PRODUCT-CODE} = &\text{PRODUCT-CATEGORY} \\
&+ \text{PRODUCT-NUMBER} \\
&+ \text{PRODUCT-CHECK-DIGIT}
\end{aligned}
$$

In the current system the product code is a simple identifier of a particular product. In the new system we have decided to add a further digit—a check digit[1]—to the product code in order to reduce the

[1] A check digit is an additional digit, usually on the end of a code, which bears a strict arithmetic relationship to the preceding digits and can be computed from them. Any simple error in writing down or entering the code—transcription or transposition—will break this relationship and cause the transaction to be rejected by the system.

185

incidence of incorrect codes being accepted by the system. This item of data is not part of the current system: it does not exist. We shall have to go through each of our product codes, calculating the appropriate check digit and adding it to the code. Mercifully, we can get the computer to help.

Another instance of the same problem is that the World's Wines stock card contains the selling price but not the cost price. Because it is a requirement of the new system to produce a monthly stock valuation, we need the cost price on the new master file. We have, therefore, the task of going through our complete set of stock cards, adding the cost price information so that it can be captured for the new stock file.

This illustrates the first problem of file creation: *completeness* of the source data. The second concern is with the *accuracy* of the data. It goes without saying that there will be discrepancies between physical stock and the stock records. The accuracy of the data is a matter of prime concern. Customers change addresses; fixed assets disappear or are written-off without the register being updated. In a system in my experience, some parts in a warehouse had three different part numbers: the original number, a partial re-coding for a NATO contract, and the legacy of an abandoned attempt to re-code all parts. The system still worked, because the people on the floor knew that a BA3076/2 was the same as a 614/21/076 which in turn could also be a 37/ZP/214/01. These anomalies had to be resolved before the job of capturing this data could begin.

Another frequent problem is *availability* of the data. Will we have access to it when we want, or are the records in constant use? Are we dealing with confidential data where special arrangements will need to be made for its storage during and after capture takes place? Is the data physically in the same place, or do we need to collect it from different parts of the organization?

Finally, there is the problem of *volatility*. If the actual records that we are capturing within a file are constantly changing—e.g., titles in a book store—we shall either have to collect all data in a very short time or resign ourselves to the necessity of maintaining the master file as we create it. However, it will be seen that these are management rather than technical problems. Forethought and planning will obviate most of them.

### User training

When I am not book-writing, my major activity is lecturing. A high proportion of this is to user management. The subject matter of this book is drawn largely from such courses. By far the most frequent comment that I receive at the end of a course is: 'We wish we'd had this course three years ago.' Regrettably, many companies wait till after the horse has bolted.

Within my own company we have a saying: *You cannot make a system foolproof because fools are so ingenious.* No system exists which an appropriate level of stupidity cannot foul up. It is vital to the success of any system that users are fully trained. As with any training, the key question is, What do people need to know? The answer to this will vary according to their involvement with the system. Within World's Wines, our main concern in dealing with George Wynne is that he knows what he wants from the system. His major area of participation was in formulating the project request. He therefore requires a familiarity with the practical implications of introducing computer systems; he needs to know how:

- to specify clear objectives;
- to identify constraints—involving personnel considerations;
- to fit the immediate application into a longer-term strategy;
- to realize what things commonly go wrong and how to avoid them.

This knowledge is consistent with his position within the organization, and with the decisions that he has to make. At the line management level the training need is more specific to the application. They need to know how:

- to specify information requirements;
- to explain clearly and comprehensively how the current system works;
- to analyse problems, originate and evaluate solutions to them;
- to ensure that the new system will be workable by the staff and acceptable to them.

Finally, we must ensure that all end-users—people whose everyday work is changed by the system—are completely familiar with their changed roles. First among these will be the stock clerks, who are now updating computer files rather than writing ledger cards. Salesmen and branch managers must familiarize themselves with the re-designed order forms. Warehouse staff must understand both the changed documents they now handle and any new procedures involved in assembling orders.

The training requirements are substantial, and vary from the strategic level of appreciation of senior management to the hands-on training of

187

those involved in data entry. The estimated training cost of £5000 in the cost–benefit analysis (if it includes the trainer's time) is almost certainly too low.

## Implementation

Once testing is completed, files are set up, stationery is delivered and users are trained, the system is ready to go live. The importance of this last phase can hardly be overemphasized. Until now, all disasters, disagreements, cost overruns, and project slippage have been kept within the organization. True, you may have estimated £100 000 for an 18-month time-scale and here you are three years on and £200 000 poorer, but such minor inconveniences pale into insignificance compared with pressing the button on a system which immediately sends out 50 000 erroneous statements, corrupts half the supplier database, or sends your customers the wrong product.

Installing a new system is disruptive and risky. There is bound to be dislocation as staff become accustomed to new procedures; there are always risks that undiscovered bugs are just waiting for the moment of maximum damage to surface. Therefore we need a strategy to minimize both dangers.

In most walks of life one minimizes both risks and dislocation by a gradualist approach—as George Wynne put it, by 'hastening slowly'. The first, and most important, decision was taken in defining the boundaries of the current project in the initial project request. The part of World's Wines' activities that fell within Stan Breagan's survey were bound to include not just order processing but also the immediately allied activities of sales ledger, purchase ledger, and stock control.

The high-risk strategy would have been to develop a system covering all these functions. This approach could have been adopted for a number of perfectly valid reasons:

- in order to look for an integrated and comprehensive package;
- because there was no obvious or convenient way of subdividing the total area;
- because of a management decision to pursue a high-risk strategy in order to realize potential benefits more quickly.

Instead, the project request carefully circumscribed the so-called 'domain of change' so as to leave sales and purchase ledger until after the order processing system has been installed and running successfully. This decision can be represented as in Fig. 21.2.

188

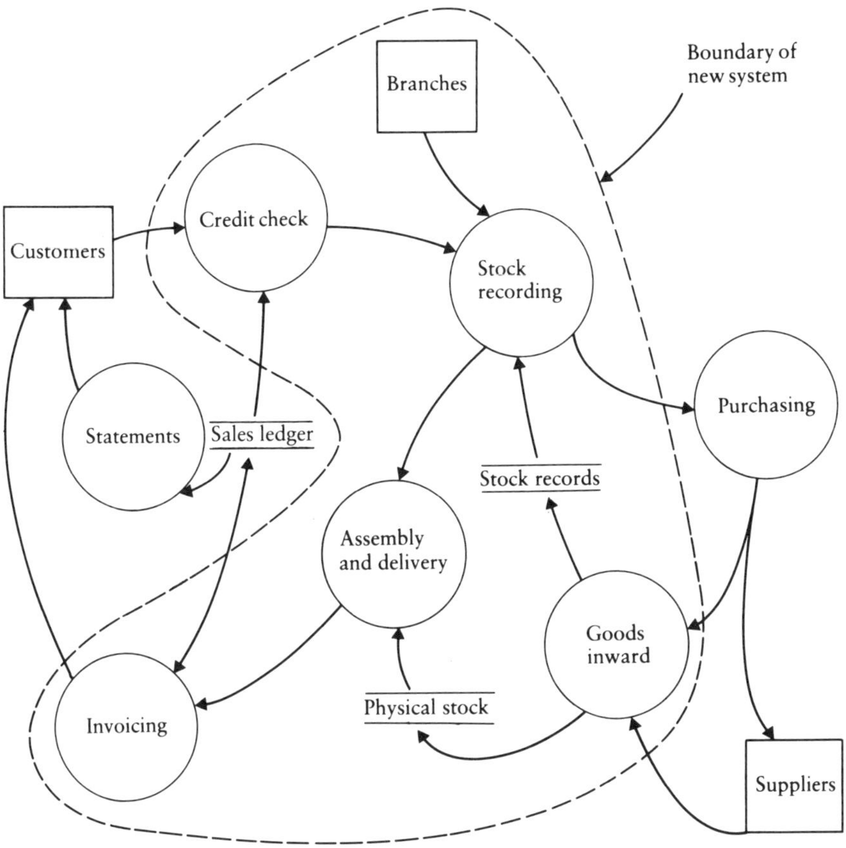

Figure 21.2   Domain of change

Partitioning in this way inevitably means the creation of interfaces between the new and unchanged parts of the complete system. Invoices will have to be posted manually to the sales ledger. Credit checking will remain a manual process until the sales ledger is computerized. We may need to create a customer file which will duplicate much of the data on the sales ledger. Such inefficiencies are a trade-off against the benefits accruing from our cautious approach; management has deemed them worthwhile.

If we step back from our immediate order processing project and look at the total system, we can identify a strategy which first computerizes order processing, then adds the sales ledger, followed by purchase ledger and automated stock control. The management decision to

189

proceed cautiously is what has enabled us to concentrate on order processing. However, our current project has always been seen in this wider context, so Stan would have been mindful of subsequent stages or enhancements when producing the specification.

Within this overall gradual plan, World's Wines, as we have seen, have gone a step further. The order processing system itself is to be developed and installed in versions.[1] These have been defined as:

Version 1    Processing of orders, including stock-updating and production of invoices; adjustments to invoices caused by amended delivery notes will be handled manually; no provision for management information.

Version 2    Automation of invoice adjustments.

Version 3    Incorporation of reporting system for management information.

Version 1 is a working subset of the order processing system. Within that, one could envisage an earlier version which could be demonstrated to the users as running successfully, although not containing sufficient functions to be used live. Typically, this could be all procedures associated with file management, e.g., new lines, new pack sizes, changes to prices or to minimum stock levels. Programs incorporating such procedures would be needed for initial file set-up and would be a useful and tangible demonstration of progress.

Versions 2 and 3 merely extend the installed system once it is working successfully. Beyond that we have made provision for planned enhancements which include:

1. automation of sales ledger with automatic updating by invoices, cash-matching, statements, and on-line credit-checking;
2. automated stock replenishment based on demand analysis, production of purchase orders and updating of the purchase ledger.

### Going live
We have identified a strategy for systems installation designed to reduce dislocation by doing it in manageable chunks. Within this, we can

[1] 'Installing' means that the company thereafter is using that part of the system to transact its business. It is possible to develop incrementally and install each version as it arrives (as in the example); however, other permutations are possible—developing the system at one go, but installing it part at a time (gradual implementation), developing increments but installing at one go, or developing and installing a complete system.

identify tactics which will minimize risks by final-testing in a pseudo-live environment. We have already noted the limitations of systems testing as a means of proving that the system works. As a final check, before entrusting the company's fortunes to the system, it is prudent to run it in as near a live mode as possible. This may, for instance, bring to light errors of omission in the original specification. These could well have escaped detection during systems testing as the latter is essentially a proof that the system works according to the specification. There are various strategies for this final check.

PARALLEL RUNNING

As the name implies, under this procedure the new system (or sub-system) is run in parallel with the old. This is the most convincing proof that the new system works, but it is only applicable in systems where the new closely resembles the old. To the extent that we have abolished or modified some procedures and instituted new ones, parallel running is unsatisfactory.

Parallel running needs careful planning. There will be pressure on staff because two systems will be being run at the same time. A variety of tasks specific to the parallel running will arise—e.g., transcription of data from one input form to another. Checking of outputs is a time-consuming task. Nevertheless, such is the confidence engendered by a successful parallel run that most organizations will opt for one whenever possible.

PILOT RUNNING

An obvious way to overcome the work pressures of a complete parallel operation is to introduce the total system in microcosm. This allows us to inspect the workings of the system in a small and easily observed environment. World's Wines may choose to implement the system in a couple of branches initially, bringing the rest of the branches in, either gradually or at a stroke, once they are satisfied with the system in its pilot form.

The best situation for pilot running is when two conditions are fulfilled:

1. *Homogeneity* If, in the new system, different branches within World's Wines are allowed to follow different procedures—e.g., those within the local telephone area can ring in their orders while those outside must mail them—then a pilot run in the latter will not prove the

191

system in the former. If, however, the new system is identical for all branches, it may reasonably be assumed[1] that, if the system works in a pilot run of four or five branches, it will work in all branches.

2. *Low connectivity* By this I mean that in a pilot run one wants to isolate the pilot area from the rest. As with a scientific experiment, we need to control the experiment by reducing the number of variables. Banks exhibit the two characteristics of homogeneity and low connectivity. First, the accounting procedures in all branches will be almost identical. Consequently, if the system works in some branches it should work in all. Second, we can control the interfaces between branches. Computerized banking is a highly centralized activity, in that all transactions are channelled through one central point. As there are no direct branch-to-branch transactions, we can isolate the pilot area from the remainder of the network.

To illustrate this in the case of World's Wines, let us consider two possible systems. Under the first, branches are allowed to get stock only from the one central warehouse. This contrasts with a more liberal, and more complex, system whereby branches are permitted to borrow stock from other branches, or to order directly from suppliers.

The virtue of simplicity in systems becomes apparent if we contemplate a pilot implementation. If there is low connectivity between branches, we can isolate the experimental area from the rest with comparative ease. It has fewer interfaces, so there is less to control. Where connectivity is higher, however, the task of isolating the test area is considerably more complex, reflecting the greater complexity of the system as a whole. The likelihood of the pilot implementation not exercising all combinations of circumstances is sharply increased. It is the complexity of the interfaces that makes pilot implementation difficult.

A final word about the incremental approach. Provided that a program has been properly specified and designed, one can easily replace existing code. In practice, this means that World's Wines could, in Version 3 of their system, use the simplest method possible for stock control, i.e., re-ordering when quantity-on-hand reaches a preset level. If the program has been constructed so that this procedure is clearly independent and self-contained, one can change the code—to introduce a more complex

---

[1] As a practising consultant, and occasional political speechwriter, I have an inexhaustible set of expressions, verbs, and adjectives, which, in subtly varying degrees of strength, imply much but promise little.

formula—without risk of introducing errors in unrelated, and unsuspected, parts of the program.

Installing a new system is a hazardous undertaking. Minimizing risk and dislocation is the prime management concern. It is irresponsible to specify, design and build a system and then think about how one is going to install it. Ease of implementation must be one of the major characteristics of a successful project, and one that is thought about at an early stage.

# 22. Reviewing the system

*... it is a custom*
*More honour'd in the breach than the observance'*

*Hamlet*

Most companies' data processing standards include a post-implementation review. Few conduct them. The standard reason, or excuse, is that they would prove little, since the implemented system bears little resemblance to that originally specified so that a retrospective examination of how well objectives were met, time-scales adhered to, and cost targets met is unproductive. Nobody likes a witchhunt, and usually all participants have something to hide. We also fail to review because we profoundly hope that we shall never have to go through a similar experience again.

Nevertheless, no activity or project that has consumed substantial company resources should escape review. To see how to go about it, we can return to Kipling's serving men (or five of them).

## 1. What are we reviewing?

It is worth identifying two separate areas for review. The first is that of the project itself. This involves examining things such as:

- Estimates of resources of manpower and machine time, their relation to actuals, and the reasons for divergence in these
- The development methods used in the project: Were data flow diagrams an aid to communication? Did the data model assist in defining the files?
- The control techniques used: Were walkthroughs an acceptable and effective way of monitoring progress and quality?
- Relationships between users and data processing staff: Was there full user involvement, and did this contribute to a better end-product?
- What level of systems maintenance was necessary in the period immediately following implementation? What type of modifications were needed and what caused them?
- How well documented is the system? Has it been updated to reflect post-operational changes?

194

Second, we review the system:

- Is it meeting the system objectives as defined in the initial project request?
- Are there any user problems, either within the new system or in its interfaces with other systems? How high are error rates?
- Is the system secure? Are audit trails, reconciliations, and other controls satisfactory?
- Are the running costs in line with those estimated in the cost–benefit analysis? If not, how great is the divergence and what is causing it?
- Are the benefits being realized? Are managers using the information produced by the system?
- Is the system effective from its operational standpoint?
- What immediate enhancements—other than those already planned—will increase the efficiency and acceptability of the system?

## 2. Why review?

This is easy. A review is not a search for the guilty—they have either left or been promoted, anyway. We review for two reasons:

- to identify any immediate problems or improvements that can be made to the system;
- to improve next time. The colloquial expression, 'we learn by experience'—as though learning is some osmotic process—is demonstrably untrue. We learn if we choose to. This means analysing what went wrong—and what went right!—with the project and modifying standards, methods, and policies for the future.

## 3. How do we review?

It is no coincidence that in this chapter I have reverted to the techniques described earlier in the book. A review is an investigation and problem analysis. We need to know what we are looking for. This should fall naturally out of our project control system.

In compiling our estimates early in the project, we would hope to have some empirical figures on which to base them. We review by collecting the actuals. In some instances a system will already be in place to capture these automatically. If not, we will have to put them together ourselves, either from figures collected but not collated, or by interviewing the people involved.

195

## 4. When do we review?

I identified two different reviews—the project review and the system review. These are best conducted at different times. The project review should be done well within the first six months after going live—in fact, as early as is consistent with the measurement of modifications necessary after implementation.

The system review should be held once any teething troubles have been overcome. Hopefully this means within the period six to twelve months after installation. If you still have significant problems after twelve months, then your project review must have made interesting reading.

## 5. Who reviews?

The principle we observed with pre-installation testing holds good here. Reviews must be conducted by people outside, and independent of, the project team. Larger installations may have a group whose function this is. More likely, an individual or *ad hoc* group will be assigned. If the latter is the case, then it should be drawn from both the user and data processing area; if the review is carried out by one person, it is preferable that he is from the user area.

The purpose of any type of review is to draw together lessons in order to influence future actions. That also describes my purpose in writing this book. Let me therefore conclude by attempting to summarize the main points.

1. *Get stuck in.* Computers affect every aspect of business life, both in operational systems and in assisting decision-making. Properly used, they are the most powerful management tool around.

The single most important factor in their successful use is you. Regard the knowledge you have gained from this book as a firm theoretical base. Build on this by examining the methods in operation within your own organization.

2. *Don't fall in love with the technology.* If you have an insatiable curiosity about how things work, buy a home computer, subscribe to a microcomputer magazine, and impress your friends with your new-found expertise in extended RAMS, asynchronous transmission, and nested DO-loops. But leave it at home. At work think logical, not physical.

196

3. *Be clear what you want.* The greatest single aid to problem solution is problem definition. If you don't know what you want, the computer can't give it to you.

4. *Don't cut corners.* The quality of an organization's information processing is rapidly becoming the single most important factor in corporate success. Employ good people. A top-class programmer is not 50 per cent better than a mediocre one: he is 500 per cent better. A poor systems analyst can cost you thousands in designing a solution to the wrong problem.

5. *Take your time.* Imposing impossible time-scales is not a sign of management virility—it is the mark of intellectual incompetence.

6. *Train people.* The mystique of computers is rapidly being dispelled. Successful use of computers results from close user involvement. To foster this, ensure that people at all levels are educated in the use and impact of this technology on their jobs.

7. *Install good standards.* This book is about systems. The most important system of all is the project control system, because that dictates how all other systems are developed and installed. This system should be a model for all others—clear objectives, good reporting, user-friendly, easily maintainable. If this system is not right, how can you hope to design others?

# Appendix A
# The problem of peaking:
# An analyst's approach

One of my basic tenets in teaching systems analysis is this:

Problems remain the same; solutions differ.

What I mean by this is that there is a high degree of homogeneity in problems across different organizations, different countries, and different ages. One could possibly develop the argument to show that, at the *logical* level, even solutions demonstrate similarities—the physical is what changes.

It follows from this that an accurate and exhaustive analysis of a common problem should lead to the identification of classes of solutions that are transportable from one organization to another. To demonstrate this analytical approach, and to explore the degree to which it logically solves a typical business problem once and for all, let us turn our attention to the phenomenon of peaking. Let us start by drawing a simple graph to represent what we mean by 'peaking' (Fig. A1.1). This graphically shows what peaking is: a temporary excess of demand for a product or service over the capacity to supply. Depending upon the nature of the product or service, the excess demand is either lost (because the product, like electricity, is not easily stored, or because the customer goes elsewhere), or it is stored up as a backlog. We can see from the figure that, in the latter situation, the area above this capacity line must not exceed the sum of the areas below the line, otherwise you never catch up.

What we have done is to analyse a peaking problem in terms of the behaviour of the two variables, demand and supply. Before tackling the problem, let us make sure that we have one. Is it worth spending money on reducing backlogs? Not necessarily, or, perhaps, not much. If your organization is a monopoly—and an uncaring one at that—just let the queues lengthen. Likewise if the cost of any solution outweighs the benefits.

However, suppose we do want to reduce backlogs: what strategies are open to us? Here is where our analysis comes in. To meet the peak demand we can work on one (or both) of the two variables. Essentially,

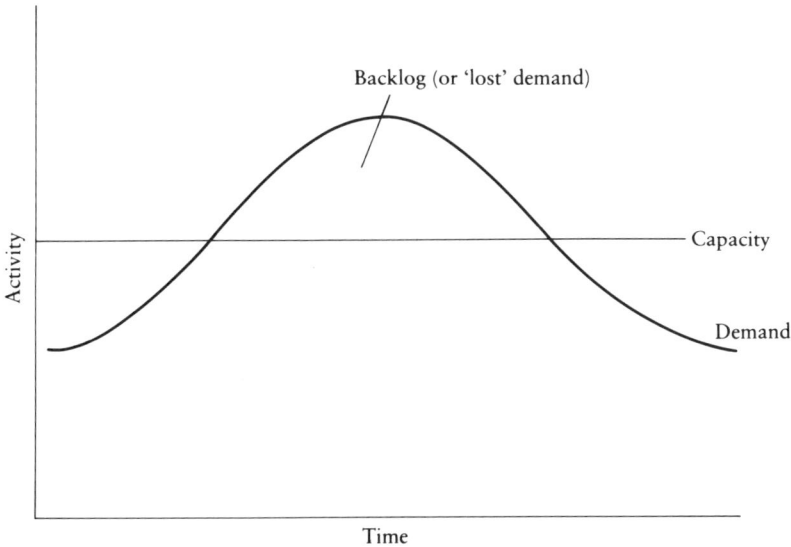

**Figure A1.1** The peaking problem

we need either to raise capacity to meet demand, or to reduce demand to match capacity. We can subdivide these two approaches into those that affect a temporary increase or decrease, and those that have to resort to a permanent one. Two basic variables, each with two options, gives us four possible solutions. We can draw them as in Fig. A1.2.

Before examining each of these possible solutions, let me make the point that none is exclusive of any other. If the Harbour Bridge problem were to become extreme, one could combine:

1a. lane-switching at peak times;
1b. a second tier;
2a. differential toll charges;
2b. encouragement of car-sharing.

Now let us attempt to validate our analysis—or rather, with Karl Popper in mind, let us see if we can invalidate, or falsify, it. We can do this by empirical observation of industries with peaking problems.

1a  Into this group fit all organizations that have the ability easily to vary their capacity. The Post Office takes on additional staff at Christmas, at which time it can easily predict a peak. Airport hotels have armies of on-call service staff who can be summoned to help

199

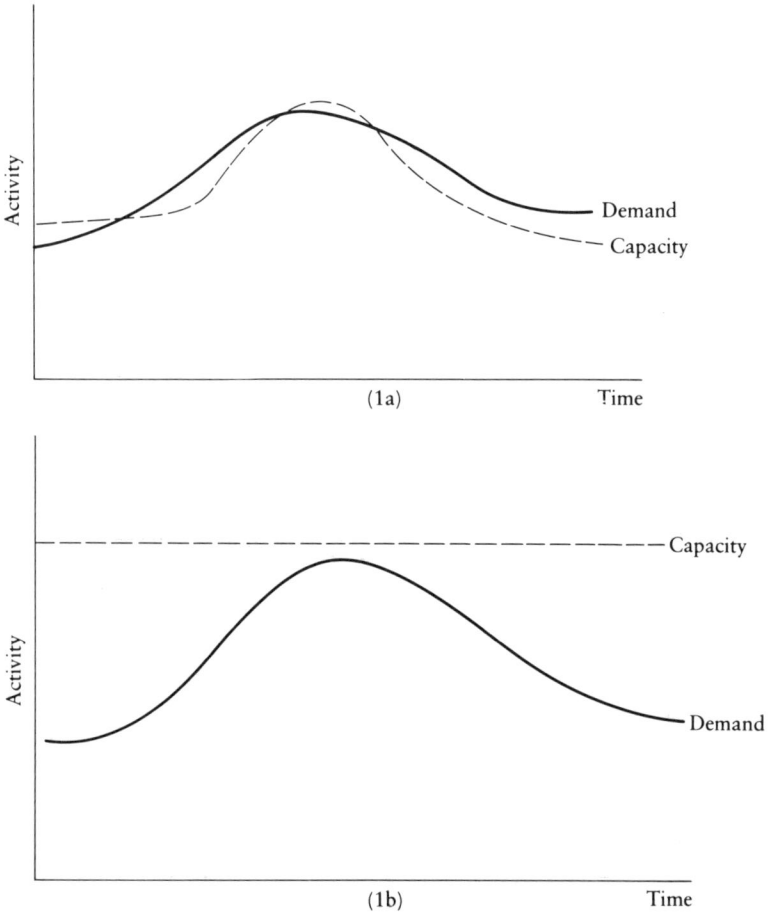

**Figure A1.2** (1a) Increase capacity at relevant time. (1b) Increase capacity permanently. (2a) Decrease demand at relevant time (smoothing). (2b) Decrease demand permanently.

with a large influx caused by the airport closing. The electricity industry negotiates facilities to meet peak loads.

1b Whereas labour is a commodity that can be adjusted to meet variations in demand, the same is less true of capital equipment. One can hire combine-harvesters, but everyone wants to do so at the same time. If supermarkets have long queues at checkouts they can vary how many are manned, but they still need to install sufficient cash registers to meet the peaks.

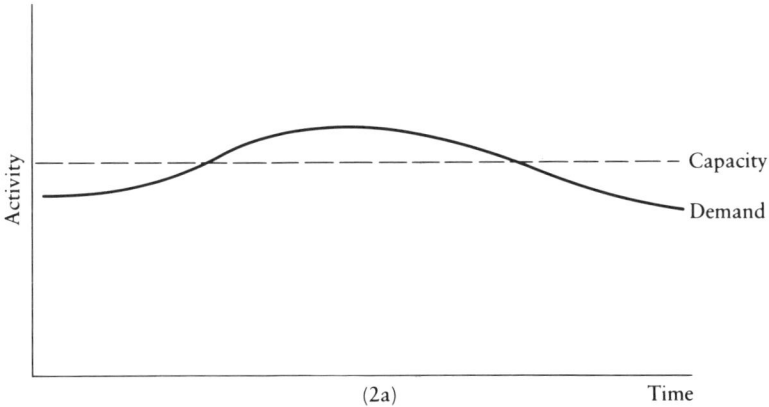

(2a)

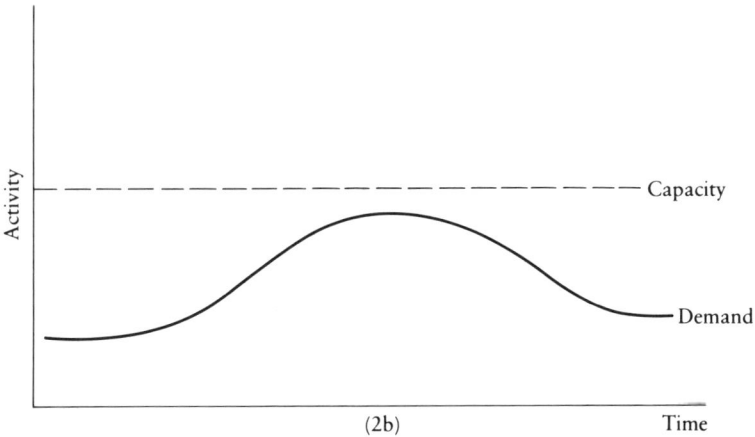

(2b)

2a Because the latter class of solutions leads to spare capacity at non-peak times, there is a natural urge to operate on the demand side. This can be seen in any organization that uses differential pricing policies—cheaper telephone calls after 6 p.m., night-time rates for electricity, and off-peak railway fares are just a few examples.

2b The final—and in many ways least attractive—option is to depress demand absolutely. This may be because a system of differential charging is too complicated to introduce in practice. As far as I am aware, parking meters have two scales of charges only, free and exorbitant: the system is not fine-tuned.

# Appendix B
# Checklist for auditing computer systems

The following checklist is illustrative rather than exhaustive. Detailed checklists can be obtained from professional audit firms or from books such as *Audit of Computer Systems* (NCC Publications).

1. Is input to be properly authorized? Does the system ensure this?
2. Will independent batch totals be input and checked by the system?
3. Are there any other input controls?
4. Are there controls to ensure that all input has been received and that it is complete?
5. Will the system detect:
   - record sequence failure?
   - missing records?
   - duplicate records?
6. Will there be an audit trail of all input records?
7. Are rejected records properly handled? Are there controls to ensure that they are re-input?
8. Are there system controls to ensure that jobs are run in the correct sequence?
9. Are there controls to ensure that all jobs and re-runs use the correct file version?
10. Any special hardware controls required?
11. Does the design conform to the specification of requirements? If not, have all the charges been agreed and documented with the user?
12. Are the re-run and re-start procedures defined?
13. Have the interfaces with other systems been designed and agreed?
14. Where re-runs and re-starts cause output files and printed output to be produced, are there controls to ensure that abortive run output is destroyed?
15. Are there progress checks to ensure that:
    - the correct files are used?
    - invalid file headers/trailers are detected and reported?
    - records sequences are correct?

- invalid/missing records are reported?
- duplicate records are detected or reported?
- controls on input and output files are made and reported if incorrect?

16. Are there sufficient controls on the master files? Are control records held in the file or on a separate control file?
17. Does the system prevent unauthorized access to master files?
18. Is there adequate fall-back on master files?
19. Is there any control to prevent files being accidentally overwritten?
20. Has the user agreed all manual checks and controls?
21. Will the user be aware if he has received all the output?
22. Are there sufficient control reports produced to the user to verify that the reconciliation procedures have worked?
23. Will the controls always be produced? Will the output always be produced? Any nil reports?
24. Are there controls on interface files?
25. Are the pages of output reports numbered? Is there an 'end-of-report' marker?
26. Are there special procedures required to ensure confidentiality
    - of input?
    - of output?
    - of printed files copies?
27. Are special programs required to handle back-up files?
28. Are there any controls and security measures required over data in transit
    - transmitted data?
    - output data?

# Appendix C
# Application packages

**Evaluating packages**

Buying a package confers the great advantage of being able to evaluate it before purchase. The secret is to know what you are looking for. Any salesman will give you a standard demonstration, set up specifically to illustrate the advantages of the package being shown. What you need is to see how the package meets your own requirements. To do this, ensure that you have sample data available of your application. This will put you in a position to evaluate the 'fit' itemized in the following checklist.

*(a) Supplier/agent*
- Financial standing
- Previous contacts with company
- Reputation
- References
- Staff expenses
- Membership of relevant trades association
- Proximity for call-out

*(b) Package—general*
- Number of users—local, world-wide
- Cost—including any hidden post-sales costs
- Delivery time
- Media on which supplied
- Quality of documentation
- Training required and available
- Compatibility

*(c) Package—systems considerations*
- Nearness of 'fit' to your problems
- If tailoring is required, is it done by:
  - (i) supplier:
    - cost
    - implications for maintenance

(ii) purchaser:
  - policy regarding upgrades
  - access to source code
  - ease of modification
- Language used
- Quality of programming
- Controls, recovery, and security
- Archiving

(*d*) *Package—operating characteristics*
- Hardware constraints:
  (i) computers on which it will run
  (ii) memory and data storage requirements
  (iii) peripherals used
- Software constraints:
  (i) operating systems required
  (ii) job control
- Volume and throughput
- Timing
- Ease of operator use

**Sample package**
MOSAIC is a modular business system package for the ICL DR520 computer equipment range. The modules, and sub-systems, may be licensed in total as an integrated system or individually and added to as and when business needs dictate. The available modules are:

1. Sales order processing, invoicing, and stock control
   Optional sub-systems are:
   - back orders processing
   - purchase order processing.
2. Sales ledger
   Options are open-item ledger or balance forward.
3. Purchase ledger
   Options are foreign currency facilities.
4. Nominal ledger

MOSAIC has facilities to handle up to nine companies, each with up to nine sites, achieved by holding separate files for companies and sites. The package is written in CIS COBOL and runs under the DRX operating environment.

205

ORDER PROCESSING, INVOICING, STOCK CONTROL
## Order processing
- Accepts sales order entry from account, cash, and casual customers.
- Automatic handling of stock items, supersessions, and alternatives.
- Addition of non-stock items to an order.
- Addition of comments to an order.
- Production of quotations and conversion to orders at quoted price or at current price.
- Credit note processing.
- Display to total order value inclusive of trade/line discounts and VAT at time of order line entry.
- Printing or picking/delivery notes and invoices immediately or in batch run.
- Stock update immediately at time or order line entry.
- Orders audit trail.
- Credit limit and account-overdue checks with warning messages displayed.
- Facility to input 'one-off' delivery address.
- Display of item stock level, on-order, and back order quantities.
- Link to back orders processing sub-system.

## Price/discount matrix
- This allows different price or discount for different groups of customers and different groups of stock. A group can be as precise as one or as general as all.
- Facilities may or may not apply to trade discount.
- Sales price may be one of three selling prices or one of three cost prices or average cost price as held on stock file, with or without percentage mark-up.
- One of up to ten discounts may be applied to item price.
- One of up to six volume discounts may be applied.
- For selected customers and/or stock items, prices may be overridden at order entry.

## Invoicing
- Transactions passed to sales ledger.
- Can be produced on demand or in batch.
- Trading report giving sales and costs accumulated from invoicing.

## Stock control
- Automatic update from order processing.

- Usage demand history for each stock item for current period and each of preceding 12 periods.
- Recommended stock re-order report by supplier including value.
- Actual-stock-ordered report by supplier including order value.
- Handling of stock movements (adjustments, issues, returns, and transfers) and goods-in (including price changes).
- Facility to generate supplier orders and accept goods-in on flexible disk.
- Optional link to purchase order processing sub-system; reports for:
  inventory list
  inventory evaluation
  stock investment (highlights overstocked items)
  goods-in/binning check list
  profit margins by stock code.

*Other reports*
- Lost sales.
- Stock adjustments.
- Profit margin by customer.
- Order status.
- Goods-in.
- Stock take.
- Back orders release.

*Back orders processing*
- Optional system for use with MOSAIC order processing and stock control modules.
- Back orders created at order entry and picking stages, listings by stock item and customer.
- Release of back orders by individual customer.
- Automatic release when sufficient stock received to satisfy demand.
- Part-allocation when limited quantities available.
- Shows items back-ordered on delivery note and invoice.
- Generates picking/delivery note and invoice showing original customer order number or date of original order.
- Combines all satisfied back orders for one customer on one invoice with appropriate references.
- Option to price at original order value or at current values.

*Purchase order processing*
- Optional system for use with MOSAIC stock control module.

- Maintains file of purchase orders by supplier created from MOSAIC re-ordering mechanism.
- Allows goods-in to be verified against purchase order, updates stock file, and adjusts on-order quantity and outstanding quantities on purchase order.
- Allows up to 99 part-deliveries to satisfy purchase order.
- Gives facilities for cancellation of order lines in part or total.
- Returns allow for items to be returned to supplier and whether or not they are to be replaced.
- Facilities for supplier invoice checking against quantities received: if purchase ledger module is in use, details are passed through to the ledger, with option to amend invoice totals if required.
- Printed report of all movements.
- Enquiry facilities to look at purchase orders: the enquiry can be made on any combination of supplier code, purchase order number, and stock code.
- Purchase order report in supplier or stock code sequence.
- Facilities to update purchase order file with supersession details so that latest stock codes are held.
- Facilities for automatic update if goods-in details received on diskette.
- Automatic adjustment and update to item stock level and on-order quantity on stock file.

SALES LEDGER
*Type*
Open item or balance brought forward.

*Transaction entry*
This is taken from the MOSAIC order processing/invoicing system and/or via direct entry of invoices, credit notes, and journals. For credit notes, and with an open item ledger, if the customer reference number equals a current invoice number and the value of the invoice is greater than or equal to the credit, automatic matching will take place.

*Transaction matching*
This allows cash, cash refunds, and unallocated cash to be entered. For balance brought forward, the cash is matched to the oldest debt. For open item, matching takes place against outstanding transactions. Specific and automatic matching facilities are provided. The automatic

process proceeds sequentially, matching entire quantities, until there is insufficient credit to match the next item.

*Enquiry*
This takes the form of a display of selected customer account details with option for further detail display of all ledger transactions for that customer. There is also:

- Display of ledger control totals.
- Display of VAT totals.

*Debtors listing and aged debt*
Debtors listing provides details by individual account, showing out-standing transaction values. Aged debt shows credit limit, outstanding balance, current and previous three period balances and whether or not credit limit has been exceeded.

*Statements*
In addition to the end-of-period runs, selected statements can be produced at any time.

*Reports*
- Day book and control.
- Period update.
- VAT.

*Labels*
Name and address labels.

PURCHASE LEDGER
*Type*
Open item.

*Transaction entry*
Direct entry of invoices, credit notes, and journals.

*Payments due*
This lists all transactions due for settlement. It allows full advantage to be taken of any settlement discounts offered.

*Payments program*
This program allows payments to be deferred, part-paid, or brought forward, recording any urgent payments which have been paid manually and any prepayments (deposits) made.

*Remittance*
All automatic payments produce a remittance advice unless the total net amount is negative. Cheques may be printed if required.

*Cash release report*
Lists all transactions actually paid for each supplier. Also reports on payments which are cancelled because total net amount is negative.

*Multi-currency*
An option is provided to enable transactions for each supplier to be in one of ten different currencies. Exchange rate differences are recorded automatically, and if a rate changes between transaction receipt and payment the difference is posted to the nominal ledger. Remittance advices are produced in the supplier's currency. Enquiries can be made in both 'native' and foreign currency.

*Day book*
This takes the form of a report on all transactions entered and on all payments made for each supplier. Control totals are printed at the conclusion of the day book.

*Other reports*
In addition to the specific reports mentioned above, the following are also produced:

- period end report,
- VAT report,
- Aged creditors report.

*Enquiry*
- Display of selected supplier account details with option for further detail display of all ledger transactions for that supplier.
- Display of ledger control totals.
- Display of VAT totals.

*Nominal ledger*
Links to nominal ledger are provided and are controlled by parameters
maintained by the user.

*Other points*
– Six-character account code.
– Three payments-due period types:
  1. discount period in months,
  2. discount period in days,
  3. discount period as day of the following month.

NOMINAL LEDGER
This is effected by direct entry of transaction data or through links from
MOSAIC sales and/or purchase ledger systems. Journals entered directly
will follow standard double entry, but the system may be overruled to
make a 'one-legged' entry.

*Day book*
This reports on all transactions entered and identifies their source.
Control totals are reported at the conclusion of the day book print.

*Trial balance*
This shows all current period transactions.

*Financial report*
This is provided as balance sheet and profit and loss. It compares
actuals with budget to produce variances and percentage variances,
both for period and year-to-date. Up to 13 periods are allowed.

*Management report*
This follows a sequence similar to that provided in financial report but
is in cost centre sequence.

*Structure*
Transactions are based upon a four-character cost centre and a six-
character nominal code.

FILE HANDLING AND ENQUIRY UTILITY PACKAGE
FILEAID is a powerful file-handling and enquiry utility available on the
DRS 20 computer range. It runs under the DRX operating environment

and is totally controlled by parameters which are easily constructed and modified. FILEAID can be used on files which are already in existence and to create, maintain, and enquire upon new files.

FILEAID functions and benefits fall in two main areas: file enquiry and file maintenance.

*File enquiry*
- Information on a file may be conditionally searched using the operators $=$, $>$, $<$, not$=$, not$>$, not$<$. These may be grouped using logical AND and OR. Comparisons may be against a literal value, another item in the file, an arithmetic expression, or a conditional expression.
- Expressions may be user-defined through numeric and/or conditional work fields. Numeric work fields can consist of arithmetic expressions involving the normal operators and item fields and/or other numeric work fields and/or constants. Conditional work fields can consist of expressions being comparisons between item fields and/or other conditional fields and/or numeric work fields.
- Fields of associated data, from each record which meets the selection criteria, may be displayed, or printed (either immediately, or spooled to a file for subsequent printing). Output may be directed to any specified printer. Fields to be displayed/printed may themselves be derived by use of arithmetic operators in conjunction with numeric/ conditional work fields and/or item fields.
- Total fields may be user-defined. The normal arithmetic operators are available, as are user-defined numeric and conditional work fields.
- Applied condition sets may be stored for re-use and automatic re-application.

*File extract*
Enquiry results may be extracted to a user-named sequential file for further processing or for transmission to remote sites. Fields of associated and/or derived data may be extracted for each record meeting the selection criteria.

*Protection*
A password may be applied to a file and/or a FILEAID function to prevent unauthorized access, and individual fields may be protected against unauthorized amendment.

FILEAID functions may be optionally suppressed from appearing on a DRS 20 terminal FILEAID menu.

*Benefits*
- The package is controlled and driven by the end-user—no programmer intervention is necessary.
- *Ad hoc* and permanent file enquiry functions are easily constructed by the user without recourse to specialized programming assistance.
- *Ad hoc* management information requests based on complex data relationships can be constructed and reported under user control, usually in a matter of minutes.

*File maintenance*
- Gives facilities for file creation and deletion, record insertion, amendment, and deletion.
- Handles single- and multi-record type files in serial or indexed form.
- Is compatible with data types under CIS COBOL and PASCAL.
- Features global file amendment facility with conditional selection of fields as per FILE ENQUIRY.
- Provides protection of fields to prevent unauthorized amendment.
- Provides password protection.

*Benefits*
- All file maintenance functions of an installation are handled with a standardized methodology, irrespective of file or application.
- The package removes the necessity for writing dedicated file maintenance programs, thereby saving programmer time and effort.
- It provides a standard and convenient method of producing test/system data files.
- Parameters devised during systems development remain, thus providing the end-user with an *ad hoc* enquiry facility and the support team with a fault diagnosis tool.
- It can be used with new and existing files.
- It gives the end-user a simple yet powerful tool with which to maintain files.

# Appendix D
# Strategic weighting of risk factors in estimating computer projects[1]

The method of adjusting a cost–benefit analysis for known risk factors consists of:

- identifying the risk factors;
- scoring the particular project against these.

## Classifying factors according to risk

HIGH-RISK FACTORS

1. *Project size*  Large projects are more difficult to estimate and manage than small ones. The money at risk is greater, as are problems of implementation and realization of benefits.

2. *Project definition*  Vagueness and poor documentation of work to date cause estimates to be poor and mean that the application logic will require re-work during implementation.

3. *User commitment and stability*  Lack of user commitment and changing staff will cause project delays.

4. *Elapsed time*  The longer a project goes on, the more things can change—business needs, staff, user management, and company policy.

5. *Number of systems interfaces*  The more interfaces there are between the new system and others, the more co-ordination and testing will be required. This causes additional work and requires continuous co-operation across departments.

MEDIUM-RISK FACTORS

1. *Functional complexity*  Complexity of actual design is often over-simplified during the feasibility study. Any suspicion of underlying complexity should be allowed for in estimating.

2. *Number of user departments*  This is the same as for interfaces, but if other users are involved in the system then the risk is slightly alleviated.

---

[1] The material for this Appendix is based on work done by John Ward of the Cranfield Institute of Management.

214

3. *Newness of technology/vendor*   The best software or hardware will contain unknowns even to the vendor. Best not to be the first, and contact other users if possible, to reduce risk.

4. *User experience of computers*   Two levels of knowledge are required: experience of automated processing, and the implications of this on the user function.

5. *The project team's experience of the user area*   Allowance must be made if the systems analysts and designers are unfamiliar with the particular application. Allowance should be made for training in this.

6. *Newness of technology to the organization*   Even if the technology itself is not new on the market, if it is new to the company then allowance has to be made for the inevitable mistakes and learning curve.

7. *Number of vendors/contractors*   Incompatibility problems and co-ordination of effort will cause time to be lost. Attention must also be paid to the interdependence of delivery dates from different suppliers.

LOW-RISK FACTORS

1. *Number of sites*   Allowance must be made where the sites involved in development and implementation are geographically scattered. Local customs, practices, and physical conditions may affect the design and implementation of a 'common' system. Training, testing, and user-liaison will carry an overhead.

2. *Functional newness*   This refers to the impact of automated techniques in an area not previously computerized.

3. *Number of project phases*   Later phases may (a) be dependent on an earlier sign-off; (b) necessitate the re-work of earlier phases as a result of testing. This risk may require higher weighting if parallel development of phases is planned.

Table D1 shows these risks weighted and scored and then translated into a risk adjustment factor. The resulting risk adjustment factor of 0.75 will subsequently be applied to the calculated net present value (NPV) of the project once operational savings have been estimated.

**Table D1**  Calculation of strategic risks: an example.
The circled items represent the World's Wines score

| Risk | Wt | Score due to project applicability | | | Wt × Score |
|---|---|---|---|---|---|
| | | 3 | 2 | 1 | |
| *(a) Highly weighted risks* | | | | | |
| 1. Project size/investment | 10 | >£250K | >£100K | (<£100K) | 10 |
| 2. Project structure/definition | 10 | Poor | Satisfactory | (Good) | 10 |
| 3. User commitment/stability | 9 | Low | (Medium) | High | 18 |
| 4. Elapsed time | 8 | >18 mths | (>6 mths) | <6 mths | 16 |
| 5. No. of system interfaces | 8 | >3 | (2–3) | 1 | 16 |
| | | | | Sub-total | 70 |
| *(b) Medium-weighted risks* | | | | | |
| 1. Functional complexity | 7 | High | Medium | (Low) | 7 |
| 2. No. of user departments | 6 | >3 | (2–3) | 1 | 12 |
| 3. Newness of technology (vendors) | 6 | All new | Some new | (All proven) | 6 |
| 4. User experience of installation sites (IS) | 5 | (Little or none) | Some/recent | Considerable and recent | 15 |
| 5. IS expertise in user area | 5 | General and/or not available | (Recent and available) | Current and knowledgeable | 10 |
| 6. Newness of technology to organization | 4 | (All new) | Some new | Well used | 12 |
| 7. No. of vendors/contractors | 4 | 3 or more | (2) | 1 | 8 |
| | | | | Sub-total | 70 |
| *(c) Low-weighted risks* | | | | | |
| 1. No. of installation sites | 3 | 3 or more | 2 | (1) | 3 |
| 2. Functional newness | 2 | All | Some | (None) | 2 |
| 3. No. of project phases | 2 | 3 or more | (2) | 1 | 4 |
| | | | | Sub-total | 9 |
| | | | | Total | 149 |

| *Factor table* | |
| --- | --- |
| *Score* | *Adjustment factor* |
| (min.)  89–100 | 1.00 |
| 101–120 | 0.95 |
| 121–140 | 0.85 |
| **141–160** | **0.75** |
| 161–180 | 0.65 |
| 181–200 | 0.55 |
| 201–230 | 0.45 |
| 231–267 (max.) | 0.35 |

Risk adjustment factor $(R) = 75$

# Bibliography

The primary objective of this book is to persuade you to involve yourself closely with any computer system that affects your working life. The secondary objective is indicating how this excellent principle can be turned into practice. Because the field is so wide, I have only been able to touch on many techniques and standards which merit much closer study. If you are inspired to look more deeply into some of them the following list will aid your search for knowledge:

### General background
Walsh, M., *Understanding Computers*, Wiley, 1981.
- A more detailed account of the physical nature of computers.

Turner, M. J., *Buying a Business Computer*, First Computer Handbook, 1980.
- A checklist-based approach to specifying requirements, cost–benefit analysis, and equipment selection.

Pannell, B., *Making a Success of Microcomputing*, Enterprise Books, 1981.
- Useful, down-to-earth introduction for the first-time user.

Berman, E. D., and Dewhurst, L., *Selecting Business Software*, Frances Pintner, 1984.
- Simple guide to spreadsheets, word processing, databases and application packages, and how to choose the right one.

Checkland, O., *Systems Thinking, Systems Practice*, Wiley, 1981.
- Stimulating book on the interaction between theory and practice of problem-solving methodology.


### Project management
Keen, J., *Managing Systems Development*, Wiley, 1981.
- Good conventional treatise covering subject in some detail. Mainly for the practitioner.

Block, R., *The Politics of Projects*, Yourdon Press, 1983.
- Instructive guide through the political minefields that beset the typical project.

DeMarco, T., *Controlling Software Projects*, Yourdon Press, 1983.
- Highly readable guide to why we are such bad estimators, and how to improve.


## Systems analysis

Pressdam, R., *Software Engineering—A Practitioner's Approach*, McGraw-Hill, 1982.
- Excellent and modern account of how systems are developed; very much for the technician.

DeMarco, T., *Structured Analysis and System Specification*, Yourdon Press, 1978.
- The definitive and clearly written book on structured analysis.

Gane, C., and Sarson, T., *Structured Systems Analysis*, Prentice-Hall, 1977.
- Same subject, almost equally readable; their data flow diagrams have rectangles rather than circles.

McMenamin, S. M., and Palmer, J. F., *Essential Systems Analysis*, Yourdon Press, 1984.
- Highly recommended book as follow-on to DeMarco. Definitely for practitioners of structured analysis.

Gause, D. C., and Weinberg, G. M., *Are Your Lights On?* Winthrop Publications, 1982.
- Short, amusing, and constructive book about problem-solving.

de Bono, E., *Lateral Thinking*, Pelican, 1977.
- Any of the de Bono series is immediately relevant to the creative aspects of systems design.


## Applications development

Martin, J., *Information Systems Manifesto*, Prentice-Hall, 1984.
- A paeon in praise of fourth-generation languages and new development methods.

Martin, J., *Application Development without Programmers*, Prentice-Hall, 1983.
- The details of how users can write, and are writing, their own systems.

219

## Programming

Metzger, P. W., *Managing a Programming Project*, 2nd edn, Prentice-Hall, 1981.
- How programs are specified, coded, and tested and the activity controlled.

Myers, G. J., *The Art of Software Testing*, Wiley, 1979.
- The strategy and tactics for testing programs and systems.

## Systems controls

Cortada, J., *EDP Costs and Charges*, Prentice-Hall, 1980.
- Guide to finance, budget, and cost control in data processing.

Thomas, A. J., and Douglas, I. J., *Auditing Computer Systems*, NCC Publications, 1981.
- Clear and informative guide to computer auditing.

Krauss, L. A., and MacGahan, A., *Computer Fraud and Counter-measures*, Prentice-Hall, 1979.
- Lengthy book on all aspects of security.

Martin, J., *Security, Accuracy, Privacy in Computer Systems*, Prentice-Hall, 1974.
- Lengthy book on all aspects of security.

Freedman, D., and Weinberg, G. M., *Walkthroughs, Inspections, and Technical Reviews*, Little Brown, 1984.
- Comprehensive and authoritative practitioner's guide to all types of reviews.

For more information on the above books, or for any queries relating to the subject matter of this book, the author can be contacted through his office:

Keith London Associates
40 Stonehills
Welwyn Garden City
Hertfordshire AL8 6PD
England
Telephone: 0707 330114/5   Telex: 291087 KLA G

# Index